Make History with this fantastic CGP book...

OK, so the new OCR B GCSE History exams are pretty tricky... but with this brilliant CGP Revision Guide, you'll be ready to go into battle!

It's packed with everything you need to get your head around the subject, including crystal-clear notes, maps, diagrams and photos for each topic.

We've also included exam-style practice questions throughout the book, plus plenty of advice on how to pick up top marks. After all that, you'll be like an heir to the throne — destined to succeed.

CGP — still the best! ☺

Our sole aim here at CGP is to produce the highest quality books — carefully written, immaculately presented and dangerously close to being funny.

Then we work our socks off to get them out to you — at the cheapest possible prices.

CONTENTS

Published by CGP

Editors:
Chloe Anderson, Emma Cleasby, Alex Fairer, Catherine Heygate,
Andy Park, Jack Perry, Rebecca Tate and Louise Taylor.

Contributors:
Peter Callaghan, Amanda Roper and Paul Smith.

With thanks to John Broadbent, Marti Cooper, Emma Crighton, Dan Heaney,
Catherine Heygate, Anthony Muller, and Rebecca Tate for the proofreading.

With thanks to Ana Pungartnik and Holly Poynton for the copyright research.

Acknowledgements:

With thanks to The Art Archive / Palazzo Barberini Rome / Collection Dagli Orti for permission to use the image on page 1.

With thanks to Historic England / Mary Evans for permission to use the images on pages 6, 9 and 90.

With thanks to Mary Evans Picture Library for permission to use the images on pages 11, 19, 21, 26, 28, 38, 39, 40, 99, 102, 103 and 106.

With thanks to Photo Researchers / Mary Evans Picture Library for permission to use the images on pages 16, 37 and 73.

With thanks to Illustrated London News Ltd / Mary Evans for permission to use the images on pages 13, 17, 25, 44 and 48.

_Image on page 41 from The College of Arms, The Westminster Tournament Roll: 1511; artist, unknown; by permission of
The College of Arms, London. E 36/214 f.109: 7 Dec 1507; author, unknown; Crown copyright._

With thanks to Mary Evans / Peter Higginbotham Collection for permission to use the image on page 45.

With thanks to Marx Memorial Library / Mary Evans for permission to use the image on page 51.

With thanks to Mary Evans / Interfoto for permission to use the image on page 58.

With thanks to Mary Evans / Classic Stock / C.P. Cushing for permission to use the image on page 61.

With thanks to Mary Evans / Everett Collection for permission to use the images on pages 65 and 119.

With thanks to The Art Archive / Granger Collection for permission to use the images on pages 68, 71, 72 and 110.

With thanks to Ashmolean Museum / Mary Evans for permission to use the image on page 82.

With thanks to Mary Evans / The National Archives, London. England for permission to use the image on page 92.

_Image on page 95 © Oliver-Bonjoch. This image is licensed under the Creative Commons Attribution - Share Alike 3.0 Unported license.
https://creativecommons.org/licenses/by/3.0/deed.en_

With thanks to Mary Evans / Iberfoto for permission to use the image on page 97.

With thanks to National Museums NI / MARY EVANS for permission to use the image on page 101.

With thanks to Mary Evans Picture Library/DOUGLAS MCCARTHY for permission to use the image on page 109.

With thanks to Photo Researchers / Mary Evans for permission to use the image on page 115.

With thanks to Mary Evans / Sueddeutsche Zeitung Photo for permission to use the images on pages 118, 120 and 127.

With thanks to Mary Evans / SZ Photo / Scherl for permission to use the image on page 122.

_Extract on page 123 from 'School for Barbarians: Education Under the Nazis' (Dover Books on History, Political and Social Science). Dover Publications Inc.;
Reprint edition (28 Mar. 2014)_

With thanks to Mary Evans / Imagno for permission to use the image on page 129.

_OCR material on pages 3, 4, 78, 79 and 135 is reproduced by permission of OCR. From OCR B, GCSE History, Paper J411,
(Sample Question Paper 2016)_

ISBN: 978 1 78294 607 6
Printed by Elanders Ltd, Newcastle upon Tyne.
Clipart from Corel®

Based on the classic CGP style created by Richard Parsons.

Sources: the Building Blocks of History

Historians have such an <u>easy life</u>. They <u>read</u> old documents and <u>rewrite</u> them... right? Actually, they do <u>a bit more</u> than that. For GCSE History, <u>you</u> have to <u>become</u> a historian, so you'd best be sure what they <u>really do</u>.

Historians use *Sources* to *Find Out about the Past*

1) <u>Sources</u> are things that historians use to <u>find out about</u> and <u>make sense of</u> the past.

2) They can be <u>written</u> (e.g. newspapers, government reports) or <u>visual</u> (e.g. photographs, maps, films).

3) Sources can be categorised as either <u>primary</u> or <u>secondary</u>:

Primary sources — evidence from the period you're studying

For example, a <u>newspaper report</u> on the First World War from 4th September 1914, or a <u>picture</u> of Henry VIII that was painted during his reign.

Secondary sources — evidence about (but <u>not from</u>) the period you're studying

For example, a <u>1989 book</u> called 'Origins of the First World War', or a <u>website</u> providing information about all the <u>portraits</u> ever painted of Henry VIII.

Historians have to *Interrogate* and *Interpret* every source

© The Art Archive / Palazzo Barberini Rome / Collection Dagli Orti

King Henry VIII, 1540

1) Historians have to be <u>very careful</u> with sources. To make sure they're using sources <u>accurately</u>, historians <u>interrogate</u> every source they use. This means they ask themselves a series of <u>questions</u> about the source's <u>background</u>.

- **What** is this source?
  E.g. It is a painting of King Henry VIII.
- **Who** made this source?
  E.g. It was produced by the King's official painter, Hans Holbein.
- **Why** did they make the source?
  E.g. He was asked to paint it by the King.
- **Where** and **when** was it made?
  E.g. It was made in the Palace of Whitehall in 1540.

2) Historians use their answers to work out <u>how useful</u> and <u>how reliable</u> a source is. For example:

- This is a <u>professional</u> painting made <u>during</u> Henry's reign (meaning the painter could have <u>met</u> Henry). So this should be a <u>useful</u> source for finding out what Henry looked like.

- BUT perhaps the painter would have been <u>punished</u> if he didn't show Henry looking good, so it may not be entirely <u>reliable</u>.

> A source that presents a one-sided view is <u>biased</u>.

3) After they've interrogated a source, historians need to <u>interpret</u> it.

> This means deciding <u>what it tells them</u> about the topic they're studying.

4) For example, Henry was probably quite a <u>large man</u> with <u>fair hair</u> and a <u>beard</u>. But the painter may have been told to make the picture to <u>Henry's liking</u> — so based on just this picture, you can't really say for sure <u>how big</u> he really was.

> Henry was the <u>king</u> — people would have <u>done</u> what he <u>told</u> them to.

5) Historians look at <u>lots of</u> sources, and <u>compare</u> them against each other. If sources <u>contradict</u> one another, they'll try to work out <u>why</u>, and what this tells them about the past.

> For example, another painting might show Henry as very <u>unattractive</u>. But a historian might <u>interpret</u> it <u>differently</u>, depending on whether Henry had <u>seen</u> and <u>approved of</u> the painting, or whether it had been made by one of Henry's <u>enemies</u> and was perhaps <u>biased against</u> him.

And if you're really good at history — they'll let you on the telly...

When you're studying GCSE History, you need to interrogate and interpret every source you see. Don't always assume what you see or read is an exact description of life way back when.

Building a Picture of the Past

Historians can use the information in <u>various sources</u> to get a better understanding of a particular period. This involves <u>linking</u> events together, and working out <u>why</u> things happened the way they did.

Historians study Change and Continuity

1) One way to get an idea of what happened in the past is to look at <u>changes</u> and <u>continuities</u> over time.

2) <u>Change</u> is when something happens to make things <u>different</u>.
   - Changes can be <u>quick</u> — e.g. a law <u>making</u> secondary education free.
   - Or they can be <u>slow</u> — e.g. a <u>gradual change</u> in a society's literacy levels.

3) <u>Continuity</u> is the <u>opposite</u> of change — it's when things stay the <u>same</u> — e.g. people believed for hundreds of years that <u>disease</u> was God's punishment for <u>sin</u>.

4) These ideas are opposites — think of <u>continuity</u> as a <u>flat line</u> going along until there is a sudden <u>change</u> and the line becomes a <u>zigzag</u>:

> The <u>most important</u> changes in history are called <u>turning points</u>. After a turning point, life might never be the same again.

5) Change and continuity can happen <u>at the same time</u> in different parts of society.
   - For example, when the <u>Normans</u> conquered England in 1066, many of the richest people in English society lost their <u>jobs</u> and <u>status</u> (= change).
   - But life didn't actually change very much for <u>peasant farmers</u> (= continuity).

6) There are <u>all sorts</u> of things that a historian might look at for change or continuity. Some things might be <u>obvious</u> (e.g. a new king or queen would be an obvious change). But historians are also very interested in whether <u>more everyday</u> aspects of society are showing change or continuity — e.g. <u>attitudes</u>, <u>lifestyles</u>, <u>beliefs</u>, <u>fashions</u>, <u>diets</u>... the list is endless.

Historians think about Causes and Consequences

1) <u>Cause</u> means the <u>reason</u> something happened — e.g. the causes of the First World War.

2) <u>Consequence</u> means what happened <u>because</u> of an action — it's the <u>result</u> of an event, e.g. a consequence of the First World War was that a lot of young men were killed.

> Any time you have an event in history, think about <u>what caused it</u> and <u>the effect it had</u> — it's a really good way to show the examiner how different historical events are <u>linked</u> to each other.

3) Causes and consequences can be either <u>short-term</u> or <u>long-term</u>.

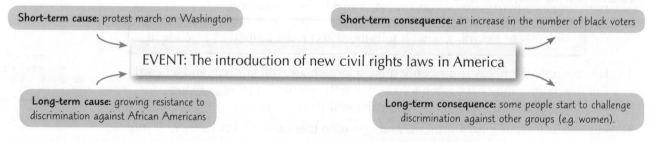

4) Historians also think about how different causes and consequences <u>interact</u>. For example, there might be a <u>chain</u> of causes that lead to an event, or one consequence of an event might be <u>more important</u> than all the rest.

You can think of these as the Four Cs of history...

As you use this book, make sure you think about 'the Four Cs' on each page. When you identify causes, consequences, changes and continuities, add them to your revision notes and learn them.

Exam Skills for the Thematic and Period Studies

These two pages are all about how to tackle the thematic and period study sections of your exam.

The Thematic Study covers a Long Period of time

1) The thematic study covers over 750 years of history, right up to the present day.
2) The study focuses on what changed (and what didn't change) over time and why.
3) You need to understand how different factors have affected the theme of your study — these are key things which have contributed towards changes and continuities throughout the period.

> If you're studying 'Migrants to Britain', this will be things like Britain's relationship with the wider world, beliefs and attitudes, government, economic forces and communications. For example, how changing attitudes towards migrants have impacted on how they're treated.

> If you're studying 'The People's Health', this will be things like beliefs and attitudes, government, science and technology, urbanisation, and wealth and poverty. For example, how improvements in science helped prevent disease.

The Period Study is all about how Events Unfolded

1) The period study covers a shorter period of history — but it still covers at least 100 years.
2) It focuses on the different events that took place during that time, as well as why events unfolded in the way they did.
3) You'll be expected to make connections between events. You must have a good grasp of cause and effect — you'll need to know what led to significant events and what their consequences were.
4) You should also have a good knowledge of the context in which these events happened — this will give you a better understanding of what happened and their impact.

There are Four basic types of exam question

The thematic studies and the period studies have the same style of exam question.

1) The first question will ask you to give three facts about your period.

> Give one way the government has tried to improve the health of the British people since 1900. [1 mark]

> This question is made up of 3 parts — a, b and c. Each one is worth 1 mark, so the question is worth 3 marks overall.

2) The next question will ask you to write a summary of something. You'll have to explain what happened and analyse it by using concepts such as cause, consequence and change.

> Write a clear and organised summary that analyses the impact of migrants on Britain in the period 1750-1900. [9 marks]

3) The third question will ask you to explain something about an event or development. For example, you might be asked about its impact or its causes.

> What was the impact of the Reconstruction era (1867-1877) on former slaves? [10 marks]

4) You'll then be given a choice of two questions — you have to answer one. Answer the one you're most comfortable with. Both questions will ask you how far you agree with a statement.

> 'Government action has been the most important factor in improvements to public health in Britain.' How far do you agree with this statement? [18 marks]

4

Exam Skills for the Thematic and Period Studies

Here is a <u>sample answer</u> to a question in the <u>thematic and period study</u> sections of the exam.

You'll need these *Skills* to answer the questions

1) Always use <u>detailed</u> and <u>relevant</u> information to support every point you make, and explain <u>how</u> it backs up the point.

2) Include specific dates, names and statistics to show the examiner you have a good <u>knowledge</u> and <u>understanding</u> of the topic.

3) Your answers should be <u>well organised</u> and <u>structured</u> — each of your points should <u>lead clearly</u> to your <u>conclusion</u>.

4) For the final question, have a <u>clear argument</u> in your head before you start writing. Even if you agree with the statement given in the question, you must consider some <u>counter-arguments</u>.

5) For more <u>general advice</u> on writing exam answers, turn to p.136.

> Make sure you get your dates right in the exam — remember that the <u>seventeenth</u> century refers to the <u>1600s</u>, the <u>eighteenth</u> century refers to the <u>1700s</u>, and so on.

Here's a Sample Answer to help you

This sample answer will give you an idea of <u>how</u> to respond to the 'how far do you agree' question. Look at the <u>points</u> that have been made and how they have been <u>supported</u> with <u>evidence</u>.

> 'Government action has been the most important factor in improvements to public health in Britain.' How far do you agree with this statement? Give reasons for your answer. [18 marks]

The action of local and national governments has played an increasingly important role in improving public health, although this role has largely been a modern one. Other factors like changing beliefs and technological improvements have also had huge impacts on public health. This answer will agree with this statement, arguing that overall, government action has been the most important factor in improving public health in Britain.

In the Middle Ages, the government did become more actively involved in the improvement of public health, but this was a very slow development. For example, while local governments made efforts to stop the spread of the Black Death in the mid 1300s, the national government only stepped in and introduced plague orders in the 1500s. These were unsuccessful nationally because the government did not enforce them and a lack of understanding of the causes of the plague meant that the orders were largely ineffective. However, some local governments had better results, such as York, which brought in taxes to support those in quarantine in 1550. Government action in the 19th century had a much bigger impact on public health. The Public Health Act of 1875 was an important turning point in efforts to improve health in Britain's growing industrial towns. For example, it forced councils to maintain water supplies and sewerage systems. This helped to prevent outbreaks of deadly diseases like cholera, which killed thousands of people earlier in the century.

> **This gives** the examiner an <u>idea</u> of how your answer will be <u>structured</u>.

> Even if you <u>agree</u> with the statement, you need to include <u>counter-arguments</u> to get top marks.

> **The answer** shows a <u>knowledge</u> of how <u>effective</u> government action has been in <u>different periods</u>.

> The answer gives examples of <u>how</u> governments improved public health.

> This is a <u>shortened example</u> — in the exam, you'll need to make <u>several more points</u> and include counter-arguments.

Make sure your response to the question is top-notch...

These long essay questions can seem really tricky at first... Always make sure you plan out your arguments before you start writing. This will help you make sure you include every point you want to make.

Exam Skills for the Thematic and Period Studies

Life in Medieval Britain, c.1250-c.1500

This page gives you a quick run down of what <u>life</u> was like for the people who lived in <u>late medieval Britain</u>.

The British Isles were split into Kingdoms

1) Medieval Britain was <u>divided</u> up into <u>individual</u> <u>kingdoms</u>. <u>England</u> and <u>Scotland</u> were run by separate monarchs and governments. This meant that there was frequent <u>conflict</u> between the two neighbours.

2) In the medieval era (sometimes called the Middle Ages) England also governed <u>Ireland</u> and <u>Wales</u> — English lords <u>controlled land</u> in Ireland and Wales for the English king.

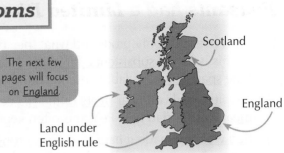

The next few pages will focus on <u>England</u>.

Scotland

England

Land under English rule

England had a Rural Economy that was based on Farming

1) About <u>90%</u> of the <u>population</u> in late medieval England lived in the <u>countryside</u>. There were a few <u>bigger towns</u> like London and York, but most towns were <u>small</u>, with fewer than <u>3000 inhabitants</u>.

2) The <u>land</u> was divided into special estates called <u>manors</u>. Each manor was <u>controlled</u> by a <u>lord</u> who was in charge of the <u>peasants</u> who lived on his land.

3) New markets started popping up in the <u>13th century</u> — locals produced things like ale, bread and textiles to <u>sell</u>. Most trade was <u>local</u>, but there were some <u>long-distance links</u> in England and with <u>Europe</u>.

Elite Landowners and the Church held lots of Power

1) Late medieval society was very <u>unequal</u> and based on a <u>social hierarchy</u>. A very small number of rich noble landowners and bishops ruled over a <u>big population</u> of poor <u>peasants</u> who worked the land.

2) <u>Political power</u> was linked to <u>land ownership</u>. The king often called on the <u>leading men</u> of the kingdom (e.g. noble landowners) to form a <u>Parliament</u> to help him rule. The <u>Church</u> owned loads of <u>land</u>, so it had lots of <u>power</u> — <u>bishops</u> often sat in <u>Parliament</u> and <u>advised</u> the king.

- England was divided into <u>local communities</u> called <u>parishes</u>. Each parish had a <u>church</u> and <u>priest</u>. Locals had to pay a special <u>tax</u> called a <u>tithe</u> (a <u>tenth</u> of what they earned) to <u>support</u> their parish priest. They were also expected to attend their <u>parish church</u> regularly.

- Few people <u>outside</u> the Church could <u>read</u> and gain their <u>own knowledge</u> about how things worked, so literate churchmen were the <u>main source</u> of people's <u>ideas</u> about things like life, death and disease.

England experienced Conflict and Disaster from the 14th Century

1) England was involved in the <u>Hundred Years' War</u> against France from <u>1337</u> to <u>1453</u>. There was also a civil war over the <u>English throne</u> between <u>1455</u> and <u>1487</u> — this is known as the <u>War of the Roses</u>.

2) There were <u>two</u> serious <u>natural disasters</u> that affected the <u>whole kingdom</u> in the 14th century:

In medieval times, Europe's climate <u>cooled down</u> — winters got <u>colder</u> and summers got <u>wetter</u>. People struggled to grow enough <u>food</u> and there was a <u>massive famine</u> across Europe after <u>crops failed</u> in 1315.

A very <u>contagious</u> and <u>deadly</u> plague called the <u>Black Death</u> spread across <u>Europe</u> in the 14th century. It reached England in <u>1348</u> and <u>killed</u> a large number of people (see p.7).

3) The <u>population declined</u> as a result of the <u>famine</u> and the <u>Black Death</u>, so there were <u>fewer people</u> to farm the <u>land</u>. As a result, peasants were able to demand <u>better wages</u> and <u>working conditions</u> from their lords. The <u>social structure</u> of England started to <u>change</u>, as lords had <u>less control</u> over peasants (p.8).

The 14th century was a bit grim...

Write a quick paragraph that explains what the economy of late medieval England was like.

REVISION TASK

Medieval Living Conditions

Life in medieval England was <u>tough</u> — many people lived in <u>poor conditions</u> that were <u>bad</u> for their <u>health</u>.

Peasants *had a* Limited Diet

1) Most peasants only produced what they needed to <u>survive</u> — this is called <u>subsistence farming</u>. As a result, there was very little <u>spare food</u> available and one bad harvest could be a <u>disaster</u>.

2) People who lived near <u>rivers</u> or the <u>sea</u> could catch fresh <u>fish</u>, but fresh <s>meat was hard to get</s>. Peasants often kept <u>cows</u> to make <u>dairy products</u>.

3) <u>Bad weather</u> made it harder to <u>grow crops</u> and could <u>damage</u> stored food (e.g. <u>poisonous fungus</u> could grow on <u>damp grain</u> and end up in <u>flour</u>).

4) Many people were <u>malnourished</u> (they weren't eating enough) and people could <u>starve</u>, especially when crop failures led to a major <u>famine</u> (see p.5).

> There was <u>no refrigeration</u>, so <u>fresh</u> <u>meat</u> and <u>fish</u> went off pretty quickly. However, they could be <u>preserved</u> with <u>salt</u> or be <u>cured</u>. Lots of peasants ate <u>preserved foods</u> like <u>pickled fish</u> and <u>cured bacon</u>.

Comment and Analysis

> Things were better for <u>wealthy</u> people — they could <u>buy extra food</u> and had a more <u>varied diet</u>.

Housing Conditions *were Very Basic*

1) Most houses were fairly <u>small</u> and only had one or two rooms. They had <u>wooden frames</u> and the walls were built using <u>sticks</u> and <u>clay</u>. Roofs were <u>thatched</u> (made using straw) and the floor was <u>hard earth</u>.

2) An <u>open fire</u> was used for <u>heating</u> and <u>cooking</u> — this was a poor source of heat and it gave off lots of <u>smoke</u> that was breathed in by people in the house.

3) <u>Glass</u> was <u>expensive</u>, so only the very <u>wealthy</u> could afford glass windows. Most houses just had <u>small openings</u> covered by <u>shutters</u>. This meant that houses were <u>dark</u>, <u>cold</u> and <u>stuffy</u>.

4) Things were different for <u>wealthy people</u>. They could afford to build <u>castles</u> or large <u>manor houses</u>. These stone buildings gradually got more comfortable as big <u>glass windows</u> and <u>large fireplaces</u> were added.

5) Most medieval homes had no <u>running water</u> or <u>toilets</u>. Most <u>water</u> for drinking and cooking came from <u>wells</u>, <u>rivers</u> and <u>streams</u>. There were <u>no sewers</u>, so most people just threw their waste into the <u>street</u> or a <u>river</u>.

© Historic England / Mary Evans

This drawing shows what the inside of a 13th century peasant's house might have been like. Many people had to bring their animals into the house at night.

Public Health *suffered because of these Poor Living Conditions*

1) People often lived in <u>cramped houses</u> with their family and <u>animals</u>, so diseases spread quickly. <u>Malnutrition</u> also made people more likely to catch <u>diseases</u> — <u>famine</u> often led to <u>epidemics</u> of serious diseases like <u>flu</u> and <u>smallpox</u>.

> An <u>epidemic</u> is when lots of people in the <u>same area</u> catch the <u>same disease</u> in a <u>short</u> space of time.

2) <u>Life expectancy</u> was very <u>poor</u>. Infections, accidents and serious illnesses (like tuberculosis) were common. Lots of <u>children</u> died young — they were vulnerable to <u>childhood diseases</u> (like measles) and <u>accidents</u> in the home.

3) People knew that <u>dirty water</u> and <u>human waste</u> were linked to <u>bad health</u>, but they thought that it was the <u>smell</u> of these things that caused illness (the miasma theory — see p.7). People <u>didn't understand</u> how important it was to have <u>good sanitation</u> (waste disposal and clean water supplies), so many lived in <u>unclean conditions</u>. Illnesses like <u>dysentery</u> were common.

4) Medieval people didn't know about <u>germs</u>, so they didn't really <u>understand</u> how to stop diseases from spreading. <u>Ideas</u> about disease were mostly based on <u>old texts</u> from Ancient Greece and Rome — these texts weren't always right, but few people <u>questioned</u> them.

Life in medieval England was no picnic...

Write an explanation of how living conditions in late medieval England contributed to poor public health. Give examples in your answer. [10]

EXAM QUESTION

Responses to the Black Death

The Black Death struck in the 14th century in Europe, and had a devastating effect. People tried to explain why it had happened, but there was little that could be done to stop the disease.

The Black Death was a devastating Epidemic

1) The Black Death was a series of plagues that swept Europe in the 14th century. It was really two illnesses:

- Bubonic plague, spread by the bites of fleas from rats carried on ships. This caused headaches and a high temperature, followed by pus-filled swellings on the skin.
- Pneumonic plague was airborne — it was spread by coughs and sneezes. It attacked the lungs, making it painful to breathe and causing victims to cough up blood.

2) The disease first arrived in Britain in 1348. Some historians think at least a third of the British population died as a result of the Black Death in 1348-50. There were further outbreaks of the Black Death throughout the Middle Ages.

3) It killed the majority of people who got infected. It also killed quickly — people were very scared.

People Didn't Know what Caused the Black Death...

No-one at the time knew what caused diseases like the plague. There were several popular theories — some of them came from Ancient Greek and Roman medical knowledge.

The Theory of the Four Humours was created by the Ancient Greek doctor Hippocrates (c.460-c.377 BC). Hippocrates believed that the body was made up of four fluids (or humours) — blood, phlegm, yellow bile and black bile. These were linked to the four seasons and the four elements. They needed to be in balance for good health.

The miasma theory is the idea that bad air (or miasma) causes disease when someone breathes it in. This bad air may come from human waste or dead bodies — anything that creates a bad smell.

Some people believed that the Black Death was a judgement from God and disease was caused by sin.

... but they tried different ways to Prevent and Treat it

1) People who thought sin was the cause tried to prevent the spread of the disease through prayer and fasting.

2) Those who blamed humour imbalances tried to get rid of the Black Death through bloodletting and purging.

3) Those who thought that the disease was caused by miasma carried strong smelling herbs or lit fires to purify the air. In 1349, Edward III sent an order to the Lord Mayor of London to remove filth from the city streets, in the hope of removing bad smells.

4) Believers in astrology carried diamonds and rubies, which they believed could protect against the Black Death. People also carried charms or used 'magic' potions containing arsenic.

> Bloodletting was the practice of removing blood from the body by making a small cut or by using blood-sucking leeches.

> Purging is the act of getting rid of other fluids from the body by excreting — doctors gave their patients laxatives to help the purging process.

Comment and Analysis

People's different beliefs about the cause of disease influenced the ways they tried to prevent or cure the plague. But because their ideas about the cause of disease were wrong, their attempts at prevention and treatment were mostly ineffective.

My oh mi-asma, the Black Death was horrible...

Think about how people's beliefs shaped their approach to plague prevention. In the exam, if you write about what people did to avoid it, try to give reasons why they took this approach.

EXAM TIP

Responses to the Black Death

Local governments stepped in to try to stop the Black Death from spreading any further. However, as the plague continued to infect more and more people, it led to a struggle between landowners and peasants.

Local Governments tried to Prevent the spread of the disease

1) Some people in Winchester thought that through miasma (p.7), you could catch the plague from being close to the bodies of dead victims. When the town's cemetery became too full to take any more plague victims, the townspeople refused to let the bishop extend the cemetery in the town centre. Instead, they insisted that new cemeteries be built outside of the town, away from the houses.

2) The town of Gloucester tried to shut itself off from the outside world after hearing the Black Death had reached Bristol. This suggests that they thought the plague was spread by human contact. Their attempt at prevention was unsuccessful — many people in the town died of the Black Death.

> 'Deadly pestilence had suddenly broken out in the said place and neighbourhood, and had daily increased in severity, so that grave fears were entertained for the safety of those coming here at the time.'
> King Edward III on his decision to close Parliament.

3) By November 1348, the Black Death had reached London. In January 1349, King Edward III took the decision to close Parliament.

4) London was particularly unclean at the time. The streets were in terrible condition — for example, there wasn't an underground sewerage system, so waste was just left in the street. But the situation only got worse when the Black Death hit. When the workers who cleaned London's streets fell victim to the plague, the King demanded that the local government do something to clean up the streets.

Comment and Analysis

The national government didn't really do anything about the plague until the 1500s (p.14). Instead, towns and citizens had to try to stop the plague from spreading any further themselves. They also had to deal with the rising death toll.

The Black Death caused Social Change

1) After the Black Death, so many people had died that there were far fewer peasants available to work.

2) Lots of villages were abandoned and many plots of land were empty because the people who had lived there had died from the plague. As a result, landowners lost income because no-one was working or living on their land.

3) It was difficult to find new peasants to farm the land because of the huge drop in population. This meant that they could demand higher wages from landowners, and move around to find better work. The cost of land also decreased, allowing some peasants to buy land for the first time.

4) The growing power of peasants threatened noble landowners. The government created laws to restrict the peasants:

- **1349 Ordinance of Labourers** — This prevented peasants from moving to look for better jobs or asking for more pay. Wages had to be the same as they were before the plague struck. This ordinance (order given by the King) turned into the 1351 Statute of Labourers.

- **1363 Sumptuary Law** — Noble landowners were worried by the growing wealth among peasants — they wanted society to stay the same. The Sumptuary Law was introduced to control what clothes peasants wore and what food they ate. However, it was difficult to make sure that people followed this law.

5) In spite of the laws, peasants still succeeded in getting higher wages. There wasn't much option for noble landowners — they needed the peasants to provide their income.

The Black Death had a big impact on Britain...

Split a piece of paper into three and write 'Winchester', 'Gloucester' and 'London'. Under each heading, summarise the action taken by the town to stop the plague from spreading.

Public Health in Towns and Monasteries

In the medieval period, how <u>healthy</u> people were had a lot do with the area <u>where they lived</u>.

Living Conditions *in Towns* were pretty Poor

1) Most towns were <u>small</u>, especially after the <u>Black Death</u> when a lot of people died (p.7-8). In 1300, London was the <u>only</u> big city — tens of thousands of people lived there.

2) Houses were usually made of <u>wood</u> and were <u>crammed together</u> — <u>overcrowding</u> and <u>fires</u> were common problems.

3) A lot of <u>towns</u> didn't have <u>clean water supplies</u> or <u>sewerage systems</u> — waste was chucked into the <u>street</u> or into <u>rivers</u> to be washed away. Sewage from <u>latrines</u> (pits with wooden seats) leaked into the <u>ground</u> and got into <u>wells</u>.

> Towns did have <u>green spaces</u> where people could grow <u>fruit</u> and <u>vegetables</u> and <u>graze animals</u>. This helped to give people a fairly <u>balanced diet</u>.

4) Businesses and homes <u>weren't separated</u> — butchers, tanners and dyers threw <u>toxic waste</u> into rivers and residential streets. People had to get their <u>drinking water</u> from rivers and wells that were <u>contaminated</u>.

5) In the 1230s, a <u>water channel</u> called the <u>Great Conduit</u> was built to bring <u>clean water</u> into London, as the Thames was getting <u>too toxic</u>.

6) In <u>1388</u>, the <u>government</u> ordered <u>town authorities</u> to keep the streets <u>free of waste</u>. Towns introduced <u>public health measures</u> to tackle waste, sewage and pollution and to create a <u>clean water supply</u>.

> Many towns, like York, ordered <u>toxic businesses</u> like butchers, tanners, fishmongers and dyers to move <u>outside</u> the <u>city walls</u>.

> York and London both <u>banned</u> people from <u>dumping waste</u> in the street. These cities also built <u>latrines</u> over <u>rivers</u> so that sewage could be <u>carried away</u>.

Comment and Analysis

The measures taken by the government show that people knew <u>living conditions</u> were somehow linked to <u>health</u>. However, many <u>regulations</u> were passed, which suggests that each regulation on its own <u>wasn't</u> very <u>effective</u>. Town authorities didn't have enough <u>money</u> or <u>knowledge</u> to <u>properly</u> fix these public health issues.

Monasteries *were* Healthier *than Towns*

Monasteries had <u>cleaner water</u> than towns and had good systems for getting rid of <u>waste</u> and <u>sewage</u>. Monks also had access to <u>books</u> on healing and they <u>knew</u> how to <u>grow herbs</u> and make <u>herbal remedies</u>.

> This is what historians think <u>Fountains Abbey</u> in Yorkshire might have been like.

> <u>Sick monks</u> were cared for in <u>infirmaries</u>. These <u>infirmaries</u> normally had their own <u>kitchen</u> that served <u>good meals</u> and <u>meat</u> to help sick monks to <u>recover</u>.

> Monasteries <u>separated</u> clean and dirty <u>water</u>. They had one water supply for <u>cooking</u> and <u>drinking</u> and one for <u>drainage</u> and <u>washing</u>, so people didn't have to drink <u>dirty water</u> like they did in towns.

> Some monasteries had <u>hospitals</u> that <u>cared</u> for <u>poor people</u> from the <u>local community</u> when they were sick and gave shelter to <u>travellers</u>. Benedictine monks believed <u>caring</u> for the sick was the <u>most important</u> Christian duty.

> Most monasteries were built near <u>rivers</u>. If there was no river, <u>man-made waterways</u> were built to supply <u>clean water</u>.

> <u>Latrines</u> were put in <u>separate buildings</u>, which were often built over streams of <u>running water</u> that <u>carried sewage away</u>.

Infirmary

Kitchen

Guest Houses

© Historic England / Mary Evans

It was <u>easier</u> to create <u>healthy living conditions</u> in <u>monasteries</u> than it was in towns.

1) Monasteries were <u>wealthy</u>, so they could <u>afford</u> to build <u>infrastructure</u> like latrine buildings and waterways to keep their water <u>clean</u>. Towns had to rely on <u>wealthy individuals</u> to <u>fund</u> these kinds of projects.

2) Monastery <u>populations</u> were <u>small</u> and had <u>one leader</u> (the Abbot) — he had the <u>power</u> to <u>enforce</u> rules about cleanliness and waste disposal. Getting <u>hundreds</u> of <u>townspeople</u> to adopt cleaner habits was <u>trickier</u> — towns didn't have one person <u>in charge</u> who could easily <u>enforce</u> public health measures.

City livin' ain't all it's cracked up to be...

Draw two boxes — one with the heading 'Towns' and the other with the heading 'Monasteries'. Fill in the boxes with bullet points about health and living conditions in each location.

Social, Economic and Cultural Changes

The <u>economy</u> changed a lot during the early modern period, and England's <u>towns</u> grew rapidly.

The Population Grew and more people started to Live in Towns

1) England's <u>population</u> grew <u>quickly</u> in the first part of the early modern period. In the <u>1520s</u>, there were about <u>2.4 million</u> people in England. By the middle of the <u>17th century</u>, the population had <u>risen</u> to about <u>5 million</u>. After this, the population stayed pretty <u>stable</u> until the middle of the 18th century.

2) Towns were also <u>growing</u>. In the <u>1500s</u>, England only had a small number of <u>large towns</u> (with a population of <u>5000</u> to <u>10,000 people</u>). Between <u>1600</u> and <u>1750</u>, the number of large towns <u>doubled</u>.

3) By <u>1750</u>, most people still lived in the countryside, but many people had <u>migrated</u> (moved) to towns to <u>find work</u>.

> 16th century towns were still pretty <u>small</u> compared to modern towns. At the time, <u>Norwich</u> was one of the biggest towns in England with a <u>population</u> of about <u>12,000</u>. Today it has over <u>130,000</u> inhabitants.

4) This had an impact on <u>public health</u>, since <u>living conditions</u> in towns could be quite bad (p.12).

Farming was More Productive in the 17th and 18th Centuries

As the <u>population</u> rose, the demand for <u>food</u> and <u>land</u> also <u>increased</u>. As a result, lots of landowners <u>increased</u> their <u>rents</u>. <u>Food prices</u> also started to <u>rise</u> quite rapidly in the <u>16th century</u>.

1) <u>Landowners</u> wanted to make as much <u>profit</u> as possible from the rising prices — they improved <u>farming techniques</u> so they could produce more <u>food</u>.

2) Open fields were <u>enclosed</u> to create <u>large farms</u>, instead of fields being shared between many farmers. <u>Poorer quality</u> land that hadn't been farmed before (called <u>marginal land</u>) was cleared and enclosed too.

> These <u>enclosures</u> of farm land meant many farmers were evicted. They were forced to <u>leave</u> their <u>villages</u> and migrate to <u>towns</u> or <u>cities</u> in search of <u>work</u>.

3) <u>New crops</u> were introduced and farmers used <u>new techniques</u> to increase the <u>fertility</u> of their land. For example, <u>water meadows</u> (land flooded with a layer of water) improved <u>hay</u> and <u>livestock</u> farming.

Britain was more Commercial by the 18th Century

1) By the 18th century, many <u>townspeople</u> worked in <u>trade</u> and <u>small industries</u> (e.g. textile production and mining). More people in <u>rural areas</u> were working in <u>industry</u> too. These people weren't producing their <u>own food</u>, so they <u>relied</u> on <u>others</u> to survive.

2) The economy became more <u>commercial</u> (it was based on buying and selling of goods). <u>Shops</u> started to open in <u>villages</u> as well as <u>towns</u>.

3) Some <u>areas</u> became known for producing <u>certain products</u> (e.g. <u>Newcastle</u> mined lots of <u>coal</u>). Some areas started to <u>farm</u> certain <u>crops</u> or types of <u>livestock</u>. This is called <u>specialisation</u>.

Comment and Analysis

Wages <u>rose</u>, but not as fast as <u>prices</u> — many people <u>struggled</u> to make ends meet, and <u>poverty</u> increased. Many people <u>couldn't afford</u> to <u>eat well</u>, which had an impact on their <u>health</u>.

4) More <u>long-distance trade</u> developed. <u>Farmers</u> and <u>local industries</u> sold their <u>goods</u> to people in <u>towns</u> across the country, instead of just their <u>local area</u>.

- <u>England</u> started to set up successful <u>overseas colonies</u> from the <u>17th century</u>, which created <u>international trade links</u>. England had been trading with <u>Europe</u> for centuries, but <u>merchants</u> started to make journeys to <u>Africa</u>, <u>Asia</u> and the <u>Americas</u> in the <u>17th century</u>.

- This created <u>jobs</u> in shipping and trade (especially in <u>ports</u>), which contributed to the <u>growth</u> of towns. <u>Industrial production</u> also increased as English manufacturers <u>exported</u> more goods <u>overseas</u>.

It was all go in early modern England...

Write a short paragraph that explains how and why towns grew in early modern England.

Social, Economic and Cultural Changes

The early modern period was a time of <u>social change</u>, <u>learning</u> and <u>discovery</u> in England.

A new Middle Class emerged in the Early Modern period

1) In the early <u>16th century</u>, people were part of classes based on their <u>status</u> and <u>wealth</u>. These classes <u>weren't equal</u> — they were part of a <u>social hierarchy</u> with the king or queen at the top.

> <u>Nobles</u> (e.g. dukes and earls) were the social elite. They owned <u>land</u> and <u>governed</u> England.

> The <u>gentry</u> were next. They <u>owned land</u> and lived off the <u>income</u> it provided.

> Most people were <u>commoners</u>. They ranged from <u>rich farmers</u> (yeomen) to <u>labourers</u> who worked for <u>wages</u>.

2) As <u>more people</u> made a living by becoming a <u>merchant</u> or <u>professional</u> (like a lawyer), these classes started to <u>break down</u>. For example, lots of successful commoners <u>bought land</u> and joined the <u>gentry</u>. This also meant that some people were able to make <u>more money</u> and lift themselves out of <u>poverty</u>.

More people were Educated in Schools and Universities

1) Lots of <u>new schools</u> were <u>built</u> between the 16th century and the early 17th century. Local schools called <u>petty schools</u> were set up all over the country (often by churchmen). They taught basic skills like <u>reading</u> and <u>writing</u>.

2) Rich commoners and the gentry often paid for <u>grammar schools</u> to be built in their <u>local area</u>. These schools taught <u>the Classics</u> (mostly things written by Ancient Romans and Greeks), as well as <u>reading</u>, <u>writing</u> and basic <u>maths</u>.

3) In the <u>16th century</u>, it became <u>fashionable</u> for children of nobles and the gentry to be taught <u>Latin</u> and <u>Greek</u> and study <u>the Classics</u>. More children from <u>richer families</u> started to go to <u>grammar schools</u> and <u>universities</u>, which was part of a <u>big increase</u> in the number of people going to university.

Comment and Analysis

Grammar schools charged <u>fees</u>, so their students were mostly children of the <u>gentry</u> and <u>rich commoners</u> (like merchants). Other children were more likely to go to <u>petty schools</u>, as they were <u>cheaper</u> to attend.

> Before the 16th century, <u>universities</u> taught <u>subjects</u> that were needed by <u>churchmen</u> and <u>professionals</u>. As more of the <u>gentry</u> started going to university, more <u>modern subjects</u> (like <u>geography</u> and <u>literature</u>) were studied.

> By the <u>17th century</u>, most <u>nobles</u>, many of the <u>gentry</u> and some <u>richer commoners</u> were <u>literate</u> (able to read and write). Literacy was <u>lower</u> among <u>the poor</u>, as many <u>couldn't afford</u> to go to school or had to <u>work</u>. While more people were <u>educated</u>, most people's knowledge about <u>health</u> and <u>medicine</u> was still limited.

Science and Technology developed in the Renaissance

The <u>Renaissance</u> was a time of <u>learning</u> and <u>creativity</u> in <u>Europe</u> that lasted from the <u>14th</u> to the <u>17th century</u>.

1) The <u>printing press</u> was introduced to England in the late <u>15th century</u>. By the <u>16th century</u>, a <u>printing industry</u> had taken off. <u>Books</u> and other <u>written materials</u> became widely <u>available</u>.

> <u>Printing presses</u> made it <u>easier</u> and <u>cheaper</u> to produce written materials. Little booklets called <u>chapbooks</u> were <u>produced</u> by printers and sold to the <u>public</u>. They included things like <u>popular stories</u> and <u>songs</u>. The first English <u>newspapers</u> were printed in the <u>17th century</u>.

An image of an early 17th century printing press.

2) <u>Vesalius</u>, an Italian medical professor, wrote books about the <u>human anatomy</u>. His works were printed and distributed around Europe, allowing <u>British doctors</u> to learn from his discoveries.

> The development of <u>printing</u> made it <u>easier</u> to <u>share ideas</u> and <u>theories</u>.

3) The <u>basic ideas</u> and <u>methods</u> of modern science were <u>developed</u> in this period. In <u>1620</u>, an English academic called <u>Francis Bacon</u> argued that <u>scientific truths</u> can only be <u>proven</u> if they are <u>tested</u> many times using <u>scientific experiments</u>. Today, experiments are <u>always</u> carried out to confirm theories.

Education was a pressing issue in early modern times...

Jot down the ways that England's society, culture and economy changed in the early modern era.

The People's Health, c.1250 to present

Early Modern Living Conditions

Living conditions in early modern towns <u>weren't great</u>, and as towns expanded things only got <u>worse</u>. People's health was <u>poor</u> because of this, so local governments tried to make towns <u>better</u> places to live.

An Increase in Population made early modern towns Worse

1) <u>Early modern towns</u> suffered from some of the <u>same issues</u> as <u>medieval towns</u> (p.9).

2) Towns were getting bigger and bigger in England (p.10) — this made living conditions <u>worse</u> than ever.

3) <u>Overcrowding</u> was a serious problem. There <u>weren't</u> any <u>restrictions</u> like there are now — people could build wherever they wanted to. This led to <u>narrow streets</u> and a lack of <u>light</u> and <u>fresh air</u> in houses.

4) <u>Streets</u> were generally in <u>poor condition</u>. They were very <u>unclean</u> and <u>animals</u> were free to walk around, adding to the uncleanliness.

5) People used to collect water from <u>rivers</u>, <u>conduits</u> (pipes for water) and <u>wells</u>. However, this water wasn't always <u>clean</u> because sanitation was poor. There were also vendors who <u>sold water</u>. <u>Water shortages</u> were sometimes a <u>problem</u> because there was so many people.

6) Town councils <u>couldn't cope</u> with the growing population and they <u>lacked</u> the <u>power</u> to enforce rules on sanitation.

> **Comment and Analysis**
>
> <u>Medieval towns</u> also had <u>difficulty</u> tackling poor conditions (p.9). <u>Growing populations</u> in towns meant that systems for waste disposal and sewerage <u>struggled to cope</u>.

Poor living conditions had a Bad Effect on people's Health

1) Since living conditions were so <u>terrible</u>, early modern towns became <u>less healthy</u> than medieval ones.

2) The <u>death rate</u> in towns was <u>very high</u>. Town populations were <u>only</u> rising because of <u>migration</u> — not because of people having families. <u>Richer people</u> tended to <u>live longer</u> than poor people though.

- The lower classes ate basic food such as <u>bread</u> and <u>vegetables</u>, but regularly there <u>wasn't enough</u> to go around. <u>Poor nutrition</u> meant that country peasants struggled to stay healthy — <u>illness</u> and <u>disease</u> were common problems.

- People in the countryside were also <u>more likely</u> to <u>survive illness</u> than people in towns.

> **Comment and Analysis**
>
> Because of the poor living conditions, <u>disease</u> spread <u>quickly</u> around towns. However, since towns were becoming more <u>closely connected</u> through commercialisation and long-distance trade, disease began to spread <u>easily</u> around the <u>country</u>.

Local Governments took steps to Improve Living Conditions

1) <u>Local governments</u> began to improve living conditions in towns in the 1600s.

2) They had the <u>authority</u> to improve many different aspects of life in town, such as <u>street paving</u>, <u>lighting</u> and <u>keeping roads clean</u>.

> At this point, the <u>national government</u> didn't have much to do with improving living conditions.

3) Several towns used Acts of Parliament to change the <u>law</u> in their <u>local area</u>:

- <u>London</u> and <u>Westminster</u> introduced a <u>town council</u> in 1662.
- <u>Bristol</u> (1701) and <u>Beverley</u> (1727) introduced <u>taxes</u> to help pay for keeping the <u>streets lit</u> and <u>tidy</u>.
- <u>Salisbury</u> used an Act of Parliament to be able to organise features such as <u>paving</u> in 1736.

4) <u>Urban Improvement Commissioners</u> were introduced in the first half of the 18th century. They were responsible for <u>carrying out</u> the work to make living conditions <u>better</u>, such as projects to <u>clean up</u> and improve the <u>condition</u> of the <u>streets</u> and get rid of <u>rubbish</u>.

Acts of Parliament paved the way for better towns...

Write down four ways that people could access water in early modern towns.

Early Modern Living Conditions

Although Acts of Parliament improved the streets, <u>housing</u> still needed to be improved. <u>Fires</u> in London and Warwick led to advances. Towns also began to give greater consideration to <u>town planning</u>.

Fires in London and Warwick led to Improvements in housing

1) <u>Houses</u> in the 17th century had <u>improved</u> for many wealthier people. They had <u>better furniture</u> and the buildings were more <u>modern</u> — glass windows and fireplaces were quite <u>common</u>.

> It's possible that some people got over illnesses <u>faster</u> because of the <u>improvements</u> made to housing.

> While conditions had <u>improved</u> dramatically between 1500 and 1700 for <u>richer people</u>, the <u>poor</u> had seen <u>little difference</u> in those two centuries.

2) However, many were still made from <u>wood</u>, so <u>fires</u> were dangerous:

- In <u>1666</u>, the <u>Great Fire of London</u> destroyed over <u>10,000</u> houses.
- To avoid a similar situation in the future, houses were rebuilt using <u>fire-proof building materials</u> such as bricks.
- Using bricks made it harder for <u>rats</u> to get into houses, which reduced the risk of <u>plague epidemics</u> (p.14-15).
- Some London streets were <u>widened</u>, but many <u>stayed</u> as they were <u>before</u> the fire — narrow and cramped. People <u>weren't willing</u> to move their homes and businesses to make way for <u>bigger streets</u>.

The Great Fire of London.

© Illustrated London News Ltd/Mary Evans

- Hundreds of buildings in <u>Warwick</u> were ruined by a <u>fire</u> in <u>1694</u>.
- The <u>town centre</u> was worst hit, which affected the <u>wealthy residents</u> and <u>important businesses</u> that were based there. Since the rich were affected, there was greater <u>urgency</u> to fix the burnt buildings and get them up and running again.
- <u>Regulations</u> were introduced which banned people from rebuilding using <u>flammable materials</u> such as timber. Houses in the town centre had to be constructed to certain <u>measurements</u>, which made the streets more <u>ordered</u> and made it harder for fire to <u>spread</u> in future.

> **Comment and Analysis**
>
> The rebuilding in Warwick highlighted the <u>differences</u> between the <u>rich</u> and the <u>poor</u>. There was a big difference between the <u>new buildings</u> in the centre and the <u>old</u>, <u>crowded houses</u> on the outskirts where the poor lived.

Local governments started to think about Town Planning

1) Local governments began to look at towns as a <u>whole</u> in the 17th and 18th centuries — how the buildings <u>looked</u> and how the streets were <u>laid out</u>. As attitudes towards <u>town planning</u> were changing, the fires in London and Warwick gave people the opportunity to try new ideas in these towns.

2) Town improvements became <u>more frequent</u> in the 17th and 18th centuries, but there were also attempts to make towns <u>more pleasant</u>. <u>Public squares</u> were a new idea that became quite popular. <u>Covent Garden</u> in London was built in the <u>1630s</u>, and more squares were later built in the capital and in towns like <u>Warwick</u> and <u>Bristol</u>.

3) Narrow streets were <u>opened up</u> and made wider, while many <u>new streets</u> were built. <u>New community buildings</u> were also constructed.

4) The streets were improved because towns wanted to seem more <u>appealing</u> to other <u>businesses</u> and <u>tourists</u> that were arriving.

> In the 1500s, London's <u>population</u> was rising so quickly that it was a <u>struggle</u> to build enough <u>housing</u> for everyone. <u>Elizabeth I</u> stepped in towards the end of the century with an order to <u>manage</u> the increasing amount of <u>construction</u>.

> Town planning helped local authorities to <u>improve living conditions</u> and reduce some of the <u>public health hazards</u> that were common in towns. For example, the new regulations introduced in <u>Warwick</u> after the fire in 1694 meant that the <u>streets</u> were <u>more open</u> — <u>fires</u> were less likely to spread and there was <u>less overcrowding</u>.

Planning is everything in towns — and exams...

Summarise town living conditions in the early modern period, using examples in your answer. [9]

Responses to Outbreaks of Plague

The plague struck early modern Britain many times. It was a deadly disease, but there was no treatment available. The government introduced some regulations to try to put an end to the outbreaks.

There were Several Outbreaks of the Plague over 300 Years

1) The first big outbreak of the plague was the Black Death in 1348 (p.7). Outbreaks continued to happen right up until 1665, when the Great Plague struck (p.15). After that, the plague was finally eradicated.

2) The plague had a devastating effect on Britain — it spread very easily and the majority of people who got infected died. During outbreaks, people were dying so quickly that it was difficult to deal with the bodies.

3) During bad outbreaks like the Great Plague, communities were hit hard and the population dropped. Business suffered greatly and some land couldn't be farmed due to a lack of workers.

4) Over those 300 years, there weren't any advances in understanding what caused the plague or how it was spread, and no new treatments were developed.

Plague Orders came into effect in London

1) In 1518, the first steps were taken by the national government against the plague when it passed plague orders in London. Straw had to be hung outside the houses that were infected, and the people that lived there had to carry a white stick so others could tell that they might have the disease.

2) 21 further plague orders were introduced in 1583. Areas where people crowded together were closed, and streets were tidied and kept in better condition.

3) However, employing enough people to enforce plague orders was a problem.

Steps were taken to Prevent the plague Nationally

1) The national government finally took nationwide action against the plague:

   - **1578** — The government issued 17 national plague orders. These orders required everyone that lived in an infected house to stay in quarantine for a minimum of 6 weeks. The government also wanted to introduce taxes to support people in quarantine.
   - **1604** — This plague act meant people could be forced to go into quarantine if they resisted.

2) The laws of 1578 and 1604 were the first attempts at a national level to prevent the spread of an infectious disease. However, the government had been late to respond to the plague in the country as a whole — its national plague orders came 240 years after the Black Death struck.

3) The government continued to introduce similar orders up until the 1660s. Because there was no progress in understanding the cause of the disease, and there were no advances in treatment and prevention, the government just published the same laws again and again.

The government was Influenced by Other Countries

1) The government's actions were based on plague prevention measures that other countries in Europe had introduced.

2) For example, pest houses were a European invention. People were confined in them until they died to stop the disease from spreading further. After the threat of another outbreak in 1630, it was recommended that pest houses be built in London too.

Comment and Analysis

England was far behind other European countries in terms of tackling the plague. Italian cities, such as Florence, were the first to come up with laws to deal with its spread.

Britain was plagued by the plague for hundreds of years...

Write down all the measures taken by the government to tackle the spread of the plague. Make sure you include the date of the law and what it did.

The People's Health, c.1250 to present

Responses to Outbreaks of Plague

While the government was trying to tackle the ongoing outbreaks of the plague, town councils and their citizens were taking matters into their own hands. They had their own ideas of how best to stop the plague.

Towns introduced Local Measures to combat the plague

Many towns took their own steps to tackle the plague and reduce the effect it would have:

People in quarantine needed food, but help from charities and family members wasn't reliable. To avoid the possibility of the infected leaving out of hunger, taxes to support quarantined people were announced in York in 1550.

Comment and Analysis

Some town policies were similar to national laws. York introduced taxes in 1550, then the government wanted to do the same nationally in 1578 (p.14). However, both local and national governments weren't powerful enough to make sure the laws were followed, so they weren't effective in stopping the plague.

In the mid 1500s, some towns tried more extreme forms of quarantine. In Gloucester and Leicester, whole parts of the towns were shut off to stop the plague from spreading to other neighbourhoods.

The village of Eyam took drastic action in 1665. After the plague arrived in a box of infected cloth from London, the inhabitants were quarantined and the entire village was closed off to stop the plague from spreading to nearby areas. A huge number of residents were killed by the plague.

The town council in Cambridge tried various methods throughout the 1500s and 1600s to stop the plague spreading. For example, they used strong smells to clear the air in official buildings, quarantined houses that were known to have the plague and opened several pest houses (which unfortunately were only finished in 1666, when the plague began to die out).

Various Ways of Controlling the Great Plague were tried in London

- In 1665, London was struck by the Great Plague. The death toll was about 100,000 — this was around 20% of the city's population.
- Fear and anxiety meant that many people fled the city, but only richer people had this option. During the 1665-66 outbreak, King Charles II, his court and Parliament all went to Oxford.
- Some of the people who left were the very people who could help — doctors and churchmen.

Local councils took measures to try to stop the spread of the plague. They were largely ineffective because they didn't know that the disease was caused by bacteria and transmitted by fleas on rats.

1) Houses that were quarantined were locked and a red cross was painted on the door, along with the words 'Lord have mercy upon us.' Some people thought God had brought the plague to punish sinners.
2) Areas where people crowded together such as theatres were closed.
3) The dead bodies of plague victims were buried in mass graves away from houses. Carts organised by the authorities drove through the city crying 'bring out your dead!', collecting corpses for burial.
4) Local councils paid for lots of cats and dogs to be killed, because they thought they carried the plague.

Individuals took their own steps to avoid catching the plague, such as trying not to touch other people. For example, if someone had to give money in a shop, the coins might be placed in a jar of vinegar. Some people carried bunches of herbs or flowers to improve the air because they thought that 'bad air' (miasma) caused the disease (see p.7).

The approaches people took reflected the range of beliefs about the cause of the plague. These beliefs were mainly based on religion or inaccurate medical theories.

Don't plague aims — this is serious stuff...
Jot down five ways that councils and individuals tried to reduce the risk of getting the plague.

The Gin Craze, 1660-1751

From 1660-1751, gin consumption reached <u>dangerous levels</u> — the government had to step in to <u>control</u> it.

Gin was Very Popular in the 17th and 18th centuries

1) In the late 1600s, there was a '<u>gin craze</u>' in Britain. Several factors led to gin being very <u>cheap</u>:

Corn	Beer	War
The <u>price</u> of corn (used to make gin) was <u>low</u>, which meant that gin was <u>cheap</u> to <u>produce</u>.	From 1688, the amount of <u>tax</u> payable on beer <u>rose</u>, but gin taxes stayed the <u>same</u>. Gin became more popular among the <u>lower classes</u> because it didn't cost as much.	At the end of the 17th century, Britain was involved in a <u>war</u> with <u>France</u>. The government passed laws to <u>stop</u> people <u>importing French brandy</u> and instead <u>promoted British alcohol</u>.

2) Since it was so cheap, gin <u>consumption</u> spiralled <u>out of control</u>, especially among the <u>poor</u>. There were growing <u>concerns</u> about the effect this was having on society.

Excessive drinking was Damaging for Health and Society

1) By the 1730s, it was very <u>easy</u> to buy gin. <u>Thousands</u> of places in London were <u>selling</u> it and every year <u>millions</u> of gallons were being <u>made</u>.

2) Excessive drinking led to a serious <u>increase</u> in <u>crime</u>, various <u>health problems</u> and population <u>decline</u>. There were several <u>campaigns</u> against gin drinking.

Demands for reform in 1736 came from <u>Parliament</u>, some <u>bishops</u> and <u>charities</u>. People were worried about the effect of gin consumption on <u>health</u> and <u>society</u>.

William Hogarth's drawing 'Gin Lane' (1751) backed the campaign against gin. It shows some of the health issues caused by drinking too much gin. For example, a woman lets her child fall from her arms, and a man sits dying, holding a glass. The image also shows other problems such as starvation and suicide.

The Government tried to Control the Sale of gin

1) To combat the negative effects of gin drinking, the <u>government</u> introduced several <u>laws</u>:

- **1729** — The government passed a law that made <u>buying</u> a £20 licence <u>compulsory</u> for gin houses and <u>increased</u> the <u>tax</u> payable on gin. However, it was <u>difficult</u> to stop illegal trade.
- **1736** — The <u>Gin Act</u> was passed, which raised <u>taxes</u> on gin again. It also increased the price of a <u>licence</u> to <u>£50</u> per year. However, the government didn't really <u>enforce</u> with the Act.

2) The laws made things <u>worse</u>. High taxes and licences encouraged the trade of '<u>bootleg</u>' gin — gin made and sold <u>illegally</u>. It was <u>dangerous</u> to drink because it was often made with poisonous chemicals.

3) In <u>1743</u>, to fund an ongoing war in Europe, Parliament passed another <u>Gin Act</u> which <u>cancelled out</u> the 1736 Act by <u>reducing charges</u> on the making and selling of gin.

The government was eventually pressured to pass the <u>1751 Gin Act</u>. This <u>restricted</u> who could sell gin (only those who paid rent and taxes) and the <u>tax</u> imposed on gin was <u>raised</u> slightly. Gin drinking had <u>fallen considerably</u> by the end of the decade.

Comment and Analysis

By the <u>1750s</u>, the gin craze was mostly <u>over</u>. Government action did help, but other factors played a part. <u>Beer prices</u> began to come <u>down</u> and <u>production</u> was <u>increasing</u>. Also, <u>corn prices rose</u> so gin became more <u>expensive</u> at a time when people had less money due to <u>lower wages</u> and an <u>increase</u> in the cost of food.

Ima-gin if the government hadn't stepped in...

Summarise the government's responses to the gin craze. Include examples in your answer. [9]

Industrialisation and Urbanisation

After 1750, Britain experienced an <u>industrial revolution</u> that caused more people to live <u>closer together</u> in <u>cities</u>. This created new deadly <u>epidemics</u>, but also new <u>attitudes</u> that would help improve people's health.

Before industrialisation Britain was a *Rural Society*

1) In 1700, the majority of Britain's population of 5 million still lived in the <u>countryside</u> or in small towns. <u>London</u> was the only city that had a population of about <u>600,000</u> people.

2) Most people still worked in <u>agriculture</u> (see p.6). Others worked in <u>cottage industries</u> — small businesses that families ran from their own homes.

3) The main cottage industry was <u>textiles</u>. Families prepared, spun and wove wool using hand and foot operated wooden <u>spinning wheels</u> and looms. They then sold the finished cloth to merchants to sell on.

New Technology *and Methods* changed everything

1) There was a lot of <u>progress</u> in the <u>agricultural sector</u>. Important changes like more people switching to <u>crops</u> that provided <u>more food</u> (e.g. wheat and barley), as well as <u>better machinery</u> made British agriculture more <u>efficient</u> — farmers could produce <u>more food</u> with <u>fewer people</u> working the land.

2) In 1775, James Watt invented a new type of <u>steam engine</u>. Before Watt, machines were mainly powered by water — steam-powered machines were slow and unreliable. Watt's machines improved on these earlier attempts, meaning <u>steam power</u> could be used in many <u>different industries</u>.

3) New inventions soon led to the <u>mass production</u> of <u>fabrics</u>.

- In 1764, James Hargreaves invented the '<u>Spinning Jenny</u>'. This hand-powered <u>spinning wheel</u> could spin much more thread than a normal spinning wheel.

- In 1769, Richard Arkwright invented a spinning machine powered by <u>waterwheels</u> that could spin many strands of wool at once. It was called the <u>Water Frame</u>.

- In 1785, Edmund Cartwright invented the <u>power loom</u> — the world's first <u>steam-powered loom</u>. Further developed by other inventors, the power loom was widely used after 1820.

<u>Factories</u> were used to house the new textile machines — some employed hundreds of people doing specific, repetitive tasks. Many of these tasks were <u>dangerous</u> and <u>injuries</u> were common. Workers also <u>breathed in fibres</u> that damaged their <u>lungs</u>.

4) <u>Mass production</u> of fabrics led to <u>prices dropping</u> significantly. (This happened in other industries, but it wasn't as drastic.) Industry <u>replaced</u> agriculture at the <u>driving force</u> of the economy.

Transportation *in Britain improved*

Britain was becoming more <u>industrial</u>, and companies needed <u>better</u> ways to <u>move products</u> around.

1) After the 1750s, Britain's <u>dirt roads</u> improved as <u>turnpike trusts</u> (businesses) were set up to build, fix and maintain them. They used <u>new techniques</u> to improve road surfaces and drainage.

2) In the 1790s, <u>canal</u> building took off in Britain — over 40 Acts were granted to build canals in the first half of the decade. The canals were used to transport <u>heavy goods</u> like iron and coal.

3) In 1825, George Stephenson completed the first public <u>steam railway</u>. It ran from Stockton to Darlington, and made use of steam <u>locomotives</u> to transport raw materials and goods.

The steam engine — not just a load of hot air...

Including background information like dates and figures in your answer is a good way to earn extra marks. Just make sure that the information you use is relevant to the question.

Industrialisation and Urbanisation

The industrial sector grew, so many people headed for the big <u>city</u> in search of <u>work</u>.

Industrialisation increased Urbanisation

1) After 1750, Britain's <u>population rose dramatically</u>, more than doubling between 1750 and 1850. The biggest rise was in <u>towns and cities</u> — in 1751-1831, Britain's urban population grew by almost 130%.

2) <u>Industrial cities</u> grew rapidly — between 1801 and 1851, <u>London</u> grew by almost 1.5 million people, while Liverpool, Glasgow, Manchester and Birmingham each grew by over 230,000 people.

3) Changes in the agricultural sector meant jobs in the countryside were <u>scarce</u> and <u>badly paid</u>, so <u>young people</u> moved to the cities to work in the new <u>industrial factories</u>.

Glasgow

Manchester

Birmingham

Liverpool

London

Comment and Analysis

<u>Urbanisation</u> was caused by both <u>push</u> and <u>pull</u> factors. People felt pushed <u>away from the countryside</u> as it no longer offered good jobs. Industrial towns offered new jobs in factories, pulling people <u>towards them</u>. As a result, urbanisation was <u>regionalised</u> — towns without industry like Norwich and York grew more slowly than others because they <u>didn't have industrial jobs to offer</u>. This also means that the <u>old ways still existed</u> in some places — there was still some small production and cottage industry, even in textiles.

The Industrial Revolution was a time of great Political Change

1) Before the industrial revolution, power was held by a <u>small elite</u> — only those with lots of <u>money</u> or <u>land</u> could vote or become a Member of Parliament.

2) In the <u>French Revolution</u> (1789-1799), the French people overthrew King Louis XVI and other members of the French elite. It <u>inspired</u> radical thinkers to demand similar changes in Britain.

3) The French Revolution <u>scared</u> Britain's elite — they thought a revolution might happen in Britain too. Large groups of people began to demand <u>political reform</u>.

> <u>Trade unions</u> were already established in the skilled trades in the 1790s. These are organised groups of workers founded to improve their members' <u>wages</u> and <u>working conditions</u>. Pitt's Combinations Acts 1799-1800 made them <u>illegal</u>, but they were so popular they were made legal again in 1824.

4) Eventually, the people's campaigns convinced the government that <u>reforms</u> were needed.

> The <u>First Reform Act 1832</u> gave the vote to small landowners, tenant farmers and shopkeepers. However, many working class people felt betrayed because the Act targeted the middle classes.

5) In 1836, the <u>Chartists</u> were founded. This popular movement wanted <u>every man over 21</u> to have the vote, and to scrap the rule that those running to be an MP had to own land.

> The <u>Second and Third Reform Acts (1867 and 1884)</u> each gave more workers the vote. After the Third Act, the majority of men had the vote. However, women and some men still did not have the vote.

Comment and Analysis

Change was slow, but ordinary people's <u>increased involvement</u> in politics (particularly after the <u>Labour Party</u> was founded in 1900) had a <u>major impact</u> on how governments approached public health over the next 200 years. Having the vote gave them a chance to <u>influence politicians</u> — they could demand better <u>living conditions</u> that would improve their <u>health</u> and <u>wellbeing</u>.

All these revolutions are making my head spin...

Make a list of the changes that took place after 1750 and write down how they helped increase urbanisation, including important examples and dates.

REVISION TASK

Urban Living Conditions

So many people moved to the towns so quickly that there was little time or space to properly house them all. The new town inhabitants had to suffer terrible conditions that helped spread disease.

Houses in the cities were very Overcrowded

1) Rapid urbanisation meant houses needed to be built quickly.

2) The government wasn't involved. Houses were built by private builders, and there were few building regulations — houses could be built without planning permission.

3) The builders were driven by profits, so they made houses as quickly and cheaply as possible, with cheap materials, poor foundations and few facilities.

4) Houses were built as close together as possible, which created crowded slums. In northern England they built back-to-back terrace houses with little outside space, no protection against damp and little fresh air.

5) Workers had low wages, so they tried to live in the smallest possible space — families with four or more children often lived in a single room. The poorest lived in cellars — in 1840, Liverpool had around 40,000 people living in cellars.

Back-to-back houses in Yorkshire in the late 1800s.

© Mary Evans Picture Library

Towns had no proper Water or Waste facilities

1) Before the Germ Theory was published (p.21), people didn't understand the need for clean water or good sewerage systems. Most houses had no bathroom — they instead shared an outside toilet, called a privy.

2) Each privy was built above a cesspit. Cesspit and household waste was collected by nightmen, who threw the waste into rivers or piled it up for the rain to wash away.

3) Water companies set up water pumps in the streets, which were shared between many houses. The pump's water supply was often contaminated by waste from the cesspits or rivers. Diseases that are passed on through dirty water (like cholera) were spread easily.

Food and Nutrition were poor

There was a lack of fresh food in the towns. The 1848 Public Health Act (p.21) introduced some measures to regulate food quality, but these were limited. There were few cooking facilities in workers' accommodation. It was also impossible to store food hygienically, so it became infected easily.

Poor Living Conditions damaged Public Health

Poor living conditions had a damaging impact on people's health, and can be linked to particular diseases. For example, tuberculosis is an air-borne disease (spread by coughing) that was common in 19th century Britain. Poor ventilation, overcrowding and poor nutrition have all been found to help spread it.

Comment and Analysis

Urbanisation meant that people had more money, but conditions were often worse than in rural areas. Health in urban areas probably got worse and then improved — e.g. life expectancy in Liverpool dropped to just 25 years in the 1860s, but rose over the next decade.

Plan your answer better than they planned those houses...

Summarise living conditions of urban workers in industrial Britain between 1750 and 1900. Use examples to back up your answer. [9]

EXAM QUESTION

The People's Health, c.1250 to present

Responses to Cholera Epidemics

Poor living conditions caused many <u>diseases</u> — <u>tuberculosis</u>, <u>influenza</u> and <u>typhoid</u> were all common. One major disease was <u>cholera</u>, which reached Britain from Asia and had a devastating impact.

Cholera epidemics Killed Thousands of people

1) <u>Cholera</u> reached Britain in 1831. By 1832, it was an <u>epidemic</u> — over 21,000 people in Britain died of cholera that year. The epidemics <u>recurred</u> in 1848, 1853-54 and 1865-66.

2) Cholera spreads when <u>infected sewage</u> gets into drinking water. It causes extreme <u>diarrhoea</u> — sufferers often die from <u>loss of water</u> and <u>minerals</u>. Both <u>rich</u> and <u>poor</u> people caught the disease.

3) At the time people <u>didn't know</u> what caused cholera — the best theory was <u>miasma</u> (see p.7). The <u>government</u> started regulating the <u>burial</u> of the dead, but this did <u>little</u> to halt the spread of cholera.

Snow linked Cholera to Contaminated Water

<u>John Snow</u> showed that there was a connection between <u>contaminated water</u> and <u>cholera</u> in 1853-54. He studied a cholera outbreak in the <u>Broad Street</u> area of London and noticed that the victims all used the <u>same water pump</u>. So he removed the <u>handle</u> from the pump and ended the outbreak.

> Snow's work received <u>little attention</u> at first. Most people still believed diseases were spread by <u>miasma</u> ('bad air').

The 'Great Stink' struck London in 1858

1) Industrial cities had <u>poor sewerage systems</u> (see p.19). In London, the introduction of <u>flush toilets</u> made this problem worse — they increased the volume of waste entering cesspits. A lot of the waste overflowed and drained into <u>the Thames</u>.

© Mary Evans Picture Library

FATHER THAMES INTRODUCING HIS OFFSPRING TO THE FAIR CITY OF LONDON

2) In the summer of 1858, hot weather caused the river's <u>water level to drop</u> and <u>bacteria</u> to grow in the waste. This produced a <u>smell</u> that was so bad it affected large parts of London and <u>stopped Parliament</u> from meeting.

3) The situation pushed the authorities in London to agree to build a new, <u>expensive sewer system</u>.

A cartoon from 1858: 'Father Thames introducing his offspring to the fair city of London — Diptheria, Scrofula and Cholera.' It suggests there was support for cleaning up the Thames, and some awareness that the sewage-filled river caused disease.

Bazalgette cleaned up London with new Sewers

1) The government knew that the sewerage system needed improving, but the 'Great Stink' persuaded them to act sooner than planned.

2) <u>Joseph Bazalgette</u> was the chief engineer of the Metropolitan Board of Works, which was responsible for public works in London.

3) To reduce the stink, Bazalgette was appointed in <u>1859</u> to build a new London <u>sewer system</u>. The sewers transported waste that was normally dumped into the Thames away from heavily populated areas to the <u>Thames Estuary</u>. About 1300 miles of sewers were built.

4) The sewer system was officially opened in <u>1865</u>.

Comment and Analysis

When Bazalgette started work on his sewers, people still <u>didn't understand</u> how diseases like cholera spread. They were trying to get rid of the <u>bad smells</u> coming from the Thames. The fact they stopped cholera by cleaning the drinking water was <u>unintended</u>.

If anyone knows the cause of cholera, John Snows...

Write a list of the important factors that helped stop cholera spreading between 1848 and 1865.

REVISION TASK

Public Health Reforms in the 19th Century

Edwin Chadwick's report was a major breakthrough in proving that poor living conditions had a negative impact on health and society. The 1848 Public Health Act was soon introduced, but it had limited success.

Chadwick's Report showed living conditions affected health

'Where those circumstances are removed by drainage, proper cleansing, better ventilation, and other means of diminishing atmospheric impurity, the frequency and intensity of such disease is abated; and where the removal of the noxious agencies appears to be complete, such disease almost entirely disappears.'
Edwin Chadwick, 1842

In 1842, Edwin Chadwick published a 'Report on the Sanitary Condition of the Labouring Population of Great Britain'. The report concluded:

- Urban living conditions were worse for health than rural conditions.
- The government should pass laws for proper drainage and sewerage.
- Improvements in conditions should be funded by local taxes.
- A healthy workforce would save money in the long term.
- Bad living conditions caused immoral behaviour, not vice versa.

Comment and Analysis

Chadwick's report was very popular — it sold 20,000 copies on top of the 10,000 that were given away. The report was also controversial, but it was significant in changing people's attitudes and beliefs about the poor. Before Chadwick's report, people thought the poor caused their bad health and living conditions through laziness and drunkenness — Chadwick proved that wasn't the case.

Chadwick's Report led to the 1848 Public Health Act

1) In 1844, the government to set up the Health of Towns Commission to investigate Chadwick's findings. The Commission confirmed Chadwick's claims were true.

2) A group called the Health of Towns Association was set up to campaign for improved public health.

3) Chadwick's report and another cholera epidemic in 1848 (which killed 53,000 people) put pressure on Parliament to pass a Public Health Act.

4) The 1848 Act set up a central Board of Health (which included Chadwick as a member) and allowed any town to set up its own local board of health as long as the town's taxpayers agreed.

Comment and Analysis

The impact of the 1848 Act was limited — towns could set up health boards but very few chose to, and those that did often refused to spend any money to improve conditions. Chadwick annoyed a lot of people, and was forced to retire in 1854. The central Board of Health was dismantled in 1858.

Louis Pasteur showed that Germs caused Disease

Advances in science in the 19th century helped people to understand what causes disease:

- The French chemist Louis Pasteur demonstrated that micro-organisms (germs) in the air cause food and drink to go off. In 1861, Pasteur published his Germ Theory, which argued that some germs cause disease.
- In 1883, the German scientist Robert Koch identified the bacteria that causes cholera.
- The Germ Theory replaced the traditional miasma theory and confirmed John Snow's findings that cholera was spread through infected water.
- These discoveries were proof that cleaner conditions would improve public health.

I hope you're not Bored of Health, as there's more to come...

Divide your page into two. On the left side, list the ways Chadwick's report and the 1848 Act improved public health. On the right side, list the public health problems they still hadn't solved.

Public Health Reforms in the 19th Century

Before 1875, there was <u>little effort</u> to improve public health. However, several developments led to a <u>change in attitude</u>, and the government and local initiatives stepped in to try to do more to <u>improve public health</u>.

Public Opinion began to Change

For most of the 19th century, people believed in a <u>laissez-faire</u> style of government — they thought the government <u>shouldn't intervene</u> in public health. But then things began to <u>change</u>.

1) <u>Snow's</u> discovery of the link between dirty water and cholera and Pasteur's <u>Germ Theory</u> (see p.21) showed that cleaning up towns could stop the spread of disease.

2) In 1867, the <u>Second Reform Act</u> was passed (see p.18). It gave an additional <u>1 million men</u> the vote, most of whom were industrial <u>workers</u>.

Comment and Analysis

Now that they had the vote, <u>workers</u> could put <u>pressure</u> on the government to listen to their concerns about health. For the first time, politicians had to address <u>workers' concerns</u> in order to <u>stay in power</u>.

The Government passed another Public Health Act in 1875

1) In 1871-72, the government followed the Royal Sanitary Commission's proposal to form the <u>Local Government Board</u> and divide Britain into '<u>sanitary areas</u>' administered by officers for public health.

2) In 1875, <u>Benjamin Disraeli's</u> government passed another <u>Public Health Act</u>. It forced councils to appoint <u>health inspectors</u> and <u>sanitary inspectors</u> to make sure that laws on things like <u>water supplies</u> and <u>hygiene</u> were <u>followed</u>. It also made councils <u>maintain sewerage systems</u> and keep their towns' <u>streets clean</u>.

3) The 1875 Public Health Act was <u>more effective</u> than the one passed in 1848 (see p.21) because it was <u>compulsory</u>.

4) Disraeli also brought in the <u>Artisans' Dwellings Act</u> in 1875. This let local councils <u>buy slums</u> with poor living conditions and <u>rebuild them</u> in a way that met new government-backed housing standards.

Comment and Analysis

There were several changes to public health during the industrial revolution, and the <u>1875 Public Health Act</u> was one of the biggest. The work of the <u>government</u> and <u>individuals</u> like Chadwick and Snow were key to these changes. <u>Technology</u> (like Bazalgette's sewers), the <u>Second Reform Act</u> and the <u>cholera epidemics</u> were other factors that prompted improvement.

There were Local Initiatives to improve public health

1) <u>Joseph Chamberlain</u>, who became Mayor of <u>Birmingham</u> in 1873, persuaded the city authorities to buy the local <u>gas</u> and <u>water</u> companies to make sure people had <u>good supplies</u> of both.

2) In <u>1875</u>, he cleared an area of the city's <u>slums</u> and built a <u>new street</u> in their place. He also <u>improved</u> some of the slum housing.

3) In <u>Liverpool</u>, <u>council housing</u> was first provided in the <u>1870s</u>. The council also set up further initiatives such as <u>health visits</u>.

At the end of the 1800s, town councils were <u>competing</u> to be better at looking after the <u>health</u> of their citizens.

<u>Philanthropists</u> showed it was possible to treat poor workers well while still making money:

- Beginning in 1879, the famous chocolate makers, the <u>Cadburys</u>, tried to provide <u>quality homes</u> and <u>improve lifestyles</u> for workers at their factory in <u>Bournville</u>, near Birmingham.

- In Merseyside, the <u>Lever Brothers</u> started building <u>Port Sunlight</u> for their workers in 1888 — a model village with <u>800 homes</u>, <u>schools</u>, a <u>church</u>, a <u>hospital</u> and even an <u>art gallery</u>.

- <u>Octavia Hill</u> was concerned with the terrible conditions in which people were living, so she developed a <u>model housing scheme</u>. Hill also believed that people should have access to <u>green spaces</u> and co-founded the <u>National Trust</u> in 1895.

Turns out laissez-faire had made things less fair...

Why were Benjamin Disraeli's 1875 reforms more successful at improving public health than the 1848 Public Health Act? Support your answer with examples. [10]

Public Health Reforms in the 19th Century

The 1875 Public Health Act, the Artisans' Dwellings Act and new technology helped to improve the living conditions of many people. However, they still left a lot of people in poverty and poor health in 1900.

By 1900, some things had Improved

1) From around the 1870s, some local councils started clearing slums and replacing them with council houses for the people living there.

2) Skilled workers gained from the improvements in housing, as they could afford the higher rents of the new, better houses.

3) The railways made towns less crowded, as they allowed the richer middle classes to move out of the towns into the suburbs.

4) Victorian engineering produced improvements in the form of brick-lined sewer networks and steam-driven pumped water systems — such as the Boughton Pumping Station in Nottinghamshire.

> **Comment and Analysis**
>
> The improvements in public health before 1900 were a result of many factors. Advances in science (e.g. Germ Theory) and technology (e.g. Victorian improvements to sewers) allowed diseases to be identified and prevented. Changing attitudes towards the role of government allowed intervention to improve public health. Finally, increased urbanisation gave intervention more urgency as more and more people became affected by the poor living conditions in towns.

Booth and Rowntree showed the effects of Poverty

1) Slums and other poor, overcrowded housing were still common in industrial towns in 1900. The poor worked long hours for low wages. Many people couldn't afford doctors or medicine — they could barely provide their children with three decent meals a day.

> There was no unemployment benefit, or pensions for the elderly. Workhouses were the only help — they provided basic food and lodging in exchange for working long hours in brutal conditions.

2) Two reports showed how widespread poverty was:

Booth's Report

Charles Booth's 1889 'Life and Labour of the People in London' showed that 30% of Londoners were living in severe poverty, and that it was sometimes impossible for people to find work, however hard they tried. He showed that some wages were so low they weren't enough to support a family.

> 'I regard these evils as being for the most part directly connected with the poverty of the sufferers and the irregularity of their employment, to be cured only by such thorough-going remedies as will strike at the causes of poverty itself.'
> Charles Booth, 1889

> 'Overcrowding and insanitary conditions of all kinds abound in the slums, and back-to-back houses in which through ventilation is impossible are common in them... Privies are usual and these, like water taps, are in many cases shared by several houses. They are particularly offensive in these over-populated and under-ventilated districts.'
> Seebohm Rowntree, 1901

Rowntree's Report

Seebohm Rowntree had a factory in York. He didn't believe the problem was as bad there as in London — so he did a survey of living conditions. His report, 'Poverty, a Study of Town Life' (published 1901), showed that 28% of people in York couldn't afford basic food and housing.

3) The lack of access to good healthcare meant that most people's health was pretty poor. When the Boer War broke out in 1899, army officers found that 40% of volunteers were physically unfit for military service — mostly due to poverty-related illnesses linked to poor diet and living conditions.

4) The government realised that it needed to improve basic healthcare in order to have an efficient army.

> **Comment and Analysis**
>
> Booth and Rowntree showed that for many families the poor living conditions in industrial towns hadn't gone away. They also made a direct link between poverty and poor health, and suggested that the way to improve public health was to tackle the causes of poverty. Rowntree's report heavily influenced the reforms of David Lloyd George (see p.29).

People's health came a long way, but still had a way to go...

'The most important improvements to public health in Britain happened between 1750-1900.'
Discuss if you agree or disagree with this statement, using examples to support your answer. [18]

A Changing Society

Britain after 1900 was a <u>rapidly changing society</u>. Every adult in Britain now had the vote and could influence the government to change public health. Changes in <u>living conditions</u> also improved health.

Women *and* Workers *gained greater influence in British Politics*

1) The British people fought in <u>two world wars</u>, between 1914-1918 and 1939-1945. The wars had a <u>major impact</u> on British society and on public health.

2) The <u>Labour Party</u>, who supported the <u>working classes</u>, became more influential, and the party gained power in 1945. It then went on to introduce a <u>welfare state</u> and the <u>National Health Service</u> (see p.29).

> The reforms of the 1945 Labour government and its successors launched the <u>welfare state</u>. This means support is given to the poorest in society through <u>council housing</u>, <u>unemployment benefit</u> and <u>free healthcare</u> on the National Health Service (NHS).

3) The Women's Social and Political Union (nicknamed the <u>suffragettes</u>) was founded in 1903 and campaigned for <u>women</u> to get the <u>vote</u> alongside other existing groups.

4) In <u>1918</u>, women who were either householders or married and <u>aged over 30</u> received the vote. <u>All women</u> over 21 finally received the vote in <u>1928</u>, bringing them in line with men.

The British Economy had Highs and Lows

In the 20th century, the types of <u>jobs</u> people did changed:

> The industries that made the British economy <u>strong</u> during the 19th century (e.g. textiles, steel and shipbuilding) continued to prosper until the outbreak of the First World War in 1914. But after the war, these industries suffered from <u>competition</u> from elsewhere in the world and began to <u>decline</u>.

> New, more <u>technical industries</u> like cars and chemicals began to overtake the older industries. They grew particularly well after 1945, but some had begun to <u>decline</u> by the 1980s.

> Since the 1960s, Britain's <u>service sector</u> has grown to be the largest employer in the country — nowadays, around <u>four out of five</u> people work in shops, hotels, restaurants, banks, schools, hospitals or other services. The number of people working in <u>manufacturing</u> has declined heavily in that time.

1) The decline of the old industries caused a lot of <u>unemployment</u> and difficulties for workers. In <u>1926</u>, workers from many different industries walked out in a <u>General Strike</u> to support British miners in their dispute with mine owners, who wanted to reduce their wages.

Comment and Analysis

In the 20th century, different types of <u>jobs</u> and <u>rising living standards</u> changed people's health dramatically. Fewer people worked in <u>physically demanding</u> and <u>dangerous</u> jobs like mining and textile manufacturing than before.

2) Things were made worse in <u>1929</u> with the <u>Wall Street Crash</u> and the <u>Great Depression</u> that followed, which left millions of people unemployed.

> The 1930s are remembered for the Great Depression, but economic hardship was fairly <u>regionalised</u>. For example, unemployment in the north-eastern town of Jarrow stood at <u>68%</u>, but was as low as <u>9%</u> in London and <u>5%</u> in Oxford.

3) During the period between 1945 and the 1970s, lots of economies around the world did very well (including Britain's) and <u>unemployment</u> was <u>low</u> — this is known as the 'post-war boom'. <u>Rising wages</u> during this boom allowed people access to <u>better homes</u> and <u>better food</u>.

4) However, economic difficulties returned, particularly in the late <u>1970s</u> and, most recently, after the <u>2008 financial crash</u>. After this, the economy <u>struggled to grow</u> again.

Booms and crashes — the economy sounds like a warzone...

Write a paragraph summarising the political changes in Britain since 1900, then do the same for the economic changes. Which do you think was most important to improving public health?

A Changing Society

British society slowly became more <u>fragmented</u> — people had less loyalty to a particular class or religion. People had an increasingly <u>liberal</u> outlook (they became <u>more accepting</u> and <u>open-minded</u>).

British Society became Better Educated and More Multi-cultural

1) Changes in the 20th century made British people <u>better educated</u>. The 1944 Butler Act made secondary education <u>free</u>, and raised the school leaving age to <u>15</u>. The 1963 Robbins Report laid the foundations for <u>new universities</u>.

2) At the start of the 20th century, Britain had a rigid, <u>class-based society</u> — there was the <u>elite</u> at the top, then the <u>middle class</u> (e.g. merchants and business owners) and the <u>working class</u> (e.g. industrial workers and farmers). But by the start of the 21st century, class identities were breaking down as British society became more <u>fragmented</u>.

3) After the Second World War, many people from countries like Jamaica, the West Indies, India and Pakistan began to <u>settle in Britain</u>. They were the first wave of immigrants to arrive in Britain since the Second World War — they helped to make British society more <u>multi-cultural</u>.

4) Steps were taken towards winning <u>equality for women</u>. The <u>Equal Pay Act</u> was passed in 1970 and prevented workers from having different salaries or conditions because of their gender. In 1975, the <u>Sex Discrimination Act</u> was passed. The Act outlawed discrimination on the basis of gender in many different areas.

> Access to <u>education</u>, improved <u>job opportunities</u> for women and the breaking down of <u>class identities</u> all meant that more people could escape <u>poverty</u> and improve their <u>living conditions</u>.

© Illustrated London News Ltd/Mary Evans

In 1948, the Empire Windrush carried the first large group of immigrants from Jamaica to Britain.

British Culture became More Liberal

1) The influence of <u>Christianity</u> decreased in public life from 1900. By <u>2011</u>, only 59% of the population said that they were <u>Christians</u>, while 25% of people said they had <u>no religion</u>.

2) People's <u>attitudes</u> became more <u>liberal</u>. Abortion and homosexuality were legalised in 1967. Before <u>abortion</u> was legalised, many women <u>died</u> during and after illegal abortions, which often used dangerous methods.

3) People became <u>less respectful</u> of public figures — politicians were highly regarded in the first half of the century, but later the public began to <u>mistrust</u> them.

4) Huge <u>scientific</u> and <u>technological</u> innovations took place in the 20th century, many of which transformed the lives of British people. Cars, phones, radios, televisions, planes, computers and the internet have <u>revolutionised</u> transportation and communication. <u>New medical devices</u> were invented, which improved the <u>diagnosis</u> and <u>treatment</u> of disease. For example, CT scanners, which were invented in the 1970s, use <u>X-ray technology</u> to create an image of the inside of a human body.

5) The economic boom of the 1950s and 1960s saw a <u>rise</u> in <u>wages</u> — people could afford to eat well and live in better housing, so <u>living conditions</u> improved. People also had much more <u>disposable income</u> — workers finally had enough money to buy <u>luxury items</u> like televisions, washing machines and vacuum cleaners.

> The rise of <u>consumerism</u> and the decline of religion was symbolised in 1994 when the law was changed to allow <u>shops</u> to open on a <u>Sunday</u>.

6) This caused a growth of <u>consumerism</u>. British people started to buy more non-essential items and shopping became a major <u>leisure activity</u>.

There was lots of change — people spent it in shops...

In the exam, remember that people's health was affected by the attitudes of the time. When giving examples, background information can be useful in showing what people thought.

Modern Living Conditions

Public health has <u>improved</u> since 1900, and this is partly because of the transformation of <u>living conditions</u>.

Since 1900 there have been dramatic Changes in public health

Public health in Britain since 1900 has <u>improved</u>.
- <u>Infant mortality</u> in England and Wales fell from around 150 deaths per 1000 children in 1901 to around 5 deaths per 1000 children in 2000.
- <u>Life expectancy</u> has increased. Only around 20% of people lived to be over 65 in 1901. In 2000, that had risen to 80%.

<u>Causes of death</u> have also changed since 1900.
- Diseases like <u>tuberculosis</u> used to kill thousands of people in the 19th century but have <u>declined steeply</u> since 1901.
- Changes in <u>lifestyle</u> and an <u>ageing population</u> have meant that deaths from <u>heart disease</u>, <u>strokes</u> and <u>cancer</u> remained high throughout the 20th century.

Housing and Living Conditions were Transformed...

1) The government traditionally <u>didn't get involved</u> in house building (see p.19). That changed during the First World War, when Prime Minister David Lloyd George promised to tackle poor-quality housing by building '<u>homes fit for heroes</u>'. The <u>1919 Housing and Town Planning Act</u> gave government subsidies to local councils to provide housing.

2) Another Housing Act in <u>1930</u> gave government grants to local councils to <u>clear slum housing</u> and to <u>build new homes</u> for the occupants. Over <u>240,000</u> slum houses had been cleared by 1939, but slums and a lack of good housing for the poor were still <u>major problems</u>.

> By 1922, around 200,000 <u>council houses</u> had been built, but they were <u>too expensive</u> for the poorest families, who still lived in <u>slums</u>.

3) During the <u>Second World War</u>, destruction from <u>bombing</u> and a <u>lack of construction</u> led to severe housing shortages, making the situation worse.

4) After the war, the Labour government built <u>800,000 homes</u> between 1945-51. In 1946, it passed the <u>New Towns Act</u> — this created completely new towns near major cities. Governments in the 1950s and 1960s <u>demolished</u> over 900,000 <u>old</u>, <u>cramped slums</u> — over 2 million inhabitants were rehoused.

A photograph of the centre of Harlow New Town in Essex, taken in the 1960s. It was designed to be extremely modern and it included blocks of flats and semi-detached houses. Other new towns built since 1946 include Basildon, Cumbernauld, Warrington, Peterborough and Milton Keynes.

© Mary Evans Picture Library

...but Improvements took a Long Time

1) Despite these changes, <u>housing problems persisted</u> into the 1960s and 1970s — in 1965 over 2 million households had <u>no hot water</u>, <u>no bath</u> or <u>no indoor toilet</u>. Many councils built <u>tower blocks</u>, but these had no outside spaces and were disliked by many of the people living in them.

2) In <u>1961</u>, a report called '<u>Homes for Today and Tomorrow</u>' gave specific <u>standards</u> for new housing, including adequate <u>heating</u>, a <u>flushing toilet</u> and <u>enough space</u> inside and outside. The suggested standards became <u>compulsory</u> for government-built housing in <u>1969</u>.

3) By the 1980s, almost every house in Britain had proper <u>heating</u>, <u>water</u> and <u>sanitation</u>.

I told a joke about a tower block, but it fell flat...

Make a timeline about housing improvements since 1900. Without looking at the page, write down next to each date why it is significant.

REVISION TASK

Responses to Spanish Influenza

In 1918-19, Britain experienced perhaps the deadliest epidemic ever recorded. Spanish Influenza affected lots of people, but no-one knew how to prevent it. The British government didn't really respond to the crisis.

Spanish Influenza caused Confusion

> 'I had a little bird,
> Its name was Enza,
> I opened the window,
> And IN-FLU-ENZA.'
> *A children's nursery rhyme from 1918.*

1) From 1918-19, a quarter of the British population caught a type of flu called Spanish Influenza, and around 228,000 people died of the disease. It killed more people than the plague outbreak of 1347-51 or the First World War.

2) The disease struck in several waves. The first was in March 1918 — it was relatively mild and the war was still being fought, so nobody paid much attention.

3) The second wave in the autumn of 1918 was the worst. It sprang up all over the world, and was quickly spread by soldiers returning home from the war and the huge crowds celebrating the end of the war in November 1918.

4) Spanish Influenza was unusual because of the types of people it affected. Normal flu tends to hit children and the elderly worst, but Spanish Influenza particularly affected fit and healthy people between about 20 and 40 years old.

OXO
Fortifies the System against
INFLUENZA INFECTION.

© Mary Evans Picture Library

An advertisement for OXO, which appeared in the weekly newspaper The Graphic on 14 December 1918.

5) At the time, no-one was sure what caused the disease, so there was a lot of confusion about how to prevent it from spreading. Doctors often contradicted one another in their advice to patients.

6) Many companies took advantage of the confusion around Spanish Influenza by marketing 'miracle cures' for the disease that didn't actually work.

The Response to Spanish Influenza was Mixed

National Responses

The government's response to Spanish Influenza was limited.

- In November 1918, the government introduced regulations to try to prevent the spread of the disease, but by this time it was already halfway through its second wave so their impact was limited.
- The government also published a leaflet, which gave people advice about how to avoid catching the disease.

Comment and Analysis

The Spanish Influenza outbreak had shown that Britain couldn't handle such a large-scale epidemic. In 1919, the Ministry of Health was established — for the first time Britain had a national organisation dedicated to health policy.

Local Responses

1) Local authorities took whatever measures they thought were best.
2) Some councils closed public buildings like schools, cinemas and libraries in order to prevent large crowds and public meetings.
3) The chief medical officer of Manchester, Dr James Niven, made people aware that crowds helped spread Spanish Influenza. He closed businesses and schools to stop the disease. Niven also sent out leaflets with advice on hygiene.

This book can't cure the flu, but it can help pass the exam...

In the exam it's important to take a couple of minutes before starting long answers to plan your writing. This will make sure that you answer the question and don't veer off topic.

EXAM TIP

The People's Health, c.1250 to present

Responses to AIDS

In the 1980s, the world was hit by another epidemic. Like Spanish Influenza, doctors were unsure of how the disease spread, but the British government soon launched several campaigns to raise awareness.

AIDS was first identified in the 1980s

AIDS (Acquired Immune Deficiency Syndrome) is caused by the virus HIV (Human Immunodeficiency Virus). It affects the immune system, severely limiting the body's ability to recover from illness. It's spread through the contact of bodily fluids, e.g. through unprotected sex or re-using contaminated needles.

1) AIDS was first identified in 1981 in California and New York in the USA. The first cases were among homosexual men and people who injected themselves with illegal drugs.
2) By 1982, AIDS had spread worldwide — cases were reported as far apart as Uganda in Africa and Haiti in the Caribbean. In 1983, AIDS was identified in women and children.
3) At the time, no-one knew how the disease spread or how to prevent it.

The Government soon Responded to the crisis

1) In Britain there was initially little action to prevent the spread of the disease. The main groups who were affected were homosexual men and drug users — there was a lot of prejudice against these groups. This meant there was a reluctance to use public money to prevent the disease.
2) But in 1985, as the number of cases was rising, millions of pounds were set aside by the government to combat the disease. It used this money to promote condom use and safer sex education, and set up needle exchanges for drug addicts (where they can dispose of old needles and get clean ones).
3) In 1986, the government ran the 'Don't aid AIDS' television campaign. This was followed by the 'Don't die of ignorance' campaign in 1987, when the government sent a leaflet about the disease to every home in Britain.
4) The campaigns were successful. They increased awareness and reduced the number of people diagnosed with HIV (the virus that causes AIDS). The campaigns were credited with helping Britain achieve lower infection rates than other countries which were slower to react.

> In 1987, the government ran a TV ad with the word 'AIDS' written across a tombstone. This was intended to shock the public and make them aware of the threat of AIDS.

There have been very few public campaigns in Britain on the issue of HIV and AIDS since 1987. It is still a serious health issue. In 2014, over 6000 people in Britain were diagnosed with HIV.

Scientists around the world tried to find a Treatment for AIDS

1) In 1983, scientists at the Pasteur Institute in France discovered the virus that causes AIDS, which would become known as HIV.
2) AZT, the first drug to combat HIV, was approved in 1987. It was quite effective, but caused harmful side effects. In 1992, a more effective combination drug therapy (several drugs used at once) was introduced.
3) In 1996, a new combination of drugs was found which completely halted the development of AIDS. This was known as ART, and became the most effective HIV treatment.
4) Science has been a major factor in dealing with HIV/AIDS.

Comment and Analysis

The British government was initially slow to react to both Spanish Influenza and AIDS, partly because they were unsure of how the diseases spread. The national government's advice on Spanish Influenza was confused, but it offered clear warnings and advice about AIDS in a strong national campaign.

Health had improved, but epidemics hadn't gone away...

Why was the response to the AIDS crisis in 1982-1987 more successful than the response to the Spanish Influenza epidemic in 1918-1919? Support your answer with examples. [10]

EXAM QUESTION

Government Involvement in Public Health

In the 19th century, the government started to get involved in public health. This continued after 1900, first with the Liberal reforms and then importantly with the Beveridge Report and the NHS.

The Liberal Reforms improved health by tackling Poverty

Booth, Rowntree and the Boer War showed that there was a link between poverty and ill health (see p.23). The newly-elected Liberal government and its Chancellor, David Lloyd George, realised it had to take action.

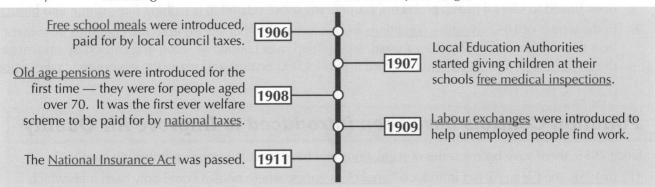

1906 — Free school meals were introduced, paid for by local council taxes.

1907 — Local Education Authorities started giving children at their schools free medical inspections.

1908 — Old age pensions were introduced for the first time — they were for people aged over 70. It was the first ever welfare scheme to be paid for by national taxes.

1909 — Labour exchanges were introduced to help unemployed people find work.

1911 — The National Insurance Act was passed.

The National Insurance Act introduced health insurance for workers — the worker, their employer and the government all contributed to a central fund that the workers could use for sick pay or to pay for a doctor.

Comment and Analysis

The Liberal reforms were the first real effort by the national government to improve people's living conditions as a way of improving their health. The reforms were a result of changing attitudes towards the role of government, and changed people's attitudes further.

The Beveridge Report led to the Welfare State

1) In 1942, during the Second World War, economist and social reformer William Beveridge published his famous report. The Beveridge Report became a bestseller — it was widely read and hugely popular.

> In his report, Beveridge called for the state provision of social security 'from the cradle to the grave'. Beveridge argued that all people should have the right to be free from want, disease, ignorance, squalor and idleness. He called these the five 'giants'.

2) In 1945, the Labour Party was elected with the promise to implement Beveridge's proposals. They passed another National Insurance Act in 1946 to cover anyone who couldn't work, whether as a result of sickness, pregnancy, unemployment or old age. This was the foundation of the welfare state.

The National Health Service was established in 1948

In 1948, the Labour government implemented Beveridge's last proposal — a National Health Service.

1) Aneurin Bevan was the Labour Minister for Health who, after a lot of negotiation, introduced the National Health Service (NHS). The government nationalised hospitals and put them under local authority control. Treatment was made free for all patients.

2) Doctors didn't like the idea of becoming employees of the government, but were wooed with a fixed payment for each registered patient. They were also allowed to continue treating fee-paying patients.

3) The NHS was extremely popular when it was established — the Conservative Party was initially opposed to the NHS, but couldn't abolish it when they came back into power in 1951 because of its popularity with voters. Over the next several decades the quality of treatment improved, and the NHS has become one of the most important factors in improving the people's health since 1900.

Beveridge Report — nothing to do with your favourite drink...

Divide your page into three, with the headings: 'Liberal reforms', 'Beveridge Report' and 'NHS'. Under each heading, explain why they were important in improving public health.

Government Involvement in Public Health

While changes in living conditions have helped people in Britain to live longer and healthier, <u>changing lifestyles</u> mean there are still a lot of <u>health concerns</u> for British people to worry about.

Poor Air Quality has damaged Public Health

1) Industrialisation has had a damaging effect on Britain's <u>air quality</u> — buildings and machines that use coal, oil or gas for power release <u>carbon dioxide</u> and other <u>harmful gases</u> into the air. Poor air quality has been linked to several health problems, particularly those related to <u>breathing</u> like <u>asthma</u> and <u>bronchitis</u>.

2) In the winter of 1952, <u>weather conditions</u> in London meant that smoke from the <u>coal fires</u> people used to heat their homes didn't disperse as usual, so it settled over London as smog (fog caused by smoke) called the <u>Great Smog</u>. The <u>air pollution</u> caused around 4,000 deaths, and made the government <u>take action</u>.

Pollution Controls have been introduced to Improve Air Quality

Since 1956, there have been a series of <u>regulations</u> that have aimed to improve British air quality.

1) In <u>1956</u>, the <u>Clean Air Act</u> introduced <u>smokeless zones</u>, where houses could only burn fuels which didn't give off lots of smoke. It also stated that <u>power stations</u> should be build <u>outside cities</u>.

2) In <u>1968</u>, the government introduced another <u>Clean Air Act</u>. This focused on the pollution caused by <u>industry</u>. Factories that burned coal, oil or gas had to use <u>tall chimneys</u> to better scatter the pollution, rather than having it concentrated over towns and cities.

3) The <u>1995 Environment Act</u> required the government to show how it was going to work towards <u>improving</u> air quality. It also set up a national system to <u>monitor air pollution</u> using data from around the country.

4) In 2015, world leaders met at a conference in Paris to try to <u>reduce</u> the amount of air pollution globally.

Changes in Food and Lifestyle have caused a Health Crisis

1) In the early 1900s, <u>poor diet</u> was a <u>serious problem</u>. Since then, there has been lots of <u>research</u> into <u>nutrition</u> people are now able to afford better <u>quality food</u> and a more <u>balanced diet</u>.

2) <u>Chemicals</u> started to be used on food so that it could be <u>stored</u> without losing its flavour or colour. However, research showed that some chemicals were <u>unsafe</u>, and they're <u>no longer used</u>.

3) Over the last few decades, Britain has been experiencing an <u>obesity crisis</u>. Obesity is a medical condition where a person has an <u>excessive amount of fat</u> in their body. It can cause serious <u>health problems</u>. In 2013, <u>24.9%</u> of British people were considered to be obese.

> There are several reasons for the obesity crisis:
> * People nowadays eat more food that's high in <u>calories</u>, <u>saturated fat</u> and <u>sugar</u>.
> * There are far <u>fewer jobs</u> which require <u>manual labour</u>. Most jobs are office-based — sitting at a desk for long hours without any <u>exercise</u>.
> * People live much more <u>sedentary lifestyles</u> — they spend a large part of each day sitting down. For example, they drive instead of walking, there are more <u>labour-saving devices</u> in the home, and children now have electronic devices to play with instead of <u>playing outside</u>.

4) Obesity can be prevented by eating a <u>balanced diet</u> with <u>very little sugar and fat</u>, as well as doing <u>regular exercise</u>. The government and food manufacturers have committed to reducing obesity, by running <u>educational campaigns</u> about the issue and <u>improving labelling</u> on food and drink products (see p.31).

Dreams of a healthy lifestyle went up in smoke...

Write a brief summary of people's living conditions and lifestyles since 1900.
Include historical evidence in your answer. [9]

Government Involvement in Public Health

As well as directly improving people's health through healthcare and poverty relief, the government has also passed legislation and run campaigns to educate the public about how to live a healthy lifestyle.

Lifestyle Campaigns aim to improve people's Health

In the 20th century, scientists showed a link between people's lifestyle choices and their health. The government ran several campaigns to make people aware of the dangers and to change their lifestyles.

1) An increase in less active lifestyles has contributed to an increase in obesity. In 2009, the government launched the Change4Life campaign, with the aim of improving diets and promoting daily exercise.

2) Excessive alcohol intake has been linked to several diseases, especially liver cirrhosis. Alcohol intake rose between 1950 and 2004, but has since fallen. This may be due to the government's Drinkaware campaign, launched in 2004. The Drinkaware logo appears on many alcohol advertisements.

The government and the NHS have also had an important role in the introduction of vaccines to prevent disease, from polio in 1956 to cervical cancer in 2008.

Comment and Analysis

These campaigns mark a big shift in the government's approach from the foundation of the NHS, and an even bigger shift from the laissez-faire attitudes of the 19th century, when people thought the government shouldn't intervene at all in public health. Not only is the government trying to treat and vaccinate against known diseases, it is now intervening in people's lives in order to stop them getting particular illnesses in the first place.

Lung Cancer can be caused by Smoking

Lung cancer was a rare disease in 1900, but became common by the 1940s. Today, around 20% of all cancer deaths in the UK are due to lung cancer. Approximately 43,500 people are diagnosed every year.

Scientists have estimated that around 90% of lung cancer cases can be linked to tobacco smoking. The popularity of smoking increased in the First World War, particularly among soldiers. Smoking soon became popular among women too.

In 1950, the link between smoking and lung cancer was proven by Richard Doll and Austin Bradford Hill.

The government has taken action to Reduce Smoking

When the link between smoking and lung cancer became clear, the government warned people of the risks.

1) In 1962, the Royal College of Physicians recommended a ban on tobacco advertising. Shortly afterwards, in 1965, cigarette adverts were banned from television. In 1971, tobacco companies were forced to put a health warning on cigarette packets.

2) In recent years, the government has put a ban on smoking in public places — this was introduced in Scotland in 2006, and in England and Wales in 2007.

3) Recent government campaigns focused on helping people to give up smoking and on discouraging people from smoking in their cars, homes and in front of children.

4) In March 2015, Parliament passed a law requiring all cigarette companies to use plain packaging on boxes of cigarettes.

These measures have contributed to a decline in smoking. The percentage of men who smoke cigarettes has fallen from 65% in 1948 to around 20% in 2010 and for women it's dropped from 41% to 20% in the same period.

Food fights — made illegal under the Food Safety Act...*

'Government involvement was the most important factor in the improvement of public health after 1900'. How far do you agree with this statement? Give reasons for your answer. [18]

*not really.

The People's Health, c.1250 to present

Revision Summary

Time flies when you're studying centuries of health. Now for some questions to see what you've taken in.
- Try these questions and tick off each one when you get it right.
- When you've done all the questions for a topic and are completely happy with it, tick off the topic.

Late Medieval Britain, c.1250-c.1500 (p.5-9) ☑

1) Which people were most powerful in medieval society? Give three examples. ☑
2) Briefly describe what a peasant's house would have been like. ☑
3) What did people think caused the Black Death? Give three examples. ☑
4) a) Explain two approaches that people took to avoid catching the Black Death.
   b) Explain two approaches that local governments took to prevent the Black Death spreading. ☑
5) Explain why public health was better in monasteries than in towns. ☑

Early Modern Britain, c.1500-c.1750 (p.10-16) ☑

6) How did early modern Britain change? Give one economic, one social and one cultural change. ☑
7) How did poor living conditions affect people's health? ☑
8) Write a brief description of living conditions in early modern towns. ☑
9) Describe two national plague orders, including the year they were introduced and what they did. ☑
10) Give two examples of local responses to outbreaks of the plague. ☑
11) Describe four laws passed by the government in response to the gin craze. ☑

Industrial Britain, c.1750-c.1900 (p.17-23) ☑

12) a) Describe one way that technology changed during industrialisation.
    b) Explain how transport improved during this time. ☑
13) Give one push and one pull factor that encouraged urbanisation. ☑
14) What were water and waste facilities like in industrial towns? ☑
15) What did John Snow discover? ☑
16) a) When did the 'Great Stink' hit London?
    b) Who was in charge of building London's new sewer system? ☑
17) What did the 1848 Public Health Act involve? ☑
18) What changes did the 1875 Public Health Act make? ☑
19) What did Booth and Rowntree's reports show? ☑

Britain since c.1900 (p.24-31) ☑

20) Briefly describe three aspects of society that have changed since 1900. ☑
21) Name two Acts passed in the 20th century to help improve housing. ☑
22) What did local authorities do to try to stop Spanish Influenza from spreading? ☑
23) How did the government respond to the AIDS epidemic? ☑
24) Give three reforms that were introduced by the Liberal government. ☑
25) When was the NHS set up? ☑
26) Name one thing the government has done to:
    a) improve air quality.
    b) reduce smoking.
    c) encourage the public to make better lifestyle choices. ☑

The People's Health, c.1250 to present

Late Medieval Britain

To understand migration to Britain in the later Middle Ages, you need to know what life was like for people back then. This page will give you a quick guide to some of the key features of Britain in the later Middle Ages.

The British Isles were split into Separate Kingdoms

1) In the later Middle Ages, the English monarch (a king or queen) ruled England, Wales and Ireland.

2) Scotland was a separate country with its own monarch and government. There were often wars between England and Scotland during the late medieval period.

> The Middle Ages began at the start of the 6th century and ended in the 15th century. This period can also be called the medieval period. The period from 1250 to 1500 is often called the later Middle Ages or the late medieval period.

Areas controlled by England

The King and the Nobility were very Powerful

1) The king was the most powerful person in late medieval England. He ruled with the support of a small group of wealthy landowners and churchmen (e.g. archbishops and bishops), who are known as the nobility. Members of the nobility sat in Parliament and advised the king.

2) The majority of the population were peasants who worked as farmers. They rented land from members of the nobility. Nobles had a lot of power and control over the peasants who rented their land.

Comment and Analysis

The king decided who could settle in England, where they could live and how much tax they should pay. This could cause difficulties for immigrants, as their lives could be hugely influenced by the beliefs and attitudes of the current king.

The Catholic Church had a lot of Influence

1) Most people in late medieval England were Catholics, and the Catholic Church was very powerful. Everyone was expected to go to church regularly. They also had to pay a tenth of what they earned to the Church (this special tax is called a tithe).

2) The Church had a lot of influence over people's attitudes and beliefs. In the later Middle Ages, churchmen were taught how to read and write, but few people outside the Church were literate. As a result, most ordinary people depended on churchmen for their knowledge about the world.

3) An important aspect of medieval Christianity was pilgrimage. People travelled to sites associated with particular saints in the hope that they would gain forgiveness for their sins, or be cured of disease. Some European migrants first came to England as pilgrims (see p.35).

Comment and Analysis

The Church could have a big influence over people's attitudes, including towards certain groups of migrants.

The English Economy was Rural and relied on Farming

1) The medieval English economy was very rural — the vast majority of people lived and worked in the countryside. There were some towns, but most were very small with fewer than 2000 inhabitants.

2) Farming improved during the late medieval period. The introduction of windmills made bread production easier, while increased sheep farming helped the English wool trade get off the ground.

3) By the 13th century, many people (including Europeans) came to buy and sell goods at the growing markets in English towns.

Good lord — it's a page on medieval England...

Remember to keep background information in your head when answering exam questions to make sure that what you're writing fits in with what was happening at the time.

EXAM TIP

Jews in England

Jews started to migrate to England in the 11th century. At first, they were protected by the kings of England, but in 1290 they were expelled from the country and banned from coming back.

Many Jews built Communities in England

1) Jews first came to England with William I from about 1070. The Jews prospered and were treated well by William and his sons, William II and Henry I, since their presence in England was good for the economy. The Jews brought over by William established good trade links with Jews in Normandy.

2) Jews were wards of the king. This meant that they were under his direct protection and authority. The king benefited from being the protector of Jews. For example, he could impose special taxes on them.

3) Jewish migrants were given certain privileges. They could hold land from the king and had a right to physical protection. If someone hurt a Jew, they were seen as harming the king's property.

4) Jews also acted as moneylenders. Christians weren't allowed to charge interest when lending money to others (they couldn't ask to be paid back more money than they'd lent to the person). However, Jews were allowed to offer loans and demand interest from people who weren't Jewish.

5) This was useful to the king, as it meant that he and his nobles could borrow money to fund wars and building projects. Many Jews became very rich by trading and lending money to English nobles and kings.

6) In the 12th century, kings realised that the growing prosperity of the Jews could be a source of income. Kings started to tax Jews. Richard I taxed them very heavily to fund his involvement in the Third Crusade.

> The Crusades were a series of wars between Muslims and Christians over control of the Holy Land (the area around Jerusalem).

Bad Feeling against Jews started to Build Up in the 12th century

1) English people resented the special position of Jews. Many were jealous of the wealth some Jews had built up, and people who owed debts to them were angry that Jews had become rich at their expense.

2) The Crusades started in the late 11th century and went on for centuries. Many people became less tolerant of non-Christians. Jews in England were increasingly persecuted (treated badly) because of their religion.

3) In the 12th century, Jews were accused of killing Christian children as part of religious rituals. This was called 'Blood Libel'. Jews were blamed for a Christian child's death in 1255. This led to Jews being killed.

The Jews began to be Persecuted in the 13th Century

1) When Richard I was crowned in 1189, a rumour that he wanted to kill all non-Christians spread around England. Many Jewish people were killed in a series of massacres. There were massacres in the 13th century too.

> Richard had banned Jews from coming to his coronation and violently sent out those that did.

2) In 1253, Henry III put restrictions on Jewish people. He introduced rules that banned Jews and Christians from mixing. Jews were ordered to only live in places where Jews had already lived. Edward I created a law that put more restrictions on Jews in 1275.

3) In 1278 and 1279, Jews were accused of coin clipping (cutting pieces off gold and silver coins). The head of every Jewish household was arrested and hundreds were executed.

4) In 1290, Edward I expelled all Jews from England. He took over their property and forced them to leave, threatening to kill them.

Comment and Analysis

The experience of Jews in late medieval England was shaped by beliefs and economic forces. The Jews had a large impact on English society and were welcomed by earlier English kings because they helped make the country richer. When religious and economic differences between Jews and their poorer Christian neighbours became more prominent, Jews became more likely to be attacked.

The Jews were shut out of England for centuries...

Scribble a summary of the experiences of Jewish communities in England in the period 1250-1290.

REVISION TASK

European Migrants

The late medieval period was a time of steady migration from parts of <u>Europe</u> to England. English <u>kings</u> were particularly <u>keen</u> for foreign merchants to migrate and contribute to the English economy.

European Migrants created Diverse Communities in England

1) Many groups of <u>European people</u> migrated to England. They did so for several <u>reasons</u>.

- Many people migrated for <u>religious</u> reasons. When the Archbishop of Canterbury, <u>Thomas Becket</u>, was murdered in his cathedral in 1170, <u>Canterbury</u> became a site of <u>pilgrimage</u> for European <u>Catholics</u>. Some pilgrims <u>stayed</u> in England after their visit.
- People also came to England to <u>work</u>. England's industries were quite <u>backward</u> compared to other European countries, so foreigners could make a lot of <u>money</u> by starting a business in England.
- England particularly needed foreign workers after <u>1348</u>, when the <u>Black Death</u> had killed huge numbers of English workers.

> After the Reformation (see p.37), England became a <u>sanctuary</u> for many European <u>Protestants</u> — e.g. French Protestants fled to England in the 17th and 18th centuries (see p.38).

2) European migrants came from <u>lots of different</u> European countries. They mainly lived in communities in <u>London</u>, but also in <u>Norwich</u>, <u>Lincoln</u> and other towns and villages.

3) European migrants had a major <u>impact</u> on late medieval England. Many Flemish migrants were skilled <u>weavers</u> and <u>cloth makers</u> — they helped grow the English <u>wool trade</u>. Flemish workers also helped build some of late medieval England's <u>cathedrals</u> and <u>castles</u>. Dutch and German <u>brewers</u> introduced <u>beer</u> into England, which soon became a major trade.

4) It is estimated that between 1330 and 1550 more than <u>64,000</u> <u>people</u> migrated to England. In 1440, it's thought that around 1% of the population in England are were <u>European immigrants</u>.

> **Comment and Analysis**
>
> In the later Middle Ages, European people migrated to Britain for both <u>religious</u> and <u>economic</u> reasons. As a result, there was a wide <u>variety</u> of people living in <u>migrant communities</u> who had <u>different skills</u> to offer and <u>different reasons</u> for coming to Britain. Religious and economic factors continued to play a key role in <u>encouraging migration</u> to Britain right up to the <u>21st century</u>.

Kings wanted Foreign Merchants to come to England

1) <u>Foreign merchants</u> brought <u>supplies</u> into England, which helped to keep <u>prices low</u>. The king could also <u>tax</u> foreign merchants <u>heavily</u>. For example, <u>all merchants</u> paid a <u>royal tax</u> on certain goods called the <u>ancient custom</u>. From <u>1303</u>, foreign merchants had to pay this tax at a <u>higher rate</u> than English merchants.

> Merchants <u>bought</u> and <u>sold</u> raw materials (like wool) and other goods to <u>make money</u>.

2) In return for paying higher taxes, kings offered <u>protection</u> and <u>special rights</u> to foreign merchants to encourage them to <u>stay</u> and <u>trade</u> in England. For example, they didn't have to pay <u>local taxes</u>. This benefited kings at the <u>expense</u> of <u>local communities</u>.

3) In <u>1335</u>, foreign merchants were given the right to <u>live</u> and <u>trade</u> freely <u>anywhere</u> in England. This caused <u>tension</u> between <u>foreign traders</u> and <u>English traders</u>. For example, many <u>London traders</u> didn't like <u>competing</u> with foreigners, so city officials tried to <u>limit</u> foreign traders. The king eventually <u>confirmed</u> the foreign merchants' right to <u>trade freely</u>.

4) In the <u>15th century</u>, attitudes towards foreigners got more <u>negative</u> (see p.36). Some <u>restrictions</u> were put on <u>foreign merchants</u> — they had to live with an <u>English host</u> who monitored what they were doing.

> **Comment and Analysis**
>
> Kings often faced <u>opposition</u> if they tried to tax <u>English</u> people too much. Making <u>foreign people</u> pay <u>high taxes</u> was a way for kings to <u>raise funds</u> without <u>angering</u> English people.

> The foreign merchants who migrated to England came from lots of <u>different</u> European countries and had a <u>variety of backgrounds</u>.

European migrants contributed to the English economy...

Under the headings 'economic forces', 'beliefs and values' and 'government actions', jot down the reasons for European migration to England during the late medieval period.

REVISION TASK

Attitudes Towards Migrants

Attitudes towards migrants varied. While the official response from the government tended to depend on England's relationship with other countries, unofficial responses were often very hostile.

War influenced Official Responses to migrants

1) Foreigners often suffered when England was in conflict with the country or place where they were born. For example, there was tension between England and Ireland in the later Middle Ages. From the 1390s, Irish people were often ordered to leave England, though some bought licences that allowed them to stay.

2) From the 1290s to the 1450s, England and France were often at war with each other. During this time, some English people became more hostile to French people, and to foreigners in general. The government responded to this growing hostility by introducing laws that penalised foreigners.

3) In 1377, the war with France was going badly and many people didn't trust foreigners (especially those linked to England's enemies). The king ordered all foreigners to leave England. However, lots of people weren't included in this order (like craftsmen and merchants). Those who proved their loyalty to England were also allowed to stay.

4) In 1436, England lost an ally — one of the Low Countries. This made England more vulnerable in the war with France. As a result, the government made migrants from the Low Countries show their loyalty to England by taking an oath of allegiance — those who refused were forced to leave the country.

5) Between 1440 and 1487, the king responded to anti-foreigner feeling by ordering all people living in England who were born in a different country to pay taxes called alien subsidies.

Comment and Analysis

During the late medieval period, the government generally encouraged migration to England (see p.34-35). However, they sometimes became suspicious of foreigners if they were from enemy countries. This pattern continued right up to more recent times. For example, during World War I and World War II, migrants from enemy countries like Germany were seen as 'enemy aliens'. They were arrested and sent to internment (prison) camps (see p.47).

Lots of foreigners avoided paying the alien subsidies, and certain groups and individuals were exempt (they didn't have to pay). This angered some English people.

Unofficial Responses to migrants could be very Hostile

The responses of English people who came into contact with migrants varied — English people were often quite hostile towards migrants, which resulted in violence.

1) There were violent attacks on Flemish immigrants in late medieval England. Many thought they were abusing their privileges as foreign traders (see p.35). Flemish weavers were killed in a riot in Norwich in 1312. In 1381, there was a big rebellion in England — Flemings were sought out and killed.

2) Bad feeling against foreigners was pretty high in the 1430s. The war with France was going badly again and the economy was struggling. Many English people were jealous of the privileges given to foreign traders.

3) In 1456, there was a violent conflict between Italian wool merchants and English traders in London. Some thought that the Italians were taking advantage of their privileges.

4) Despite all of this hostility towards them, many immigrants integrated (mixed) well into English society. Some married English people. They also traded with the English and contributed towards the prosperity of English towns, cities and ports.

Comment and Analysis

Historians think that foreigners made up at least 1% of the population of England and maybe even 6% of London's population in the 15th century. Since foreigners were widespread in England by this time, many English people probably came into contact with foreigners in their daily lives.

Feelings about foreigners changed with the war...

Explain the impact that European migrants had on Britain in the period 1250-1500. Give examples to support your answer. [10]

Early Modern Britain

Early modern times could be quite exciting — the Reformation brought new values and attitudes, and there were also new discoveries and innovations. There was still lots of war and conflict, though.

The Reformation led to Religious Instability

1) In the 16th century, groups of Christians (known later as Protestants) were questioning the teachings and practices of the Catholic Church. They eventually broke away from the Catholic Church and formed their own Protestant churches. This religious revolution is called the Reformation.

2) England started the process of becoming a Protestant country in the 1530s, when Henry VIII broke away from the Roman Catholic Church and made himself head of the Church of England. This led to 30 years of religious instability in England, which was brought to an end by Elizabeth I in second half of the 16th century. She reformed the English Church and England became a Protestant country for good.

3) The Reformation led to a lot of conflict between Protestants and Catholics in Europe. As a Protestant country, England offered a refuge to Protestants fleeing Catholic persecution in other European countries. As a result, more migrants came to England from Europe in this period (see p.38).

The early modern period was a time of Exploration and Trade

1) England became increasingly involved in international exploration and trade. From the late 1500s, English sailors travelled to the Americas, Africa and Asia, and began to trade with these regions.

2) English ships brought sugar and tobacco from the Americas, spices from south-east Asia, cotton textiles from India (see below), and tea, silk and porcelain from China. They also became involved in the slave trade (see p.41), taking African people to North America and the Caribbean, where they were forced to work on plantations (large farms) growing crops like sugar, tobacco, rice and cotton.

3) By 1700, England had become a very successful trading nation. The growth of England's international trade network caused increasing immigration from around the world, especially from India (see p.40) and Africa (see p.41).

> **Comment and Analysis**
>
> Advances in shipbuilding and navigational techniques in the early modern period allowed ships to travel longer distances and carry more cargo and crew. This made it easier for migrants from around the world to travel to England.

The East India Company was formed by English Merchants

1) The East India Company was established in 1600, when Queen Elizabeth I gave permission to a group of English merchants to sail to the Indian Ocean to trade. The Company's ships first reached India in 1608. They traded many goods, but the most important was cotton textiles.

© Photo Researchers / Mary Evans Picture Library

East India Company ships in the 17th century.

2) The East India Company established trading posts on the Indian coast. As trade with India grew, the Company took control of more and more Indian territory.

3) The East India Company was no ordinary business. It had its own army, and its trading posts developed into Indian cities like Calcutta (modern-day Kolkata).

4) The East India Company had a lot of employees, and they often brought their families with them to India. They employed Indian ayahs (see p.40) to look after their children. Some ayahs came to Britain.

The ships pressed on in search of new lands...

Spelling is really important in the exam — whether it's a word you'll use a lot, like 'migration', or a more specific word like 'Reformation', make sure that you're able to spell it.

EXAM TIP

Protestant Refugees

After the <u>Reformation</u> (see p.37), there was often <u>conflict</u> in Europe between <u>Catholics</u> and <u>Protestants</u>. Some Protestants facing <u>religious persecution</u> or <u>financial difficulties</u> migrated to Britain.

Huguenots were Protestants fleeing Persecution

1) <u>Huguenots</u> were <u>French Protestants</u>. France was a mainly <u>Catholic</u> country, but the Huguenots were allowed to <u>live</u> in France and practice their <u>religion</u>.

2) This <u>changed</u> in the 17th century, when the Huguenots began to face growing <u>persecution</u>, which caused many to flee to Protestant countries, including <u>England</u>. Persecution reached a peak in 1685, when King Louis XIV <u>outlawed Protestantism</u>.

3) By 1700, there were around <u>50,000</u> Huguenots living in England. Most Huguenots settled around <u>London</u>, or in small villages on the banks of the <u>River Thames</u>. The village of Wandsworth, just outside London, had a <u>French school</u> and <u>cemetery</u>.

Huguenots arrive in Dover in 1685.

© Mary Evans Picture Library

> The Huguenots formed <u>separate communities</u> at first, but gradually became <u>more integrated</u> into English society.

4) However, Huguenots also had to follow <u>strict rules</u>. The government made Huguenots pay <u>more taxes</u> than everyone else, and <u>restricted</u> the types of <u>job</u> they could do.

5) Huguenots also faced <u>opposition</u> from many people. In the 1680s, English craftsmen wrote <u>petitions</u> to try and <u>stop</u> Huguenots from working in their industries.

> Many of the Huguenots were <u>skilled</u> and <u>wealthy</u>. They brought new <u>methods</u> and <u>technologies</u> with them from France, which helped transform the English <u>wool</u> and <u>silk</u> trades into the most successful in the world and <u>boosted</u> the English economy.

The 'Poor Palatines' migrated for Financial and Religious reasons

1) <u>Palatines</u> were <u>Protestant farmers</u> living in the <u>Rhineland</u>, in modern-day Germany. They came to England for several reasons:

> Both the Huguenots and the Palatines fled to England for <u>religious reasons</u>. But <u>economic factors</u> meant that the Huguenots integrated into English society more successfully.

- In 1708–9, the Palatines faced a <u>very cold winter</u>, which spoiled their crops and caused many people to fall ill.
- The Palatines were under the threat of <u>invasion</u> from French Catholic armies.
- The <u>success</u> of the Huguenots in England persuaded Parliament to pass the 1708 <u>General Naturalisation Act</u>, which allowed <u>all Protestants</u> the right to settle in England without restrictions. This <u>encouraged</u> the Palatines to make the trip to England.

2) By summer 1709, there were <u>13,000</u> Palatines living in London. The government tried to settle them around the country, with small groups of Palatines in <u>villages</u> across England.

3) People hoped the Palatines would <u>benefit</u> the English <u>economy</u>, as the <u>Huguenots</u> had done — a <u>relief fund</u> was set up to help the refugees.

4) However, it became clear that this <u>wasn't</u> the case — the Palatines had <u>few skills</u> apart from farming, so they were soon seen as a <u>burden</u> on the country. This caused bad feeling towards Palatines — Palatine houses in Kent were <u>surrounded</u> by a mob, which <u>threw stones</u> and shouted at the Palatines to leave the country.

5) In 1710, the government decided to <u>expel</u> the Palatines and <u>resettle</u> them elsewhere. Over 5000 Palatines were sent to <u>Ireland</u>, where they found that the living conditions were very similar to those they had left in the Rhineland — many <u>went back home</u>. A further 3000 went to <u>New York</u> in America.

6) In 1711, the General Naturalisation Act was <u>withdrawn</u> — the idea of letting all Protestant refugees into the country had become <u>too unpopular</u>.

Huguenots how they improved the economy so much...

Write a list of the similarities and differences between the experiences of the Huguenot refugees and the Palatine refugees.

REVISION TASK

Gypsies and Jews

Early modern England welcomed <u>diverse</u> groups of migrants from Europe, including Dutch, Flemish, French, German and Italian migrants. Two important groups that came during this period were <u>Gypsies</u> and <u>Jews</u>.

The Government passed Harsh Laws against Gypsies

1) <u>Romani people</u> are a group of travelling people who share a common language and culture. They are believed to have originally come from <u>Northern India</u>.

2) Some groups of the Romani people came to Europe, and are thought to have first migrated to England during the <u>late 15th</u> or <u>early 16th centuries</u>. They were given the name '<u>Gypsies</u>', which comes from the word '<u>Egyptians</u>' — many people in England thought Gypsies came from Egypt.

3) Gypsies in early modern England lived in both the <u>countryside</u> and the <u>towns</u>. They found ways of making money, for example through <u>casual farm work</u>, <u>trading</u> or entertainment, like <u>palm reading</u>. Gypsies were often given places to stay by <u>landowners</u> eager for <u>cheap workers</u>.

4) However, the government <u>disliked</u> the Gypsies — they were suspicious of the fact that the Gypsies <u>travelled around</u> rather than having one fixed address. They began to pass <u>anti-Gypsy laws</u>.

5) England's first anti-Gypsy law was the <u>Egyptians Act</u>, passed in 1530 by <u>Henry VIII</u>. The Act <u>banned</u> any more Gypsies from coming to England, and forced those already in the country to <u>leave</u>.

6) In 1554, Queen <u>Mary</u> passed an even harsher <u>Egyptians Act</u> — people couldn't travel without a <u>license</u> and a Gypsy who stayed in England for over a month could be punished by <u>death</u>. Anyone caught <u>talking</u> to somebody from the Gypsy community could also be <u>executed</u>.

The Readmission of Jews allowed them a Safe Refuge

1) In 1648, a series of <u>attacks against Jews</u> took place in Eastern Europe, which killed around 100,000 people. European Jews were looking for a <u>refuge</u>. Although England had expelled their ancestors in 1290 (see p.34), they thought it could be their answer.

2) In 1655, <u>Rabbi Menasseh Ben Israel</u>, a Jewish leader based in the Netherlands, asked England's ruler, <u>Oliver Cromwell</u>, to formally <u>allow Jews</u> back into England. Cromwell <u>supported</u> the proposal, but passed the request on to a committee, which <u>failed</u> to come to an agreement.

3) In March 1656, <u>twenty Jewish refugees</u> took their chances and came to Britain anyway. Cromwell <u>welcomed</u> them — they were given permission to <u>practice Judaism</u> and to build a <u>synagogue</u>.

Jewish Communities began to grow in England

1) Though they could live in England, Jews were still <u>banned</u> from taking up jobs in many areas of work, including the army and the law. Many became <u>bankers</u>, <u>money lenders</u> and <u>businessmen</u>.

> In 1753, Parliament passed the <u>Jewish Naturalisation Act</u> to remove these barriers, but it was so controversial it was withdrawn one year later.

The entrance to Leadenhall Street Synagogue in London in the 1700s.

2) Jews built up large <u>communities</u>, particularly in the <u>East End</u> of London. In this way, many Jewish communities became <u>self-sufficient</u> — once they arrived, very few Jews needed help from England.

3) Many Jewish bankers and traders were extremely <u>successful</u>, and had a major impact on Britain. For example, they helped build the <u>City of London</u> into the <u>financial centre</u> that we know today.

4) Jews were met with <u>anti-Semitism</u> (anti-Jewish prejudice) from many Londoners — they were blamed for the city's <u>poor living conditions</u> and <u>dirty streets</u>.

The Jewish refugees had a big impact on Britain...

In the exam you'll get a couple of questions that just ask you to give factual information. If you learn your stuff now, then these questions will be the perfect place to pick up some lovely marks.

EXAM TIP

Early Indian and African Migrants

The growth of the East India Company (see p.37) meant that trade links developed between England and the Indian subcontinent. This brought many migrants from Asia to England — including ayahs and child servants.

Ayahs *looked after English Children in India*

1) Ayahs were the servants, nurses and nannies who looked after the children of East India Company employees in the 18th and 19th centuries. Ayahs tended to be poor Indian Hindu or Muslim women employed by the English wives of East India Company employees.

2) English nurses were scarce in India. East Indian Company employees were wealthy, so hiring an Indian nurse was easy.

3) Ayahs could be employed with a family throughout their lives, starting as young women and working into old age, and often brought up several generations of the same family.

A drawing of an ayah caring for the children of an English family in India.

4) English parents in India were largely absent, so their children spent most of their time among ayahs. Many English children born in India were closer to their family's ayahs than to their parents. This could cause tensions with the children's parents, who didn't like the idea of their children picking up the Indians' language or way of life.

> Ayahs were in a confusing position. To East India Company officers they were just servants, but they also had influence over the children they cared for.

Ayahs *sometimes came to England*

1) If East India Company officials, merchants or soldiers were sent abroad, their families and ayahs would often go with them. Ayahs would also travel back to England with the families they were employed by to look after the children on the long sea crossing.

2) English families often promised to take their ayahs back to India, but some ayahs continued to work for their family in England, or were abandoned upon arrival. Abandoned ayahs often had no money, so they tried to get work as domestic servants or resorted to begging.

> Ayahs rarely travelled using their own name — they instead had to take the name of the family they were attached to. This showed a lack of respect for the ayah's culture or personal identity.

3) Ayahs had to overcome a lot of racism. English families looked down on them and English people often used the offensive term 'natives' to describe Indians.

> Ayahs are thought to have had a big impact on the English language. Ayahs taught the children they looked after Hindi. It is likely that Hindi words like 'mama' and 'papa' became part of the English language due to the influence of ayahs. Other Hindi or Urdu words that have entered the English language include 'bungalow', 'chutney' and 'pyjamas'.

Comment and Analysis

As Britain's Empire grew, people from all over the world were brought to Britain, where they were often abandoned with little support or protection. Despite the fact that British ships and British families had left these migrants stranded, most people made little effort to help them.

Indian *and* African Children *were often used as* Servants

1) Many children were taken from their homes in India and Africa to work as messengers, craftsmen and dressmakers. They were also brought to England by families to work as domestic servants — children as young as six were made to work in this way.

2) It became quite fashionable to have an Indian or African child servant. They were often dressed in exotic clothing and treated as decorations. Many nobles and monarchs (e.g. Elizabeth I) hired African children as part of their household staff.

Ayahs cared for a family — the family didn't care for them...

Give one example of the hardships that ayahs faced when they came to Britain in the 18th century. [1]

Early African Migrants

Africans started to <u>migrate</u> to England in the <u>16th century</u> when <u>trade routes</u> opened between Africa and England. Later, Africans were brought to England <u>against their will</u>, following the founding of the <u>slave trade</u>.

Africans *came to England for* Different Reasons

1) Many Africans were brought to England to work as <u>servants</u> in the households of English nobles and tradesmen. <u>Catherine of Aragon</u> (one of the six wives of Henry VIII) brought <u>black servants</u> with her from <u>Spain</u> in 1501.

2) Africans also came to England when <u>trade routes</u> between <u>England</u> and <u>Africa</u> opened up in the <u>16th century</u>. Some Africans came to England on merchant ships as <u>sailors</u> and many Africans ended up working in <u>merchants' households</u>. Five Africans were brought to England by merchants in <u>1555</u> to <u>learn English</u> — three went back to Africa and worked as <u>interpreters</u> for English traders.

3) Between <u>1585</u> and <u>1604</u>, England was at <u>war</u> with <u>Spain</u>. English <u>ships</u> captured the <u>crews</u> of many <u>Spanish ships</u> during the war. These crews included <u>Africans</u>, who were brought to England when the <u>English ships</u> returned to <u>port</u>.

Free Africans *worked in lots of* Different Professions

1) By the <u>end</u> of the <u>16th century</u>, there were <u>hundreds</u> of Africans living in England. Many <u>Africans</u> settled in <u>London</u>. There were also Africans in <u>big towns</u> like Bristol, Plymouth, Southampton and Leicester.

2) Some had <u>high status</u> jobs working for the <u>king</u>. A <u>black musician</u> called <u>John Blanke</u> worked for Henry VII and Henry VIII from <u>1507</u>.

3) Many African <u>servants</u> and <u>workers</u> depended on their <u>employers</u> for their <u>livelihood</u>, but others were <u>independent</u>. For example, there were successful African craftsmen in England who <u>supported themselves</u>.

This is part of a manuscript made in 1511 to mark the birth of Henry VIII's son. Historians think that the black trumpeter is John Blanke.

4) Africans appear in many 16th century <u>parish records</u> (church records of burials, marriages and baptisms). These records suggest that many African migrants were <u>integrated</u> into <u>local communities</u> — they <u>mixed</u> with <u>English people</u> and lived and worked alongside them.

5) For example, several Africans were <u>baptised</u> as Christians or <u>buried</u> in English churchyards in the <u>16th century</u>. Some Africans had <u>relationships</u> and <u>children</u> with English people.

6) In <u>1596</u>, a merchant was given permission by Elizabeth I to take <u>Africans</u> from England to <u>Spain</u> (probably to <u>sell</u> or <u>exchange</u> for prisoners of war), as long as their employers agreed — he <u>failed</u> when their employers <u>refused</u> to let them be taken. This suggests that the employers <u>valued</u> their African workers.

Britain sold *African People into* Slavery

1) In 1660, <u>King Charles II</u> founded the Company of Royal Adventurers Trading to Africa. In 1672, it became the <u>Royal African Company</u> — the company that managed the <u>slave trade</u>.

2) Ships from British ports (e.g. <u>Liverpool</u>, <u>London</u> and <u>Bristol</u>) went to the <u>West African coast</u>, where traders bought slaves. They took the slaves to North America or the Caribbean, where they were <u>sold</u> to plantation owners.

> Thousands of African people were transported on British ships <u>every year</u>. By 1807 (the year the slave trade was abolished) <u>over two million</u> African people had been transported from Africa to the Caribbean and America.

3) Some slaves were brought to <u>Britain</u>, either by returning <u>British Empire officers</u> or by <u>farm owners</u>.

Life could be hard for Africans in Britain...

To what extent do you agree that migrants coming to Britain in the period 1500-1750 had a negative experience? Give reasons to support your answer. [18]

Industrial and Imperial Britain

Britain was very wealthy and powerful in this period. The <u>industrial revolution</u> made Britain the 'workshop of the world', and the <u>British Empire</u> created a global trading network. Both <u>encouraged migration</u> to Britain.

The Industrial Revolution transformed Britain's economy

1) The invention of <u>machines</u> like the Spinning Jenny (which made it easier to spin yarn) in the 1760s made British textile manufacturing more efficient — cloth could be made by a machine, rather than by hand in people's homes.

2) Machine owners built large <u>factories</u> to house their machines, and <u>employed workers</u> to operate them. From the 1780s, <u>steam</u> was used to help power these machines, which made them even <u>more efficient</u>.

3) Britain was the <u>first</u> country in the world to industrialise, and it soon became a very <u>large manufacturer</u> of textiles and other goods.

4) The industrial revolution caused a lot of <u>internal migration</u> (people moving around within the same country). People moved from the British <u>countryside</u> (where farming jobs were decreasing) to the new <u>industrial towns</u> to work in the factories.

> The industrial revolution encouraged the development of new methods of <u>transport</u>, including <u>canals</u>, <u>railways</u> and <u>steamships</u>. These improvements in transport made it <u>easier</u> for people to <u>migrate</u>.

> **Comment and Analysis**
>
> The industrial revolution was a major <u>pull factor</u> for migrants — it provided new <u>jobs</u>, not only in the <u>factories</u> but also in the <u>towns</u> that built up around them.

Britain established Colonies all over the world

1) Between about 1750 and 1900, the British empire <u>grew rapidly</u>:

> Britain also had US and Canadian colonies in <u>North America</u>, but it <u>lost</u> its US colonies in <u>1783</u> after the American War of Independence.

- Most of Britain's colonies in the <u>Caribbean</u> had been founded in the <u>17th century</u>. The colonists created <u>sugar</u>, <u>tobacco</u> and <u>cotton</u> plantations. They used <u>slave labour</u> (see p.41) until the abolition (banning) of slavery in 1833.

- After victory in a war against France, Britain took control some of <u>Canada</u> in 1763. Another victory over France in the same year gave the East India Company (see p.37) <u>more control</u> over <u>India</u>.

- In the late 18th century, <u>Australia</u> and <u>New Zealand</u> were brought under British control.

- By the mid-19th century, the East India Company controlled large areas of India. However, in 1857, Indian people <u>rebelled</u> against the company's rule (this is known as India's <u>First War of Independence</u>). In response, the British government passed a law in 1858 which brought India under the <u>direct control</u> of the British Empire.

- In the late 19th century, the 'Scramble for Africa' began, with European countries competing for control over large parts of <u>Africa</u>. Britain set up many colonies, including <u>Kenya</u> and <u>Uganda</u>.

2) Britain operated a worldwide <u>shipping</u> and <u>trade</u> network between its colonies, transporting <u>raw materials</u> and <u>manufactured goods</u> between the different parts of the British Empire. This vast <u>international network</u> made a huge contribution to the <u>growth</u> of the <u>British economy</u>.

The Growth of the British Empire encouraged Immigration

1) The <u>slave trade</u> led to African and Caribbean migration to Britain. Some <u>slaves</u> were brought to Britain with British Empire officers or Caribbean plantation owners. Some African and Caribbean people came as <u>domestic servants</u>. Former slaves who were now <u>free men and women</u> also came — some <u>wrote books</u> about their experiences and <u>campaigned</u> to end the slave trade.

2) Many African and Asian people worked on British Empire <u>ships</u> as sailors (see p.44). Some sailors <u>stayed in Britain</u> between voyages, while others settled in Britain <u>permanently</u>.

Imperial ambitions on an industrial scale...

Split your page in two. On one side, list all of the ways the industrial revolution caused migration to Britain. On the other side, list all of the ways the British Empire caused migration to Britain.

Irish Migrants

The <u>industrial revolution</u> caused a lot of migration to Britain. People arrived from all over the world, but many of the migrants during this period came from just across the water, in <u>Ireland</u>.

Many people from Ireland built Communities in Britain

1) During the <u>industrial revolution</u> (see p.42) there was large-scale migration from <u>Ireland</u> to industrial towns in Britain. Irish people migrated for <u>several reasons</u>:

- In the 1840s, <u>potato harvests</u> in Ireland <u>failed</u>, causing <u>mass starvation</u>. This left thousands of people with no choice but to <u>flee the country</u>.
- The <u>industrial towns</u> offered many <u>job opportunities</u> for Irish migrants, particularly in <u>factories</u> and on the <u>railways</u>.
- Ireland became part of the United Kingdom in 1800, meaning that Irish migrants in Britain could enjoy the <u>same rights</u> as other UK citizens.

> By <u>1900</u>, the majority of Britain's Irish population had been <u>born</u> on the British mainland — <u>permanent Irish communities</u> were firmly established in Britain by this time.

2) The number of Irish in England more than <u>doubled</u> from nearly 300,000 in 1841 to over 600,000 in 1861. <u>Liverpool</u> was one of the busiest areas for Irish migrants, as it was one of the major ports for ships from Ireland. There were also large Irish communities in <u>Glasgow</u>, <u>Manchester</u>, <u>Dundee</u> and <u>Bradford</u>.

3) <u>Whole families</u> sometimes travelled from Ireland to England, while other Irish migrants joined <u>family members</u> who'd already migrated to British towns and cities. <u>Irish communities</u> sprang up in certain <u>areas</u> of these towns and cities.

4) The Irish migrants were mostly <u>Catholic</u>. As Irish communities grew, they helped to found <u>Catholic churches</u> and <u>schools</u> in England.

Comment and Analysis

Until the late 18th century, Catholics in Britain were severely <u>restricted</u> — they couldn't buy <u>property</u>, stand as an <u>MP</u> or practise their <u>religion</u> in public. Changes to the law from the 1770s onwards made life easier, but it was <u>Irish migration</u> that caused a <u>Catholic revival</u>, as it dramatically increased the Catholic population of Britain.

Irish Migrants faced Poor Living Conditions

1) Like many <u>poor people</u> in towns and cities during Britain's industrial revolution, many Irish migrants lived in <u>poor conditions</u> in slums. The Irish often had to live in the <u>dirtiest</u> parts of towns — in Liverpool many lived in <u>cellars</u>, some of which were infested with rats.

2) Most Irish migrants worked in <u>manual</u> jobs in factories, coal mines and docks. They often worked long hours for very little money. Irish migrants also worked on the new canals and railways in Britain — these people soon became known as <u>navvies</u>.

3) They worked for <u>low pay</u>, so they were a source of <u>cheap labour</u> for rich business owners. However, they were <u>disliked</u> by Britain workers because they undercut their <u>wages</u>.

4) Irish migrants were <u>stereotyped</u> by locals as violent and drunk, and were <u>unfairly targeted</u> by the <u>police</u>. There were also <u>anti-Irish riots</u> during the 1850s in towns across the north of England.

5) The Irish migrants' arrival led to a rise in anti-Catholic <u>discrimination</u> — the Protestant locals thought they were <u>morally superior</u> to the Catholic Irish.

> However, the <u>high intermarriage rate</u> between Irish and locals suggests many were able to <u>integrate</u> relatively <u>easily</u>. There were also many <u>successful</u> Irish migrants, who took up important roles in law, acting and other areas.

Comment and Analysis

While many <u>ordinary people</u> were <u>upset</u> by increased migration into Britain between 1750 and 1900, the <u>government</u> took very little action to try and control it. It was only in the <u>20th century</u> that the government began to introduce increasingly strict controls to limit migration.

Irishmen, Scotsmen and Englishmen walk into a factory...

Write a leaflet for potential Irish migrants during the industrial revolution.
In your leaflet, outline the pros and cons of migrating to an English factory town.

Asian and African Migrants

As the British Empire grew, so did its navy. Britain didn't have enough sailors, so it often recruited them from Asia and Africa. Some of these foreign sailors settled in Britain and built up their own communities.

Sailors *from all over the world worked on British Ships*

Many foreign sailors worked for the British Empire. They came from all over the world:

1) Sailors from the Indian subcontinent and south-east Asia were known as lascars. They initially worked for the East India Company (see p.37), and later worked on ships throughout the British Empire. They were known for their hard work and sailing skills.

2) Sailors of African descent from the Caribbean and West Africa also worked on British Empire ships. The British Empire liked to recruit sailors from these regions because of their local knowledge.

3) Chinese sailors worked for British merchant companies like Blue Funnel Line. Many Chinese sailors came from Shanghai — the city was a major international trading port in the late 1800s.

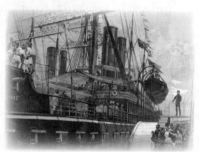

The steamship 'Rome' in a London dock in 1886, manned by lascars.

Sailors' Communities *grew in British Port Towns*

1) In the mid-19th century, there were around 12,000 foreign sailors working on British ships, and at least half of them spent time living in British port towns. Sailors came to Britain for several reasons:

- Poor sailing weather meant sailors had to stay in British ports for months on end before their next journey.

  Improvements in shipping made it easier for migrants to travel to distant countries by sea.

- British ships sometimes abandoned their crew in Britain, without any money or support.

2) Sailors settled in the port towns that they arrived in. London and Liverpool were the two most popular destinations. Other sailors settled in Hull and Bristol.

3) Migrant groups built their own communities to serve the sailors — some ran restaurants and hostels for the migrant population.

A large group of lascars, particularly from the Bengal and Goa areas of India, formed a community in eastern London.

There was a big African sailor community in Liverpool. Many African sailors married African or local women and African communities started to grow.

Cardiff, Liverpool and London had large Chinese communities. These became known as 'Chinatowns'. Many Chinese migrants ran laundry businesses where sailors could have their clothes washed. Later in the 20th century, lots of Chinese migrants worked in the food industry.

Life *in Britain was* Difficult *for migrant sailors*

1) Many sailors lived in slums and other poor areas of the port towns. They often had to live in dirty and freezing conditions — each year, at least 100 foreign sailors died during England's harsh winters.

2) Some abandoned sailors found work on other ships, but others had to resort to begging. Some were helped by British people — some British women ran shelters for homeless sailors.

3) The sailors were mainly men, and there were few south Asian or African women in Britain at that time. Many sailors married British women.

4) The sailors had to face widespread racism in Britain at the time. Many popular writers and newspapers spread false ideas that England was being taken over by immigrants. They particularly didn't like the idea of relationships between Asian or African men and British women.

Foreign sailors faced further opposition. British ships paid their foreign crew less than their English sailors, so local sailors disliked their foreign counterparts for undercutting their wages. There were attacks on foreign sailors, particularly at times of high unemployment.

Asian and African sailors were all at sea in Britain...

There was a lot of variation in the experiences of different groups of immigrants at different points in time, so in the exam make sure you're clear about which group you're describing.

EXAM TIP

Migration from Italy and Eastern Europe

War, famine and persecution in Europe caused many migrants to come to Britain. Among these were Italians and Eastern European Jews — both built large communities in British towns, but both faced opposition.

Italian Migrants had a large Impact on Britain

1) Between around 1800 and 1900, many Italians migrated to Britain. They did so for several reasons:

- In the period 1803-15 there was a major war in Europe involving many countries. This affected Italian farmers, who lost family members, livestock and crops in the war.
- People in Italy experienced a series of epidemics, including typhus (in 1816) and cholera.
- Europe was going through an agricultural revolution as well as an industrial revolution. This meant farming could be done with fewer people, putting many farm workers out of a job.
- Between 1815 and 1861, the different Italian states became united. This caused instability in Italy, so some Italians decided to migrate.

2) Italians migrated to a range of cities in Britain, including Glasgow and Newcastle. The largest Italian community was in Clerkenwell, London — this area became known as 'Little Italy'.

3) Italian migrants built schools, hospitals and shops to support the community. Italian newspapers and political groups were also set up. In 1863, the Italian community in London built St Peter's Roman Catholic Church in Holborn. The church is still known as St Peter's Italian Church.

4) The Italian migrants often had very little money — like lots of workers in industrial cities, many lived in poor conditions.

5) Some of the Italians who arrived in Britain established businesses, including road-building and ceramics. Others became street salesmen, for example as ice cream sellers or organ grinders.

> Italian migrants also faced opposition — people often used negative stereotypes to describe them, and there was a general suspicion of them because they were Catholics.

6) Italians' introduction of ice cream to Britain had a big impact on Britain's food industry, with hundreds of ice cream parlours and ice cream carts springing up across the country. Italian immigrants also opened restaurants, which introduced British people to other Italian dishes.

Jews came to Britain from Eastern Europe

1) In the late 19th century, thousands of Jews migrated to Britain. This was partly to escape disease and hunger — in 1866, there was a cholera epidemic in Poland and a famine in Lithuania. Jews also fled persecution in Germany and Russia. Many went to America — others went to Britain as it was relatively close and cheap to travel to.

2) Most Jewish immigrants worked in the clothing industry, mainly by managing or working in sweatshops — small, unregulated factories where they worked in cramped conditions for long hours and little pay.

3) New Jewish communities began to grow in some British cities, including London, Manchester and Hull. They developed their own shops, restaurants, theatres and other venues, completely run and attended by members of the community.

4) Unlike previous Jewish refugees (p.34 and p.39), Eastern European immigrants lived in closed communities. This, along with their distinctive language and appearance made them targets for anti-Semitic abuse.

A photograph from 1902 of a shop in London with both English and Hebrew words in its window. There was conflict between Jewish and Christian businesses — the Jewish holy day is Saturday, so Jewish businesses opened on Sundays when Christian businesses were closed, drawing away customers.

Italian migration raspberry rippled throughout Britain...

Explain how far you agree with the following statement: 'Economic forces were the most important factor influencing migration to Britain'. [18]

Britain since c.1900

A lot of things happened after 1900, including <u>two World Wars</u> and a <u>Cold War</u>. Britain's relationships, meanwhile, began to shift away from its former colonies in the <u>Commonwealth</u> and towards <u>Europe</u>.

Britain and the Empire fought in two World Wars

1) The <u>First World War</u> broke out in <u>1914</u>. Many countries became involved in the fighting, including <u>Britain</u> and its <u>Empire</u>. The war caused <u>heavy losses</u> — over <u>900,000</u> British and Empire soldiers died in the war, and around <u>2 million</u> were wounded. The war ended in <u>1918</u>.

2) Just two decades later, in <u>1939</u>, the <u>Second World War</u> broke out. Thousands of <u>refugees</u> fled to Britain during the war (see p.47-48), and Britain also became an important <u>haven</u> for defeated governments.

3) Once again, Britain called on its <u>Empire</u> to fight in the Second World War. Many Empire soldiers were temporarily <u>stationed in Britain</u>, and some decided to <u>return</u> once the war was over.

Britain saw the Rise and Fall of its Empire

1) The British Empire was at it's <u>largest</u> in <u>1922</u> — that year, the empire covered almost a <u>quarter</u> of the world's land and around a <u>fifth</u> of the world's population.

2) However, <u>independence movements</u> were gaining support across the Empire. <u>Ireland</u> gained independence from Britain in 1922. In <u>India</u>, campaigners like <u>Mahatma Gandhi</u> led the Indian independence movement — India became <u>independent</u> in <u>1947</u>.

3) Many countries in the <u>Caribbean</u> and <u>Africa</u> gained independence from Britain in the <u>1960s</u>. The British-held territory of <u>Hong Kong</u> was returned to China in <u>1997</u>.

> Britain kept ties with old colonies through the <u>Commonwealth</u> — an <u>international organisation</u> that includes many countries that were in the British Empire. Many <u>Commonwealth migrants</u> came to Britain <u>after World War II</u> (see p.49).

Britain's Relationships with other European countries Improved

1) After the Second World War, European policy makers tried to prevent another war by <u>strengthening the ties</u> between their countries. They formed the <u>European Economic Community</u> (EEC) in 1957, which aimed to maintain peace in Europe through <u>trading</u> and <u>sharing resources</u>.

2) Britain joined the European Economic Community in <u>1973</u>, hoping to <u>improve</u> its <u>economy</u> by increasing its trade with other European countries. This helped <u>strengthen</u> Britain's ties with other European nations like France and Germany.

3) Britain's connections with these countries were strengthened further when the EEC became the European Community, which became part of the new <u>European Union</u> (EU) in 1993.

> One of the main principles of the EU is the <u>free movement of people</u> — citizens of the EU are allowed to <u>live</u> and <u>work</u> in another European country <u>without visas</u>. This helped <u>increase</u> migration to Britain from the continent.

> New methods of <u>communication</u> like the phone, TV and the internet made the world <u>more connected</u> in the 20th century. <u>Instant communication</u> meant that <u>distance</u> between countries seem <u>less important</u>, which removed a barrier that might have stopped people from migrating in the past.

The Cold War divided the world until 1991

1) Between around 1945 and 1991, much of the world was divided into <u>two sides</u> — those who supported the Soviet Union and those who supported the United States. This was known as the <u>Cold War</u>.

2) Europe was particularly <u>divided</u> — Western Europe, including Britain, was on the USA's side, while Eastern Europe was under the Soviet Union's influence. There was very <u>little chance</u> for people to move between West and East Europe.

3) In 1991, the Cold War came to an <u>end</u>, and people were able to move between East and West Europe for the first time in decades. This helped <u>increase</u> migration from Eastern Europe to Britain.

Some relationships thawed during the 20th century...

Remember to support your argument with background information, but only if it's relevant.

The First and Second World Wars

Many refugees came to Britain during World War I. At the same time, people became suspicious of immigrants already in Britain, and some were imprisoned. These events were repeated in World War II.

German Immigrants were Attacked during the First World War

1) Britain declared war on Germany on the 4th August 1914. The next day, Parliament passed two Acts. The Aliens Restriction Act made immigrants register with the police. The Trading with the Enemy Act gave the government the power to confiscate German-owned businesses.

2) German immigrants were accused of aiding the enemy or not being patriotic to Britain. British people in towns across the country assaulted German immigrants and ransacked their businesses.

3) In 1915, the government began taking German immigrants away from their homes to prisoner of war camps or other temporary facilities.

> During the two World Wars, immigrants from Germany and other countries fighting against Britain were described as 'enemy aliens'.

Lots of people came to Britain during the Second World War

People from all parts of the world came to Britain during the Second World War. Some came as refugees, others came to help with the war effort.

1) Six European armies were based in Britain during the war, bringing huge numbers of Polish, Dutch, French, Norwegian, Czech and Belgian troops to the country.

2) British Empire troops also came to Britain during the war. They included soldiers from the West Indies, parts of Africa and around three million soldiers from India.

> In October 1939, the government lifted its colour bar in the armed forces — the military could promote non-white soldiers to officer rank for the first time.

German and Italian immigrants were sent to Internment Camps

1) When the Second World War broke out, the government once again arrested German immigrants it suspected of being 'enemy aliens' and sent them to internment (prison) camps.

2) In April 1940, Britain's campaign to take Norway from the Nazis failed. British newspapers and politicians blamed German spies for the defeat. This caused 'spy fever' — almost all German immigrants and their descendents were suspected of being spies.

3) In June 1940, Italy joined the war on Germany's side. Mobs of British people attacked Italian people living in cities around the UK. The police arrested the Italians, and sent them to internment camps. By the end of June, thousands of Italians had been taken away from their homes.

4) The Prime Minister, Winston Churchill, was keen to expand the internment programme — by August 1940 around 27,000 people of German or Italian origin had been arrested. Most were taken by ship to camps on the Isle of Man, Canada or Australia.

5) The conditions on some ships were terrible. The HMT *Dunera* set out for Australia in July 1940. The passengers were put in rooms with little air and no facilities to wash. Some were assaulted by the crew members.

6) The horrors of the HMT *Dunera* forced the government to rethink. In August 1940, it announced that all internees would be released. By the summer of 1941, only 5000 people were left in the internment camps.

Comment and Analysis

During the Second World War, immigrants were seen as guilty until proven innocent. The government even sent many Jewish refugees to internment camps (which they had to share with Nazi prisoners of war) just because they spoke German or had come from Germany.

HMT Done-an-error would've been a better name...

Draw a spider diagram of the experiences of different groups of immigrants in Britain during the Second World War. Try to include as many dates and other facts in your diagram as you can.

REVISION TASK

Jewish Refugees

When <u>Adolf Hitler</u> became Chancellor of <u>Germany</u> in 1933, <u>Jews</u> began to leave the country in fear.

Jewish Refugees fled Nazi Germany

1) Thousands of Jews left Germany after the Nazis <u>came to power</u>. Some of them fled to <u>Britain</u>.

2) Early in 1938, Germany took over <u>Austria</u>, so Austrian Jews also fled their homes. Many countries, including Britain, responded by <u>restricting how many more refugees</u> they would accept.

3) 1938 saw a series of <u>anti-Semitic acts</u> by the Nazis. The worst were the attacks in November known as <u>Kristallnacht</u> (the 'Night of Broken Glass'). This drove more migration — at least <u>100,000 Jews</u> left Germany and Austria between 1938 and 1939.

4) Kristallnacht <u>changed</u> British public opinion. The government <u>relaxed restrictions</u> for some Jewish refugees. By the outbreak of the Second World War in September 1939, at least <u>40,000</u> Jewish refugees had arrived in Britain.

The Kindertransport rescued Jewish children

1) After Kristallnacht, the British government allowed unaccompanied <u>children</u> to enter Britain on <u>temporary visas</u>.

2) Some British individuals and charities came forward to help organise an <u>evacuation</u> of Jewish children from Germany, Austria and Czechoslovakia. This was known as the <u>Kindertransport</u>.

3) Groups of children travelled from European cities by train to ports in countries like the <u>Netherlands</u>, where they then got a <u>ship</u> to a British port, like <u>Harwich</u>.

4) From there, children who were <u>sponsored</u> by charities went to live with their <u>foster families</u>. Those without sponsors went to live in temporary shelters, like <u>schools</u> or <u>farms</u>.

5) The first transport arrived on <u>2nd December 1938</u> and the last left Germany on <u>1st September 1939</u>. Over 7000 Jewish children were rescued as part of the programme.

> The development of <u>railways</u> in <u>Europe</u> made migration a lot easier. Without the railways, it would have been <u>more difficult</u> and <u>expensive</u> for European migrants to reach <u>ports</u> and sail to Britain.

© Illustrated London News Ltd / Mary Evans

A Kindertransport ship arrives in Harwich in December 1938.

Kindertransport children had Mixed Experiences of Britain

1) Children who were <u>fourteen or older</u> were often put to <u>work</u> in order to help Britain's war effort, for example by helping on farms or as domestic workers.

2) The <u>living conditions</u> of the Kindertransport children depended on their <u>foster families</u> or hosts — some were treated as a new member of the family, while others were <u>treated very poorly</u> and <u>abused</u>.

3) During the 'spy fever' of 1940 (see p.47), around <u>1000 children</u> from the Kindertransport programme were <u>imprisoned</u> as '<u>enemy aliens</u>' by the British government. They were <u>set free</u> by the end of 1940 and many of them went on to join the British army.

4) The Kindertransport was set up with the expectation that the children would eventually go back to their <u>parents</u>. At the end of the war, it became clear that this wasn't possible — many of the children's parents had been <u>murdered</u> by the Nazis in the <u>Holocaust</u>.

5) Some Kindertransport children left for America or Israel, while others <u>stayed</u> in Britain. Many Jewish refugees and their descendents became very <u>successful</u> in Britain after the war, in areas such as <u>science</u>, the <u>arts</u>, <u>politics</u> and the <u>media</u>.

> A large proportion of the Kindertransport children went on to make a huge <u>contribution</u> to Britain — several of them even won <u>Nobel prizes</u>.

Britain saved a lot of people, but it was a reluctant refuge...

Write a summary that analyses why migrants came to Britain in the period 1900-1980. Make sure your summary is clear, organised and supported by examples. [9]

EXAM QUESTION

Commonwealth Migration

After the <u>Second World War</u>, the British Empire <u>declined</u> as more countries gained <u>independence</u> from Britain.

The British Nationality Act was passed to stop Labour Shortages

1) After World War II, Britain didn't have <u>enough people</u> to fill the <u>jobs</u> needed to <u>recover</u> from the war.

2) There was growing <u>confusion</u> about whether people living in the <u>Commonwealth</u> were British citizens.

3) These problems caused the government to pass the <u>British Nationality Act</u> in <u>1948</u>. The Act gave <u>British citizenship</u> to <u>all people</u> living in British colonies and the Commonwealth, allowing them to <u>enter Britain freely</u>. It was hoped that this would <u>encourage</u> Commonwealth migrants to come and work in Britain.

4) Britain was <u>attractive</u> for migrants for different reasons:

The growth of <u>air travel</u> in the second half of the <u>20th century</u> made it <u>easier</u> for migrants to travel to Britain.

For economic reasons

Britain had lots of jobs and some British companies ran campaigns to encourage migration. Many people from the <u>West Indies</u> fought for Britain in <u>World War II</u>. After the war, they returned to countries with <u>poor economies</u> and <u>few jobs</u>. Many decided to <u>work in Britain</u> instead.

For political reasons

For example, in 1947, India gained <u>independence</u> from Britain, and was <u>split</u> into two countries — a Hindu-dominated <u>India</u>, and a mainly Muslim <u>Pakistan</u>. Many <u>Hindus</u> and <u>Muslims</u> found themselves on the wrong side of the border, and left for Britain. India's <u>Sikhs</u> felt they didn't fit on either side, so many of them they also left.

To escape persecution

Many people of <u>Asian descent</u> lived in Britain's African colonies. When <u>Uganda</u> and <u>Kenya</u> became independent in the 1960s, both nations wanted to become <u>more 'African'</u>. They began to persecute their Asian citizens and forced them to leave. When the <u>persecution</u> began, the British government tried to <u>resist</u> taking in these refugees (see p.50). However, many eventually settled in Britain.

These migrants had an Impact on Culture and the Economy

Commonwealth migrants worked in different industries

1) Most <u>West Indians</u> worked in areas where there were lots of jobs, particularly in factories, the transport system and hospitals.

2) <u>Indian</u> and <u>Pakistani</u> migrants settled in British cities, including <u>London</u>, <u>Leeds</u> and <u>Bradford</u>. They worked in <u>factories</u> and the <u>transport system</u>. They immediately faced <u>racism</u> — some companies tried to ban Sikhs from wearing <u>turbans</u> at work.

3) Some <u>Asian migrants</u> from Britain's African colonies founded <u>successful businesses</u> in Britain.

Many companies hired Commonwealth migrants because they were <u>cheaper to hire</u> than British workers. This caused <u>tension</u> in <u>local communities</u>, as many British people didn't want to <u>compete</u> for jobs with migrants, who they saw as <u>culturally different</u> to British people. There were <u>riots</u> and <u>violent attacks</u> on migrants in the second half of the 20th century because of this tension (p.50).

Comment and Analysis

In the <u>1950s</u>, many migrants from the Commonwealth were <u>single men</u> who came to Britain to <u>work</u>. By the late <u>1960s</u> and <u>1970s</u>, more and more <u>families</u> had migrated to Britain and set up <u>permanent homes</u>. This meant that migrant communities <u>grew</u>, bringing new <u>foods</u>, <u>fashions</u> and <u>cultural values</u> to Britain. However, <u>racism</u> and <u>prejudice</u> meant that migrant communities <u>weren't properly integrated</u> into British society until later in the 20th century.

Some Commonwealth migrants tried to integrate into British communities

1) Many <u>West Indians</u> tried to <u>integrate</u> into British society, but they faced <u>opposition</u>. Banks <u>wouldn't</u> lend them money so they couldn't start <u>businesses</u>. Restaurants and shops sometimes <u>refused</u> to let them in because of their skin colour. They also faced <u>racial abuse</u> on the street and on buses.

2) Many <u>Indian</u> and <u>Pakistani</u> migrants <u>didn't try to integrate</u> (partly because they faced racism). They built their <u>own communities</u> and set up a <u>banking system</u>, <u>law firms</u>, <u>schools</u> and <u>places of worship</u>.

3) Many people of <u>Asian descent</u> from Britain's African colonies settled in <u>London</u>, <u>Leicester</u> and <u>Birmingham</u>. <u>Charities</u> helped them settle, and they soon built up large <u>communities</u>.

Diverse groups with diverse experiences of Britain...

Write a paragraph about the impact of Commonwealth immigrants on Britain.

Immigration Legislation

The arrival of Commonwealth migrants and their poor treatment by locals led to <u>social instability</u> in some areas. Migrants dealt with <u>racism</u> from locals, and the government saying they were <u>part of the problem</u>.

Immigrants were the victims of Race Riots

1) From their arrival in Britain, many Commonwealth immigrants had to deal with <u>racism</u> — they were often <u>refused jobs</u> or <u>accommodation</u> because of the <u>colour of their skin</u>.

2) In the 1950s, gangs of violent young British men <u>attacked immigrants</u> from the West Indies. The attacks grew into <u>race riots</u>, in which the gangs <u>assaulted</u> West Indian immigrants and <u>ransacked</u> their businesses.

3) The worst riots took place in <u>August 1958</u>, when violence broke out in <u>Nottingham</u>, as well as the <u>Shepherd's Bush</u> and <u>Notting Hill</u> areas of London. In Notting Hill, around 400 white men attacked West Indian businesses and houses.

> The first <u>Notting Hill Carnival</u> took place in 1959. This was partly a response to the riots. It became an annual <u>celebration</u> of <u>West Indian</u> and <u>African culture</u>.

The government introduced a law to Reduce Immigration

1) Politicians <u>condemned</u> the white rioters, but also suggested that the riots were in part caused by <u>too much immigration</u>. As a result, <u>immigration laws</u> were changed. In 1961, the government announced a law that would <u>limit</u> Commonwealth migration. It was passed in <u>July 1962</u> as the <u>Commonwealth Immigrants Act</u>.

   - The Act tried to <u>control</u> the number of immigrants coming to Britain from the Commonwealth.
   - Immigrants had to apply for a <u>work voucher</u> before coming to Britain. The <u>fewer skills</u> and qualifications they had, the <u>less likely</u> their application for a work voucher was to succeed.

2) The Act caused a <u>fall</u> in Commonwealth migration. However, some historians have argued that <u>controlling immigration</u> did <u>not</u> help deal with <u>violence</u> and <u>racial discrimination</u>.

Comment and Analysis

The 1962 Act was a <u>big change</u> from the 1948 British Nationality Act (see p.49). After the 1962 Act, the success of a Commonwealth migrant's application depended on how much they could <u>contribute to the country</u>, rather than the <u>historical ties</u> that had existed between Britain and its former colonies.

Race Relations laws and Immigration Controls were introduced

1) The government wanted to tackle the type of racism that had led to the 1958 riots. In 1965, it passed the <u>Race Relations Act</u>. This outlawed <u>racial discrimination</u> and set up a <u>Race Relations Board</u> to deal with race-related complaints. However, the board was <u>weak</u> so the Act wasn't properly enforced. In 1968, the powers of the Race Relations Board were <u>extended</u>.

2) In 1968, many people from the Asian population in <u>Kenya</u> (see p.49) tried to flee their country and come to Britain. Fearful that more migration would increase racial tensions, the government decided to <u>increase controls</u> on Commonwealth migration. It passed another <u>Commonwealth Immigrants Act</u> in <u>1968</u>.

3) Under the 1968 Commonwealth Immigrants Act, only those with a British-born <u>parent</u> or <u>grandparent</u> could claim full British citizenship. The Act was followed by an even more restrictive Immigration Act in <u>1971</u>.

> <u>Immigration laws</u> are about stopping people from <u>coming into the country</u>. <u>Race relations laws</u> are about stopping <u>discrimination</u> against immigrants who are <u>already in Britain</u>.

Racism was a persistent problem in Britain...

Dates are particularly important when you're writing about different laws. With so many Acts with similar names, adding the Act's date makes sure the examiner knows exactly which law you mean.

Racist and Anti-Racist Movements

The <u>political</u> and <u>social impact</u> of Commonwealth immigration was quite serious. <u>Racial tensions</u> came to a head in the 1960s and 1970s, when conflict between <u>racist</u> and <u>anti-racist</u> groups turned into <u>violence</u>.

Racist and Anti-racist Movements began to gain support

1) In 1967, the <u>National Front</u> (NF) was founded. The NF was <u>racist</u> — it only let <u>white people</u> join, and believed that only white people should be allowed to migrate to Britain. Other similar racist groups, like the <u>British Movement</u>, began at around the same time.

2) In 1968, the Conservative politician <u>Enoch Powell</u> made his famous '<u>Rivers of Blood</u>' speech, in which he made <u>racist remarks</u> and <u>criticised</u> the government's <u>race relations</u> laws. He was <u>sacked</u> from his position in the party, but his comments encouraged further racist language and actions.

3) In August 1977, the NF planned a <u>march</u> in <u>Lewisham</u> — an area of London with a large black population. The police <u>refused</u> to ban the march, so several <u>anti-racist groups</u> took matters into their own hands. The NF and the anti-racist groups met in Lewisham, and the march descended into <u>violence</u> between the two groups — this became known as the <u>Battle of Lewisham</u>.

4) After the Battle of Lewisham, the anti-racist protesters came together to form the <u>Anti-Nazi League</u> in 1977. This became one of the main British <u>anti-racist movements</u> in the late 1970s.

5) Other <u>anti-racist groups</u> were founded, including <u>Campaign Against Racism and Fascism</u> (CARF) and <u>Anti-Fascist Action</u>.

> The NF had <u>over 300 candidates</u> in the 1979 general election, but hardly anyone voted for these candidates — the party <u>split</u> in 1980. Some members formed the <u>British National Party</u> in 1982.

© Marx Memorial Library / Mary Evans

Thatcher's government passed a new British Nationality Act

1) <u>Margaret Thatcher</u> became Prime Minister in 1979. In 1978, she had given a TV interview in which she said that people in Britain felt '<u>swamped</u>' by immigrants. She believed in <u>stricter</u> immigration controls.

2) In 1981, with fears that rates of immigration were still rising, Thatcher's Conservative government passed a new <u>British Nationality Act</u>. This created <u>three different levels</u> of citizenship:

- <u>British citizenship</u> was given to people who were <u>already</u> British citizens and had the <u>full right to live and work</u> in Britain. British citizens kept <u>all their rights</u>.

- <u>British dependent territories citizenship</u> was given to people who were already British citizens but came from one of Britain's <u>overseas territories</u>, like the Falkland Islands or Gibraltar. They were allowed to hold a <u>British passport</u>, but had to have a <u>work permit</u> or <u>visa</u> before entering Britain.

- <u>British overseas citizenship</u> was given to people who were British citizens before the act came into effect, but who <u>no longer fitted</u> into either of the other two groups. They now had to apply for a <u>visa</u> before entering Britain.

Comment and Analysis

The British Nationality Act <u>restricted immigration</u> by limiting what counted as being <u>British</u>. This was the end of a <u>process</u> that started with the <u>1962 Commonwealth Immigrants Act</u> (see p.50) — the right to live in Britain was <u>taken away</u> first from <u>Commonwealth citizens</u>, then from <u>overseas citizens</u> still under <u>British rule</u>. British nationality became <u>exclusive</u> to people who lived in Britain itself.

The Act was tested in 1995–97 when people in the British overseas territory of <u>Montserrat</u> were left homeless after a volcano eruption. When they asked Britain for help, the government initially <u>refused</u>, and only reluctantly gave them refuge in Britain <u>two months later</u>. When they arrived in Britain, the Montserrat people were given <u>very little help</u> to find jobs or homes. They had gone from being <u>British citizens</u> before 1981 to <u>unwanted refugees</u> by 1997.

British citizenship was becoming an exclusive club...

To what extent do you agree that migrants coming to Britain after 1900 had a positive experience? Give reasons to support your answer. [18]

EXAM QUESTION

Migration since the 1980s

People from around the world have continued to migrate to Britain since the 1980s. Some have come to escape war or persecution in their home country, while others have come to find work.

There are Different Types of Migrants

> By the late 20th century, a complex international network of air, sea, rail and road links had developed, so it was easier for migrants to travel to Britain.

Most migrants since the 1980s fall under one of three categories:
- A refugee is someone who has fled their home country to escape war, persecution or natural disaster.
- When they come to Britain, refugees have to apply for permission to stay (asylum). While they're waiting for their application to be processed, they're known as asylum seekers.
- An economic migrant is someone who migrates for economic reasons, e.g. to find work.

Many Refugees applied for Asylum in Britain

1) Since the 1980s, war and persecution have created new groups of refugees, for example:

   - In the early 1990s, Yugoslavia in south-eastern Europe broke apart into several countries. This led to a series of wars, which forced millions of people to leave their homes.
   - In 1991, civil war broke out in Somalia, a country in eastern Africa. Many people fled the country and applied for asylum in Europe.
   - Persecution and civil war caused thousands of Sri Lanka's Tamil minority group to flee.
   - Many people fled Afghanistan after the USA and other countries invaded in 2001.
   - Between 1983 and 2005, there was a civil war in Sudan, which caused many to flee. The war ended with part of the country breaking away to form South Sudan, which itself plunged into civil war, creating even more refugees.
   - In 2011, an uprising in Syria led to a civil war. Many Syrians fled the conflict.

   > Not all asylum seekers are successful. Those who are successful are allowed to stay in Britain as refugees. Unsuccessful asylum seekers are sent back to their country of origin.

2) Many people from these areas applied for asylum in Britain. Asylum seekers mainly settled in London and the south-east of England. In 1999, the government began to spread asylum seekers around the country, e.g. to Manchester, Glasgow and Leeds.

3) Asylum seekers were often housed in poor accommodation. It was also difficult for them to find jobs — from 2002, they were banned from working without the permission of the government.

4) In general, asylum seekers were not welcomed by locals. Sometimes they were even attacked — in 2000, a group of asylum seekers had to move from where they'd been placed in Hull due to frequent attacks.

5) Some asylum seekers were even worse off — the government housed them in detention centres (e.g. Yarl's Wood in Bedfordshire) while their claims were processed. Campaigners criticised some of these centres for their poor living conditions and the way the detained asylum seekers were treated.

Economic Migrants came to Britain for a range of reasons

1) Some economic migrants came from the European Union (see p.46). Economic migrants from EU countries can move freely within the EU in order to work. Many economic migrants came from countries that joined the EU after 2004, for example Poland and Hungary.

2) Other economic migrants came from the Commonwealth (see p.49) and other parts of the world. Unlike EU migrants, most needed to apply for a visa before working in Britain. They often worked in jobs where Britain had major labour shortages.

3) Though they have faced opposition from some politicians and newspapers, economic migrants have contributed significantly to British society and Britain's economy.

All these people are keeping things moving...

Explain how far you agree with the following statement: 'The government was the most important factor influencing migration to Britain'. [18]

EXAM QUESTION

Revision Summary

That section didn't know whether it was coming or going. Keep your brain cells moving with these questions.
- Try these questions and <u>tick off each one</u> when you <u>get it right</u>.
- When you've done <u>all the questions</u> for a topic and are <u>completely happy</u> with it, tick off the topic.

Late Medieval Britain, c.1250-c.1500 (p.33-36) ☑

1) Briefly describe England's economy in the later Middle Ages. ☑
2) Give two examples of the persecution of Jews before their expulsion from England in 1290. ☑
3) List three reasons why many European people migrated to England in the later Middle Ages. ☑
4) How did late medieval English kings encourage migration from Europe? ☑
5) Give two official and two unofficial responses to European migration in late medieval England. ☑

Early Modern Britain, c.1500-c.1750 (p.37-41) ☑

6) What was the East India Company and when was it founded? ☑
7) Explain why Huguenot refugees migrated to Britain. ☑
8) List three reasons why the Palatines migrated to Britain. ☑
9) How did the government respond to Gypsy immigration in the 16th century? ☑
10) When were Jews readmitted into England? ☑
11) Describe the experiences of Jews who arrived in England after readmission. ☑
12) What is an ayah? How did they end up in Britain? ☑
13) Give three reasons why Africans migrated to England during the 16th century. ☑

Industrial and Imperial Britain, c.1750-c.1900 (p.42-45) ☑

14) How did the Industrial Revolution affect migration to Britain? ☑
15) Describe what life was like for Irish migrants living in English industrial towns. ☑
16) What is a lascar? Why did they come to Britain? ☑
17) Describe two difficulties that foreign sailors faced when they settled in Britain. ☑
18) Describe the impact that Italian migration had on Britain. ☑
19) Give three reasons why Jews migrated from Eastern Europe to Britain in the late 1800s. ☑

Britain since c.1900 (p.46-52) ☑

20) Describe Britain's changing connections with the wider world in the 20th century. ☑
21) Around how many German and Italian immigrants were imprisoned during the Second World War? ☑
22) What was the Kindertransport programme? ☑
23) For each of these groups, give one reason for migrating and describe their experiences of Britain:
   a) people from the West Indies.
   b) people from India and Pakistan.
   c) people of Asian descent from Uganda and Kenya. ☑
24) How did the government respond to racial tension in Britain in the 1960s? ☑
25) Give the names of one racist and one anti-racist movement since the 1960s. ☑
26) What is an asylum seeker? ☑

Early Territorial Expansion

When America gained <u>independence</u> from Britain in 1783, westward expansion began almost <u>immediately</u>.

Most of the American population used to live along the East Coast

1) From the 15th century, European countries such as Britain, France and Spain <u>colonised</u> America. By the 18th century, Britain had <u>13 colonies</u> on the <u>east coast</u>. After winning the <u>Seven Years' War</u> against France in <u>1763</u>, Britain gained the <u>Northwest Territory</u> and became the <u>dominant</u> power in North America.

2) <u>Tension</u> grew in the British colonies over increasing British <u>interference</u>, e.g. tax and trade regulations and outlawing <u>migration</u> into the Northwest Territory.

3) The colonies declared themselves the independent <u>United States of America</u> in 1776 and fought the <u>Revolutionary War</u> against Britain (1775-1783) to gain their <u>independence</u>.

4) Britain <u>recognised</u> the independence of the United States in <u>1783</u> and the war <u>ended</u>. The United States also gained the <u>Northwest Territory</u> from Britain.

5) In 1789, the American <u>Constitution</u> came into force and <u>George Washington</u> became the first <u>president</u> of the United States. By 1790, each of the 13 former colonies had been admitted as <u>states</u>.

> The <u>Northwest Ordinance</u> of 1787 agreed that in time the Northwest Territory should be cut up into <u>states</u> and that these should be admitted to the Union (the United States of America).

Comment and Analysis

The Northwest Ordinance was important because it laid out <u>plans</u> for <u>westward expansion</u> into the Northwest Territory (Ohio was the first state to be created in the Territory). It also established a <u>process</u> for adding <u>new states</u> to the Union.

The Louisiana Purchase Doubled the size of America

1) In 1803, the US bought the Louisiana Territory from France — it covered <u>over 800,000 square miles</u> of land, but its boundaries <u>weren't clear</u>. It was a <u>vast</u> amount of land — all or part of <u>15 states</u> would be formed from it.

> The US claimed that the Louisiana Purchase included <u>West Florida</u>, which belonged to <u>Spain</u> — but Spain <u>disagreed</u>. In <u>1810</u>, the people of West Florida <u>revolted</u> against Spanish rule — US soldiers <u>occupied</u> the area and President Madison declared it to be part of the <u>US</u>. Spain officially gave Florida to the US in the <u>Adams-Onis Treaty</u> of <u>1819</u>.

2) The Louisiana Purchase encouraged westward <u>migration</u>. Settlers had already started to move westwards, but the Purchase provided even <u>more land</u> for people to settle on.

3) It gave the US control of the <u>Mississippi River</u>, which was important for <u>trade</u>, especially as the nation expanded westwards.

4) President Thomas Jefferson commissioned the <u>Lewis and Clark Expedition</u> in 1803 to <u>explore</u> the Louisiana Territory and the land beyond. The group reached the <u>west coast</u> in <u>1805</u> and returned with their findings.

> The expedition resulted in greater <u>geographic</u> and <u>scientific</u> knowledge of the West.

Comment and Analysis

The Louisiana Purchase helped the US <u>establish</u> itself as a nation. The Louisiana Territory was a huge amount of land, which increased the <u>confidence</u> of the USA and its <u>power</u> on the world stage.

Justifies giving Independence Day another watch I reckon...

It's important to be familiar with the stuff that went on in America before 1789 — you won't be tested on it but it will improve your grasp of the topic and give you more confidence in the exam.

Early Territorial Expansion

A second war with Britain in 1812 made expansion <u>easier</u> for the US. Many US citizens <u>supported</u> expansion.

War Weakened Native American Resistance to western expansion

1) America <u>declared war</u> on Britain in <u>1812</u>. The government was angry that the British were <u>restricting</u> American trade, <u>forcing</u> American sailors to join the British Navy and <u>supporting</u> the Native American fight against western expansion.

> America <u>asserted</u> itself during the war — it was seen as a <u>second war of independence</u>.

2) The war ended in 1815. There was <u>no clear winner</u> and neither side <u>lost territory</u> — the <u>Treaty of Ghent</u> agreed to return things to how they were <u>before</u> the war.

3) However, <u>Native Americans</u> in the East were <u>badly affected</u> by the war:

- Native Americans felt <u>threatened</u> by westward expansion. Britain <u>supported</u> them in halting expansion, but at the end of the war Britain <u>withdrew</u> this support.
- The Shawnee war chief <u>Tecumseh</u> managed the difficult task of <u>uniting</u> different Indian tribes. But he <u>died</u> helping the British in the war and there was no-one to replace him.

> **Comment and Analysis**
>
> After the war, the Native Americans were <u>less able</u> to resist expansion — they were no longer united and had lost their external ally. Following Tecumseh's death, the USA made more than <u>200 treaties</u> with eastern tribes, which resulted in the tribes <u>losing</u> their <u>land</u>.

White Americans wanted to Expand Westwards

1) The US government and American people increasingly believed that it was America's <u>duty</u> to expand westwards. Thomas <u>Jefferson</u>, president from 1801-1809, believed that land ownership and farming would create a <u>healthy</u>, <u>virtuous</u> population. To American people, expansion promised <u>freedom</u>, <u>independence</u> and <u>opportunity</u>.

> The population of America was <u>growing</u> — people wanted <u>more</u> land to farm.

2) Better <u>transport links</u> were created which enabled western expansion.

- Construction of the 620 mile long <u>National Road</u> began in 1811, connecting the <u>east coast</u> to <u>Illinois</u>.
- The 353 mile long <u>Eerie canal</u> opened in 1825, connecting <u>New York</u> to the <u>Great Lakes</u>.

3) These transport links connected <u>farmers</u> who had moved westwards with <u>markets</u> in the <u>East</u>, creating profit-making opportunities for them.

> <u>Steamboats</u>, introduced in 1807, provided <u>faster</u> transportation along waterways.

4) <u>New technology</u> also made farming <u>profitable</u> and <u>attracted</u> settlers to move westwards, e.g. the <u>mechanical grain reaper</u> was invented in 1831, which allowed farmers to harvest crops more <u>efficiently</u>.

By 1838, <u>26 states</u> had been created from territory belonging to the United States.

CANADA

Oregon Country (shared between US and Britain)

Mexico

Unorganised Territory

Disputed between Mexico and Texas

Republic of Texas (1836)

MEXICO

New Hampshire
Vermont (1791)
Massachusetts
Maine (1820)

Wisconsin Territory (1836)
Michigan (1837)
Iowa Territory (1838)
New York
Rhode Island
Connecticut
New Jersey
Pennsylvania
Delaware
Maryland

Illinois (1818)
Indiana (1816)
Ohio (1803)
Virginia

Missouri (1821)
Kentucky (1792)
N. Carolina
S. Carolina

Arkansas (1836)
Tennessee (1796)
Mississippi (1817)
Alabama (1819)
Georgia

Louisiana (1812)
Florida Territory

ATLANTIC OCEAN

— National Road
— Eerie Canal

Things were already going badly for the Native Americans...

Make a timeline of the important events from 1789 to 1838. If you're feeling adventurous, keep adding to it throughout this section all the way up to 1900 — you know you want to.

The Making of America, 1789-1900

Cotton Plantations and Slavery

As cotton became more and more <u>profitable</u>, cotton plantations and slavery <u>expanded</u> in the South.

Cotton and slavery Weren't always Dominant in the South

1) <u>Plantations</u> were established in the South of America in the <u>17th century</u>. Plantations were large farms which harvested crops such as <u>sugar</u>, <u>tobacco</u> and <u>cotton</u> — these were <u>labour intensive</u> crops, so <u>large</u> numbers of workers were needed to harvest them.

2) At first, <u>indentured servants</u> were the main source of labour on these plantations, but they were gradually replaced by <u>African slaves</u>. Plantation owners got these slaves through the <u>Atlantic slave trade</u> — Africans were <u>forced</u> into slavery and <u>transported</u> to America on ships where they would be <u>bought</u> at market.

> Indentured servants agreed to work for a certain number of <u>years</u> in return for <u>passage</u> to America from <u>overseas</u>.

3) <u>Tobacco</u> was more profitable than cotton in the <u>18th century</u>. Cotton picking was a <u>time consuming</u> business — the cotton fibres had to be separated from the seeds <u>by hand</u>.

Technology increased the importance of Cotton and Slavery

1) Britain experienced an <u>industrial revolution</u> in the early 19th century. New <u>machines</u> were developed which allowed factories to <u>process</u> much <u>more</u> cotton. As a result, <u>demand</u> for cotton in Britain <u>increased</u> enormously, which meant US planters could <u>export</u> much larger quantities of cotton to Britain.

> Cotton fuelled <u>westward expansion</u> because people wanted <u>more land</u> to farm cotton.

2) In the US, the <u>mechanical cotton gin</u> was invented by Eli Whitney in 1793. It removed the cotton fibre from the seeds <u>mechanically</u>.

3) The cotton gin hugely increased the <u>speed</u> at which cotton on plantations could be processed. This allowed planters to <u>expand</u> their cotton production. They increased their labour force, which resulted in the <u>expansion</u> of <u>slavery</u>.

4) Cotton became the South's <u>most important crop</u> — the economy of the South came to <u>rely</u> upon cotton <u>exports</u> and the South became <u>dependent</u> on slavery.

> The end of the Atlantic <u>slave trade</u> in <u>1808</u> meant that the price of existing slaves in the US <u>increased</u>. (Although the slave trade ended, slavery and slave trading <u>continued</u> in the USA.)

5) Only a <u>small</u> number of <u>wealthier</u> southerners owned plantations and slaves, but many southerners saw slavery as part of their <u>way of life</u> — they called it their 'peculiar institution'.

Slaves were Treated Badly on plantations

1) Many white Americans saw black Africans as <u>inferior</u> to white people. African slaves were seen as <u>property</u> of the planters and had <u>no rights</u> or <u>freedom</u>.

2) <u>Cheap</u> labour was needed for plantations to be <u>profitable</u>, which meant that slaves had <u>poor living conditions</u>. They worked <u>long</u>, <u>hard hours</u>, were <u>not fed well</u> and lived in small, poorly built <u>cabins</u>.

3) Treatment of slaves on plantations <u>varied</u>, but was often <u>inhumane</u> and <u>cruel</u>. Owners tried to maintain <u>strict discipline</u> of slaves by <u>whipping</u> and <u>beating</u> them. <u>Sexual abuse</u> of female slaves was common.

> <u>Frederick Douglass</u> was a slave who was born on a plantation in 1818. He <u>taught himself</u> to read and write and managed to <u>escape</u> to the North where slavery was banned. His autobiography is a <u>useful source</u> for showing the <u>treatment</u> of slaves — he writes about his <u>separation</u> from his mother at an early age and the <u>brutal whippings</u> and <u>beatings</u> he suffered on one plantation.

Comment and Analysis

It's important to recognise slaves' efforts to <u>resist</u> this inhumane treatment. Some <u>ran away</u> and some even <u>rebelled</u>. Others worked <u>slowly</u>, <u>damaged</u> farm machinery and kept African <u>culture</u> alive through religion and music.

> Plantation owners tried to keep slaves like Douglass in <u>ignorance</u> by not allowing them to learn to <u>read</u> or <u>write</u>.

Cotton plantations and slavery went hand-in-hand...

You'll need to understand the relationship between the expansion of cotton and the expansion of slavery for the exam. The success of cotton meant that slavery became a way of life in the South.

EXAM TIP

The Removal of Indigenous People

A number of <u>Native American</u> tribes lived on <u>land</u> in the East which US citizens <u>wanted</u> to settle and farm on.

Washington aimed to 'Civilise' eastern Native American tribes

1) President <u>George Washington</u> pursued a policy of '<u>civilising</u>' Native Americans living east of the Great Plains (see below) — many US citizens saw Native American society as <u>inferior</u> and <u>savage</u> and believed that they needed to be <u>taught</u> how to live like white settlers.

2) Washington claimed he wanted to <u>respect</u> the Native Americans' <u>right</u> to their homeland as long as they <u>assimilated</u> into society.

> This meant changing their <u>lifestyle</u> to fit in with that of white Americans.

3) <u>Five tribes</u> were considered '<u>civilised</u>' as a result of this policy, because they took on aspects of white culture — the <u>Cherokee</u>, <u>Chicksaw</u>, <u>Choctaw</u>, <u>Creek</u> and <u>Seminole</u>.

Jackson Moved eastern tribes on to the Great Plains

1) Some of the land that settlers wanted to farm was <u>occupied</u> by Native American tribes. The five 'civilised' tribes lived on land in the <u>South</u>, which settlers wanted for growing <u>cotton</u>. Settlers <u>harassed</u> these Indian tribes and <u>pressured</u> the government to take their tribal land.

> The <u>Cherokee</u> lived in European-style <u>houses</u> and published their own <u>newspaper</u>, but people still didn't see them as <u>equal</u>.

2) In 1830, the <u>Indian Removal Act</u> was passed under President <u>Andrew Jackson</u> — this authorised the president to grant tribes land on the <u>Great Plains</u> in <u>exchange</u> for their land <u>in the East</u>. Jackson claimed that it would <u>benefit</u> the tribes to be moved <u>away</u> from settlers where they could live in <u>peace</u>.

> The Great Plains were a huge, flat expanse of <u>grassland</u>. The weather there was often <u>extreme</u> — e.g. <u>droughts</u> and heavy <u>snow</u>.

3) The Removal Act was supposed to be <u>voluntary</u>, but when some tribes in the south-east <u>resisted</u>, the US government <u>forced</u> them to leave:

- The <u>Cherokee</u> resisted removal through <u>legal</u> means, but they were eventually <u>forcefully</u> marched by US soldiers to the Plains in 1838. It was <u>winter</u> and it's been estimated that <u>4000</u> Cherokee out of around 15,000 died on the march. This journey became known as the <u>Trail of Tears</u>.
- The <u>Seminole</u> fought a guerilla war against the US army from <u>1835-42</u>. The war was <u>costly</u> for both sides, but the Seminole eventually <u>surrendered</u> and were moved onto the Plains.

4) By 1840, most of the eastern tribes had been moved onto the Plains — around <u>70,000-100,000</u> people in total.

5) The intention was that Native Americans would live on the Great Plains, while settlers farmed land in the East — the Plains would be like one <u>large Indian reservation</u>. The boundary between the two regions was known as the <u>Permanent Indian Frontier</u>.

6) At this point, white Americans viewed the Plains as '<u>The Great American Desert</u>'. They believed that its <u>harsh</u> climate and lack of <u>wood</u> and <u>water</u> made it unsuitable for settling.

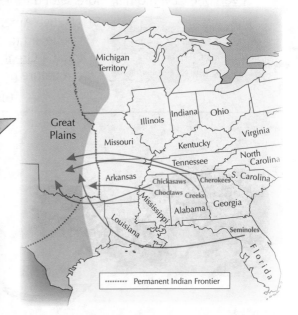

Comment and Analysis

The government gave the Native Americans the Great Plains, but <u>only</u> because white settlers <u>didn't</u> want the land themselves. Because they saw Native Americans as <u>inferior</u>, they felt it was <u>acceptable</u> to give them land they themselves didn't think was <u>fit</u> to live on.

'Here you are, you can have this lovely desert to live in...'

Use this page to understand how and why the Permanent Indian Frontier was created. It was actually a lot less permanent than the name suggests... more about this later.

The Plains Indians

Other Native American tribes already lived on the Great Plains — they're known as the <u>Plains Indians</u>.

The Plains Indians lived in different groups called Tribes

1) The Plains Indians weren't a single group with a single culture — there were many <u>different</u> tribes.

2) These tribes had things in <u>common</u>, but they were <u>diverse</u> in appearance, lifestyle and language.

> E.g. The <u>Cheyenne</u> led a <u>nomadic</u> lifestyle — they regularly moved from place to place, following the buffalo which they hunted for food. In contrast, the <u>Mandan</u> farmed and lived in <u>permanent</u> villages.

The Plains Indians led Very Different Lifestyles to white settlers

The <u>Lakota Sioux</u> are an example of a nomadic Plains Indian tribe who lived very <u>differently</u> to settlers. They had broadly <u>similar</u> beliefs and practices to other nomadic Plains Indian tribes.

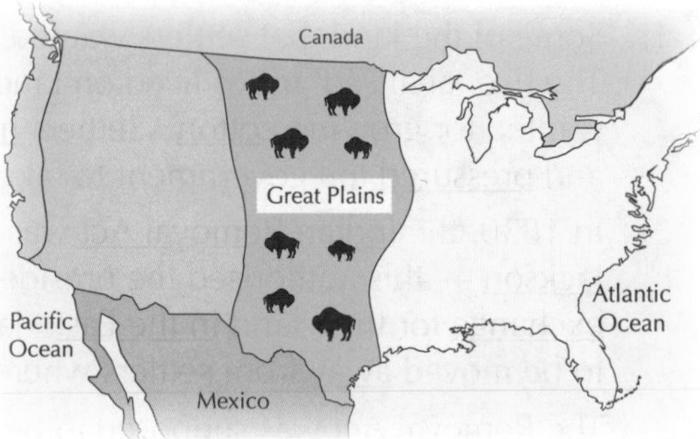

1) The Lakota Sioux were the <u>largest</u> of the <u>three</u> Sioux-speaking tribes and were split into <u>seven bands</u>. Each band had a <u>chief</u> and a <u>council</u> of elders. The chief didn't have complete control, but he would have earned <u>loyalty</u> over the years by demonstrating <u>courage</u> and <u>generosity</u> — this gave him <u>influence</u> over the tribe.

(Map showing: Canada, Great Plains, Pacific Ocean, Atlantic Ocean, Mexico)

2) Buffalo were <u>vital</u> for the Lakota Sioux. They used almost <u>every</u> part of the animal — <u>meat</u> for food, <u>skin</u> for clothing and tents, and <u>bones</u> for weapons and tools. Living in <u>tipis</u> (family tents) allowed the Lakotas to <u>quickly</u> follow buffalo herds — tipis are <u>easy</u> to take down and put back up.

3) <u>Tribal warfare</u> was common — it was a way for men to gain <u>prestige</u>. The aim wasn't necessarily to <u>kill</u> or <u>seize land</u>, but to perform acts of <u>bravery</u> such as <u>stealing horses</u> or <u>counting coup</u> (getting close enough to an enemy to touch him). The Lakota Sioux were <u>skilled</u> warriors. Their main enemies were the Crow and the Pawnee.

> Taking the <u>scalp</u> of an enemy was important to the Lakota Sioux for <u>religious</u> reasons. But scalping and killing were <u>less important</u> to them than counting coup.

4) The Lakota Sioux <u>didn't</u> see land as something that could be <u>bought</u> and <u>sold</u> — land belonged to <u>everyone</u>. Even other, more settled tribes believed agricultural land belonged to the tribe as a whole.

> The Lakota Sioux performed <u>rituals</u> such as the Vision Quest, Sweat Lodge Ceremony and Sun Dance to <u>contact</u> the spirits.

5) Native American religion was closely linked with <u>nature</u> — humans were believed to be <u>part of</u> nature, not masters over it. The Lakota Sioux believed that a <u>Great Spirit</u> called Wakan Tanka created the world, and that <u>everything</u> in nature contained <u>spirits</u> which they needed to keep on their side.

6) Women did most of the <u>work</u> in the village or camp, while the men <u>hunted</u> and <u>fought</u>. The Lakota Sioux were a <u>male-dominated</u> warrior society and men were the <u>heads</u> of their families, but women were <u>respected</u>. They owned the tipi and its contents, which gave them <u>status</u>.

> The Lakota Sioux practiced <u>polygamy</u> (having more than one wife) — the dangers of hunting and warfare meant there were often <u>more women</u> than men in tribes.

> Hunting became <u>easier</u> for the Lakota Sioux when they began to use <u>horses</u>, which were brought over by the Europeans in the <u>16th century</u>.

Comment and Analysis

Settlers <u>failed to understand</u> the culture of the Plains Indians because it was so <u>different</u> to their own. This led to <u>tension</u> and <u>conflict</u>.

I don't think they're going to get along, do you...?

When answering exam questions, it's important to understand the cultures and perspectives of different groups of people in order to explain how they interacted with each other.

The Journeys of the Early Migrants

Gradually, US citizens began to move <u>across</u> the Great Plains to reach the fertile land on the <u>west</u> coast.

Settlers started to move to the west coast in the late 1830s

1) The first people to explore the West were <u>mountain men</u> who hunted animals in the <u>1820s</u> and <u>1830s</u> to sell their skins. They <u>didn't settle</u> in the West, but established westward <u>trails</u> that settlers would later use.

2) <u>Missionaries</u> were among the earliest settlers on the <u>west coast</u> in the <u>1830s</u>. The aim was to <u>convert</u> the Native Americans there to <u>Christianity</u>.

3) Later, <u>larger</u> groups of people who wanted to make new lives for themselves went to the west coast. The first of these was the <u>Peoria Party</u> in 1839. Others followed in the 1840s — their routes became known as the <u>Oregon and California Trails</u>.

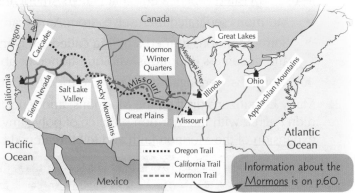

Information about the <u>Mormons</u> is on p.60.

4) <u>The Great Migration</u> of <u>1843</u> saw a sudden <u>increase</u> in settlers — a party of around <u>1000</u> people moved to the west coast.

Settlers had many Different Reasons for heading west

Life in the East was <u>hard</u>, and there was promise of <u>better</u> things in the West.

Problems in the East

- <u>Economic</u> problems — <u>Recession</u> in 1837 caused <u>low wages</u> and high <u>unemployment</u>.
- Overpopulation — European immigration led to <u>overcrowding</u> and <u>fewer jobs</u>.
- <u>Disease</u> — There were <u>yellow fever</u> epidemics.

Attraction of the West

- <u>A new start</u> — Land was <u>fertile</u> and <u>cheap</u>.
- <u>Government encouragement</u> — They wanted people to settle in the West to <u>strengthen</u> America's <u>claim</u> to the land there.
- <u>Gold</u> — Gold was discovered in California in 1848 (p.61). People hoped to make their <u>fortune</u>.

'Manifest Destiny'

- Many <u>white Americans</u> believed they were destined to <u>occupy</u> and <u>govern</u> all of <u>North America</u>. They saw it as their <u>God-given right</u>. John L. O'Sullivan coined the term '<u>Manifest Destiny</u>' in <u>1845</u> to describe this belief.
- They believed they were <u>superior</u> to Native Americans and that they should '<u>civilise</u>' the <u>continent</u>.

Reasons why people went west can be split into <u>push and pull factors</u> — things that pushed them <u>out</u> of the <u>East</u> and things that pulled them <u>to</u> the <u>West</u>.

The journey to the west coast was Difficult

1) It took around <u>5 months</u> to complete the <u>2000 mile</u> journey to the west coast. The journey had to be completed <u>before</u> winter. People travelled in <u>wagons</u> and formed wagon trains with other settlers.

2) The journey was <u>dangerous</u> — as many as <u>10%</u> would die on the way.

- There were <u>mountains</u> and <u>rivers</u> to cross — this was difficult with <u>heavy</u> wagons.
- People suffered from <u>food</u> and <u>water</u> shortages, and <u>diseases</u> such as typhoid and cholera.
- <u>Accidents</u> were common, such as falling under wagon wheels and accidental shootings.

In 1846, the <u>Donner Party</u>, heading for California, tried a short cut but they ended up <u>trapped in deep snow</u> in the Sierra Nevada. Of the <u>87</u> emigrants, less than <u>50</u> survived... by <u>eating</u> those who had died.

<u>Half</u> of the estimated <u>100,000</u> people who went to California during 1849 did so by <u>sea</u>. This journey also took around <u>5 months</u> and had its own <u>difficulties</u> — <u>crowded</u> conditions, <u>sickness</u> and <u>storms</u>.

To be fair, the grass on the west coast probably <u>was</u> greener...

Make a list of the difficulties the early migrants faced on their journey to the West.

The Making of America, 1789-1900

The Mormons

Another group of settlers were the Mormons — members of 'The Church of Jesus Christ of Latter Day Saints'.

The Mormons were Persecuted because of their beliefs

1) This religion was started by Joseph Smith, who published the Book of Mormon in 1830. It claimed that Jesus had visited America and that Native Americans were descended from the lost tribes of Israel.

   • Mormons separated themselves from American society and called non-Mormons 'gentiles'.

   • Some Mormons formed a militia called the Danites and there was violence against non-Mormons and dissenters (Mormons who questioned or abandoned the Mormon faith).

   • Mormons were against slavery and tried to convert Native Americans to Mormonism.

2) Many US citizens disliked the Mormons, and repeatedly drove them out of their homes. They didn't agree with the Mormon practice of polygamy (having more than one wife), feared the expansion of the Mormon faith and felt threatened by the Mormons' political and economic power.

> **Ohio, 1831**: The Mormons first settled in Kirtland, Ohio. They faced violence — Joseph Smith was tarred and feathered in 1832. The bank which Smith founded collapsed in 1837 — users of the bank were angry and drove the Mormons to Missouri.

> **Missouri, 1837**: The Mormons' anti-slavery stance annoyed slave-owners, and the Danites were suspected of plotting with Native Americans. Many leaders were arrested, so Brigham Young led the Mormons to Illinois.

> **Illinois, 1839**: The Mormons created their own city called Nauvoo, with its own army and laws. Joseph Smith declared his candidacy for President. Smith was eventually killed in jail by an angry mob and Brigham Young took over as leader.

They moved West and eventually settled in Salt Lake Valley

1) Brigham Young decided to move the Mormons further west. He wanted to create an independent Mormon state where they could live freely. He chose Salt Lake Valley — conditions there were dry and harsh, but it was 'a place on this earth that nobody else wants' and it was part of Mexico, not the US.

2) The Mormons planned to leave Illinois in the spring of 1846, but due to an increase in anti-Mormon violence they had to leave in February. This rushed departure meant that they left supplies behind and were disorganised. Conditions were hard — it was a cold winter and there was deep mud.

3) Their progress was very slow, which meant they couldn't complete the journey that year. They stayed in Winter Quarters by the Missouri River over winter (see map on p.59) — by the spring of 1847, around 400 Mormons had died from disease, the cold and lack of supplies.

> Although the journey was hard, the Mormons planted crops and built way stations along the trail to feed and help later travellers.

4) They set off again in April 1847 and organisation improved. They were divided into groups led by captains under the strict overall command of Young. They finally reached Salt Lake Valley in July.

5) The conditions in Salt Lake Valley were tough, but Young led the Mormons in solving their problems:

   • There was little rain or other water sources, so they dug irrigation ditches.

   • There were no trees for wood, so they built houses from bricks of earth.

   • They needed to become self-sufficient but there weren't enough of them, so Young encouraged Mormons from all over the world to move to Salt Lake.

6) In 1848, Mexico gave Salt Lake City to the US — it became the territory of Utah and was subject to American laws. The Mormons ignored these laws and the Danites attacked US officials. In 1857, the US appointed a non-Mormon governor who arrived with 2500 US troops.

> Tensions were high — later in 1857, 140 non-Mormon settlers were massacred. Mormons blamed the Indians, but others suspected the Danites.

> The American government put pressure on the Mormons to abandon polygamy. The US only allowed Utah to become a state in 1896 after the Mormons had abandoned polygamy in 1890 — the Mormons successfully settled Salt Lake Valley, but they had to compromise their beliefs.

The Mormons had their own reasons for moving west...

Make sure you understand that different groups of people had different experiences.
The Mormons went west to escape persecution — a very different motivation to other settlers.

EXAM TIP

Gold Miners

Migration to the west coast during the 1840s was <u>gradual</u>, with most people heading to <u>Oregon</u>. But the California Gold Rush <u>changed</u> this — in just a few years, <u>huge</u> numbers of travellers journeyed to <u>California</u>.

Gold was found in California in 1848

1) <u>James Marshall</u> found gold while working at John Sutter's sawmill in January <u>1848</u>. News of this spread <u>slowly</u> to the <u>east coast</u>, until President Polk made a speech in December <u>confirming</u> that gold had been found. As a result, <u>tens of thousands</u> of people made the journey west during <u>1849</u>.

2) People were <u>excited</u> at the prospect of making their <u>fortune</u>. Many hoped to find gold and then return <u>home</u>.

> James Carson, an army sergeant in California, abandoned his post to look for gold, writing later that he had 'a very violent attack of <u>gold fever</u>.'

3) People came to California from all over the <u>world</u> — e.g. China, Mexico and South America, as well as from other parts of North America.

A miner panning for gold.

© Mary Evans/Classic Stock/C.P. Cushing

The California Gold Rush presented many Challenges

1) Life as a miner was <u>hard</u>, even before reaching California. There were many <u>deaths</u> from <u>cholera</u> on the journey to California between 1849 and 1853.

> Some people ran <u>service</u> industries, e.g. <u>stores</u> and <u>saloons</u>. Unsuccessful miners often stayed on in California as <u>farmers</u> and <u>merchants</u> and started <u>families</u>.

2) Only a <u>lucky few</u> found gold in California. Surface gold (found using the simple method of panning) was <u>limited</u> and soon grew <u>scarce</u>. Some miners returned <u>home</u>, but others couldn't <u>afford</u> to.

3) Living and working conditions were <u>poor</u>. There was little <u>hygiene</u>, <u>disease</u> was common and <u>nutrition</u> among miners was poor. Miners who couldn't find gold worked for mining companies in <u>dangerous</u> conditions for <u>low</u> wages. When not working, people turned to <u>drinking</u> and <u>gambling</u> which often led to <u>trouble</u> in mining towns.

4) The <u>rapid</u> migration of mostly <u>male</u> gold seekers and the quick <u>development</u> of <u>mining towns</u> meant that society was <u>unstructured</u> — there were no stable <u>families</u> or <u>communities</u>. There were <u>no laws</u> at first — miners had to enforce the law themselves but their justice wasn't always <u>fair</u>.

5) There was frequent <u>racial conflict</u>. White Americans considered themselves <u>superior</u> to foreign miners and more <u>entitled</u> to the gold, especially when it began to grow scarce.

> Native American tribes living in California suffered as a result of the Gold Rush. The <u>Native American</u> population in California <u>dropped</u> from around <u>150,000</u> to less than <u>30,000</u> during 1845-1870. This was the result of <u>violent attacks</u>, <u>epidemics</u> and being <u>driven off</u> their land.

California and the US as a whole felt the effects of the rush

1) Mining harmed California's <u>environment</u>. Timber for mine supports used up <u>forests</u>, chemicals such as mercury caused <u>pollution</u>, and the technique of <u>hydraulic mining</u> (the use of powerful jets of water to wash away hillsides and reach the gold beneath) <u>destroyed</u> the landscape.

2) But mining also kick-started California's <u>development</u>. The non-Native American population rose from around <u>14,000</u> to about <u>225,000</u> between 1848-1852. Mining towns such as <u>Sacramento</u> and <u>Stockton</u> expanded. <u>San Francisco</u> became the <u>economic centre</u> of California.

3) The Gold Rush <u>accelerated</u> the economic growth of the US. The wealth generated by gold mining gave America an important role in <u>world trade</u>. Settlement in California increased the need for <u>better links</u> between the east and west of the country. This led to improved <u>mail services</u> and a <u>transcontinental railroad</u> (see p.68).

Comment and Analysis

Mining had a <u>negative</u> impact on many individuals, especially the <u>Native Americans</u>, but it played an important role in the <u>expansion</u> of the US.

Use your judgement to answer this exam question...

'The California Gold Rush had a positive impact on America.'
Do you agree with this statement? Explain your answer. [18]

EXAM QUESTION

The Clash of Cultures

As more <u>settlers</u> started to <u>cross</u> the Great Plains, <u>tension</u> grew between them and the <u>Plains Indians</u>.

There was a *Lack of Understanding between settlers and Indians*

1) To settlers, it seemed that the Plains Indians had no system of <u>government</u>, that their warfare was <u>cowardly</u> and their religion just <u>superstition</u> (see p.58).

2) They had different views on <u>land ownership</u>. Native Americans believed that the land was for <u>everyone</u>, but settlers wanted to <u>own</u>, farm and exploit it. Settlers thought the Plains Indians' nomadic lifestyle was <u>uncivilised</u> and that they <u>wasted</u> the land. Native Americans thought that the settlers <u>ruined</u> the land.

> **Native Americans and settlers increasingly came into contact...**
> * Significant numbers of settlers moved <u>beyond</u> the Permanent Indian Frontier and across the Plains to reach lands in the West from 1843. Many <u>more</u> came with the California Gold Rush of 1849.
> * The settlers disrupted <u>buffalo</u> herds which the Plains Indians <u>relied</u> on, and <u>polluted</u> water sources.
> * As a result, Plains Indians became more <u>hostile</u>. They sometimes <u>attacked</u> wagon trains, increasing the settlers' <u>fear</u> and <u>distrust</u>. The settlers also felt <u>threatened</u> by the Indians' inter-tribal conflict.

The Reservation System *replaced the Permanent Indian Frontier*

1) The government wanted to <u>reduce</u> conflict on the Plains. It decided to pursue a <u>policy of concentration</u> — the Plains Indians would be concentrated onto <u>specific areas</u> of the Plains called <u>reservations</u>.

2) The <u>Fort Laramie Treaty</u> (1851) was the government's <u>first</u> attempt to concentrate the Plains Indians in certain areas. It defined the <u>territory</u> of each tribe to try to minimise inter-tribal conflict.

3) Tribes agreed to <u>remain</u> in their territory, allow settlers to <u>cross</u> the Plains, and allow the government to build <u>roads</u> and <u>forts</u> along the trails. In return, the government promised the tribes that they would have <u>permanent</u> rights to their lands, and that tribes would receive <u>$50,000</u> of goods a year for 50 years.

4) Neither side kept to the treaty. Not all tribes <u>agreed</u> with it and many didn't even know it <u>existed</u>. The US government didn't keep its side of the deal either — it couldn't ensure <u>settlers</u> kept to the agreement, and in 1852 it <u>reduced</u> the yearly payments from 50 years to 10.

5) The treaty had a large <u>impact</u>:

> * <u>Settlement increased</u> in California and Oregon.
> * <u>Restricting</u> Native Americans to reservations <u>threatened</u> their way of life, as did the building of roads and forts in their territory.
> * <u>Broken promises</u> increased Native American <u>resentment</u> towards the government and settlers.

> **Comment and Analysis**
>
> The Fort Laramie Treaty marked the <u>end</u> of the <u>Permanent Indian Frontier</u> — Native Americans could no longer live <u>freely</u> on the Plains. It paved the way for <u>further</u> treaties in the 1850s and 60s which resulted in tribes <u>losing land</u>, e.g. in 1853 treaties were made with tribes in <u>Kansas</u> and <u>Nebraska</u> to make room for settlers — these tribes lost nearly <u>17 million acres</u>.

The Pike's Peak gold rush brought about New Conflict

In 1858, gold was discovered in Colorado near <u>Pike's Peak</u> (in the Rocky Mountains). The discovery sparked a <u>gold rush</u> which <u>renewed tensions</u> between the <u>Plains Indians</u> and the <u>settlers</u>.

> The discovery of gold led thousands of people to <u>move</u> to Colorado. New towns like <u>Denver</u> and <u>Boulder</u> emerged, which helped Colorado to develop <u>socially</u> and <u>economically</u>. Colorado's <u>population growth</u> also helped it to become officially recognised as a US <u>territory</u> in 1861.

> These settlers occupied land promised to the <u>Arapaho</u> and <u>Cheyenne tribes</u> in the <u>Fort Laramie Treaty</u> of 1851. Instead of upholding the treaty, the government negotiated a <u>new one</u> in 1861 called the <u>Fort Wise Treaty</u>. This <u>restricted</u> the territory of both tribes, giving more land to the <u>settlers</u>. The treaty <u>increased</u> <u>tensions</u> between the Plains Indians and the settlers, which contributed to the <u>Cheyenne Uprising</u> and the <u>Sand Creek Massacre</u> in 1864 (see p.72).

'Well, when we said you could have all this lovely desert...'
Summarise what each side agreed to in the Fort Laramie Treaty.

The Causes of the Civil War

The North and the South developed in <u>different</u> ways and had different attitudes towards slavery.

The North and South had Different Economies

1) In the early 19th century, the <u>South's economy</u> was heavily based on <u>cotton exports</u>. Cotton was produced <u>cheaply</u> using slave labour on <u>plantations</u> (p.56).

2) Slavery wasn't as important in the <u>North</u> — it had a more <u>diverse economy</u> that was based on lots of <u>different industries</u> and <u>agricultural crops</u>.

3) By <u>1804</u>, all of the <u>northern</u> states had <u>abolished slavery</u> (banned it). This created a <u>division</u> between southern '<u>slave states</u>' and northern '<u>free states</u>'.

4) As time went on, the North became even <u>more industrialised</u>, while the South <u>relied</u> more and more on <u>cotton cultivation</u>. By the <u>1860s</u>, the <u>North</u> had <u>six times</u> as many <u>factories</u> as the South.

5) The North was <u>more wealthy</u> than the South as a result of its <u>diverse</u> and <u>industrialised</u> economy.

> The North didn't necessarily want <u>racial equality</u>. They were more worried about the South gaining political power and spreading slavery into new territories (see below).

> Not <u>all</u> southerners were slave owners — in <u>1860</u>, only about <u>5%</u> of southerners <u>owned</u> slaves. <u>Less than 1%</u> of these slaveholders had <u>large slave plantations</u> with 200 or more slaves. However, because the southern <u>economy</u> was based on slave labour, southerners saw it as part of their <u>way of life</u>.

> **Comment and Analysis**
> Some historians point out that the <u>South</u> didn't <u>need</u> to <u>industrialise</u>, because they made lots of money out of <u>plantation agriculture</u>. This might have been true, but it was a bad idea to <u>rely</u> on <u>one industry</u> (cotton) to keep the economy going.

The North had a Bigger Population than the South

1) The <u>North's</u> population was <u>bigger</u> than the South's. A <u>big proportion</u> of the <u>South's population</u> were <u>slaves</u> — by <u>1860</u>, there were almost <u>4 million slaves</u> in the <u>South</u> compared to <u>8 million</u> free white Americans.

2) The North's population gave it more <u>political power</u>, as states with a bigger population could have <u>more representatives</u> in the <u>lower house</u> of Congress.

> <u>Slaves</u> were counted as <u>three-fifths of a person</u>. This gave southerners <u>more power</u> than they would've had if only <u>free people</u> were counted.

3) The <u>South</u> still had lots of <u>political power</u>, though. Each state had <u>two</u> representatives in the <u>Senate</u> (the upper house of Congress). Each <u>new state</u> that applied to join the Union had to <u>decide</u> whether to allow or ban slavery. As long as the number of <u>free</u> and <u>slave</u> states in Congress was <u>balanced</u>, the <u>South</u> could use its votes in the <u>Senate</u> to <u>protect slavery</u>.

Westward expansion Increased the Tension over Slavery

1) <u>Slavery</u> became so important in the <u>South</u> that many southerners believed there would be <u>economic</u> and <u>social chaos</u> if it was abolished. They were keen to <u>protect</u> their way of life.

2) As <u>westward expansion</u> continued, <u>northern senators</u> tried to stop <u>new states</u> becoming slave states. They wanted to use <u>land</u> in the West for their <u>own economic development</u>.

3) This caused <u>tension</u> between the North and the South, which came to the surface when <u>new states</u> asked to join the Union.

> The <u>southern states</u> feared that admitting more free states would give the North enough <u>power</u> to pass a law abolishing slavery in <u>all</u> <u>states</u>. The <u>northern states</u> worried that they would be <u>outvoted</u> in the Senate if <u>too many</u> <u>slave states</u> were admitted. Both sides wanted the <u>balance</u> to tip in their <u>own favour</u>.

> In <u>1820</u>, the <u>Missouri Compromise</u> was created to try and <u>reduce tension</u> over slavery. An <u>imaginary line</u> was drawn from the southern border of Missouri to the western edge of US territory. All <u>future states</u> that formed <u>north</u> of the <u>Missouri Line</u> were to be <u>banned</u> from becoming <u>slave states</u>.

> **Comment and Analysis**
> The North and the South were <u>suspicious</u> of each other. They both feared that the other's way of life would be <u>forced</u> upon them.

4) The <u>Missouri Compromise</u> worked well for about <u>twenty years</u> and Congress stayed balanced. However, the debate started up again in <u>1846</u> after the USA gained <u>more territory</u> in the West.

And I thought the UK had a North/South divide...

Describe the differences in economics, population and political power between North and South.

The Causes of the Civil War

Tensions continued to <u>build</u>, and <u>Lincoln's election</u> as President was the <u>final straw</u> for the South.

Free State Abolitionists wanted Slavery to End

Some people in northern free states campaigned for slaves to be <u>freed</u> — they were called <u>abolitionists</u>. At first, abolitionists wanted slavery to be <u>ended slowly</u> and for owners to be <u>compensated</u> for losing their slaves.

1) Opposition became more <u>radical</u> in the 1830s — abolitionists began to call slavery a moral evil which should end <u>immediately</u>. They became more organised, forming the <u>American Anti-Slavery Association</u> in <u>1833</u>.

2) Abolition gained <u>some support</u> in the <u>North</u>. However, many northerners <u>didn't support</u> abolition — they worried about the impact of <u>freed slaves</u> coming to the North in big numbers. <u>Southerners</u> felt that their <u>way of life</u> was being attacked, so there was <u>little support</u> for the movement in the South.

3) In <u>1851</u>, abolitionist Harriet Beecher Stowe wrote a novel attacking slavery called '<u>Uncle Tom's Cabin</u>'. It sparked <u>support</u> for abolition by making many in the <u>North</u> more aware of the <u>immorality</u> of slavery.

Comment and Analysis

<u>Attitudes</u> to slavery <u>varied</u> in the North — not everyone was opposed to it. But this didn't make the South feel any less <u>threatened</u> — they believed that the North was <u>united</u> against them to <u>end slavery</u>.

The Missouri Compromise was Broken in 1854

1) The <u>Kansas-Nebraska Act</u> of 1854 <u>ended</u> the Missouri Compromise. Under the Compromise, slavery had been <u>outlawed</u> in the Kansas-Nebraska territory — but when the Act admitted Kansas and Nebraska to the Union, it allowed settlers to <u>vote</u> on whether they were to become free or slave states.

2) Many northerners were <u>angry</u> with the Act. The <u>Republican Party</u> was formed as a result of this discontent — it aimed to stop the <u>spread</u> of slavery. By 1856, the Republicans had gained much support in the <u>North</u>, but the <u>Democrats</u> stayed popular in the <u>South</u>. This created more <u>tension</u>.

The Act was designed to <u>reduce</u> tension, but it actually made things <u>worse</u>. Many in the North saw it as <u>giving in</u> to the South.

Lincoln's Election as President in 1860 triggered Secession

1) In 1860, Republican Abraham Lincoln won the presidential election. He thought slavery was <u>immoral</u> and opposed its <u>spread</u> into new territories, but said he didn't want to <u>interfere</u> with it in areas where it already <u>existed</u>.

Lincoln was a <u>minority</u> president — he only got 40% of the overall vote and he didn't get <u>any votes</u> in <u>10</u> of the <u>southern states</u>.

2) Many Southerners felt that they <u>didn't</u> owe any <u>loyalty</u> to a man who <u>threatened</u> their way of life. His election triggered the secession (withdrawal) of seven states, and in <u>February 1861</u> these states formed the <u>Confederate States of America</u> with <u>Jefferson Davis</u> as their <u>president</u>.

3) When <u>Lincoln</u> was sworn in as Union president in <u>March 1861</u>, he said that he <u>wouldn't</u> <u>accept secession</u>. Davis thought that <u>states</u> had the <u>right</u> to <u>secede</u> — he <u>didn't</u> want the Union to <u>break up</u>, but he also believed in the <u>South's freedom</u> to own slaves.

4) Lincoln <u>refused</u> to withdraw US government <u>troops</u> at <u>Fort Sumter</u> in South Carolina — the Confederates saw this as a lack of respect for their independence. Lincoln sent more <u>supplies</u> to the fort, but said that he would only attack if the South did so <u>first</u>. In <u>April 1861</u>, Confederate troops attacked the <u>fort</u>.

5) This <u>triggered</u> a Civil War between the <u>Union</u> and the <u>Confederates</u>. By <u>August 1861</u>, <u>11 southern states</u> had seceded from the Union. Lincoln declared that the Confederate states were in <u>rebellion</u>.

Lincoln insisted that the <u>aim</u> of the war was to <u>preserve</u> the <u>Union</u> rather than abolish <u>slavery</u> — he knew that many <u>northerners</u> and citizens in the remaining <u>loyal</u> southern states <u>wouldn't</u> <u>support abolition</u> as a war aim.

- The <u>aim</u> of the war <u>changed</u> with Lincoln's <u>Emancipation Proclamation</u> in <u>1863</u> — all slaves in rebellious states were to be <u>emancipated</u> (freed). This made <u>ending slavery</u> an aim of the war (in addition to preserving the Union).
- Emancipation made <u>military</u> sense because it would <u>strengthen</u> the northern army. It also tied in with the <u>moral</u> beliefs of Lincoln, who was facing increasing <u>pressure</u> from fellow Republicans to make the war about slavery.

Lots of tasty marks to have a go at here...

Do you agree that Lincoln's election was the main cause of the Civil War?
Explain your answer. [18] (Use the information from page 63 in your answer too).

African Americans in the Civil War

The Civil War was fought from <u>1861 to 1865</u>. The <u>North</u> won — seceded states <u>returned</u> to the <u>Union</u> and <u>slavery</u> was <u>abolished</u>. The Civil War had a <u>huge impact</u> on the lives of African Americans.

Many African Americans wanted to Serve in the Union Army

1) Many African Americans tried to join the army (enlist) at the outbreak of war, but they were <u>rejected</u>. Those who tried to enlist included <u>freemen</u> in the North and <u>slaves</u> who <u>escaped</u> from the South after the war started.

> Lincoln was worried he would lose the <u>support</u> of the remaining <u>loyal</u> southern states if he <u>allowed</u> African Americans to join the Union Army.

2) African Americans were eventually accepted into the Union Army with the <u>Emancipation Proclamation</u> of 1863 (see p.64). Thousands enlisted and formed <u>all-black</u> units. One of the first of these was the <u>54th Massachusetts Infantry Regiment</u>.

3) Around <u>180,000 African American soldiers</u> had joined the Union Army by the war's end.

4) African Americans also helped the war effort in <u>other</u> ways, e.g as blacksmiths, nurses and cooks. Some served as <u>guides</u> and <u>spies</u> for the Union Army in the South.

> **Comment and Analysis**
>
> After the Emancipation Proclamation, the aim of the war became about <u>ending slavery</u> as well as preserving the Union — African Americans now had a <u>chance</u> to fight for their <u>own freedom</u>.

They faced Prejudice from northerners

1) Although there was opposition to <u>slavery</u> in the North, many northerners <u>didn't</u> see African Americans as <u>equal</u>. Black people faced <u>racism</u> and <u>discrimination</u> in the Union Army:

- They fought in <u>segregated</u> regiments led by white officers.
- Many people didn't believe that black men were as <u>skilled</u> or <u>brave</u> as white men — they were often given <u>menial</u> jobs.
- Black soldiers were paid <u>$10</u> a month — <u>$3</u> less than white soldiers.
- African Americans were given <u>poorer supplies</u> and worse <u>rations</u>.

2) Black soldiers faced more <u>danger</u> than white soldiers if they were <u>captured</u> by the South in battle — the Confederates threatened to <u>enslave</u> them.

The assault on Fort Wagner

© Mary Evans / Everett Collection

> But black troops proved their <u>bravery</u>, e.g. the 54th Massachusetts Infantry Regiment's 1863 assault on <u>Fort Wagner</u> in which <u>half</u> the troops were killed.

> There was <u>racial tension</u> in the North. When <u>conscription</u> was introduced in 1863, many northerners were <u>angry</u> — they didn't want to be <u>forced</u> to fight to <u>free</u> slaves. This led to <u>riots</u> in New York in which African Americans were <u>killed</u>.

Many African Americans Unwillingly helped the South

1) As white men left to fight in the Confederate Army, <u>discipline</u> on some plantations was <u>relaxed</u>. Many slaves began to <u>resist</u> by working at a <u>slower</u> pace, refusing to obey <u>orders</u> and breaking <u>rules</u>.

2) Many slaves and free African Americans were <u>forced</u> to support the Confederate war effort. They were made to build <u>fortifications</u>, work in <u>factories</u> or work as <u>nurses</u> and <u>cooks</u>.

3) Some free African Americans in the South did <u>volunteer</u> to help the Confederates — usually as skilled or manual <u>labourers</u> — but they were in the <u>minority</u>.

4) Confederates were <u>unwilling</u> to arm slaves because of fears of slave <u>rebellion</u>. Slaves were only accepted as troops in <u>1865</u>, when the South was coming close to <u>losing</u> the war.

The Civil War changed the lives of African Americans...

Make sure you understand the effect of the Civil War on African Americans. Many fought for their own freedom. But many faced prejudice — their next battle would be one for equality.

EXAM TIP

The Reconstruction Era

The Reconstruction Era was the period after the Civil War when efforts were made to rebuild the United States.

Slavery was Formally Abolished after the War

After the Union won the war in 1865, over four million slaves were freed and the South's plantation economy was destroyed. Politicians started to rebuild the South and help freed slaves to become part of free society.

1) Securing freedom for African Americans was a key part of Reconstruction. Many slaves in the South had already been freed by the Emancipation Proclamation in 1863, but slavery still existed in the border states (the slave states of Delaware, Kentucky, Maryland and Missouri which remained loyal to the Union).

> Lincoln was assassinated in April 1865, but it was his government that laid the groundwork for the 13th Amendment.

2) The 13th Amendment was introduced by Lincoln when he was re-elected in 1864 — it formally abolished slavery in all states. It was ratified by most northern and border states, and some southern states, in December 1865.

> Ratification is when states formally accept changes to the Constitution. An amendment is ratified once three-quarters of states have agreed.

> The 13th Amendment freed slaves, but it didn't give them equal rights. There was a debate during the Reconstruction Era over how far African Americans should be given civil rights.

3) The Freedmen's Bureau was set up in March 1865 to help freed slaves and poor southerners to rebuild their lives. It provided food and shelter, and legal and medical aid. It also helped communities to establish new schools. It was poorly funded and limited by political issues (see below) — it closed in 1872.

Andrew Johnson began Presidential Reconstruction in 1865

1) Andrew Johnson took over as President in April 1865 after Lincoln was assassinated. He took a lenient approach to the South.

> Andrew Johnson was a Democratic senator from Tennessee. He was pro-slavery but strongly disagreed with southern secession.

- He pardoned all white southerners except Confederate leaders and wealthy planters, but many later received individual pardons.
- Some of the southern elite regained power — many had been in the Confederate government and army.
- Property was returned to its original owners instead of being redistributed. Many African Americans rented land from white people (sharecropping) — sometimes they rented from their former masters.
- Some southern states created the Black Codes, which limited the freedom of African Americans. For example, South Carolina made black people pay a tax if they were not farmers or servants.

2) Johnson didn't support equal rights for African Americans, so he did nothing to stop the Black Codes.

3) In 1866, he vetoed (rejected) the Civil Rights Act, which gave equal rights to African Americans. He also tried to stop the Freedmen's Bureau from continuing its work.

> **Comment and Analysis**
>
> Although sharecropping gave black people more freedom and independence than under slavery, many sharecroppers got into debt and poverty.

Some Republicans disagreed with Johnson's Approach

1) Some radical Republicans wanted racial equality and greater punishment of Confederate leaders.

2) Moderate Republicans didn't agree with Johnson's vetoes of the Freedmen's Bureau Bill and the Civil Rights Act. They created an alliance with the radicals and overturned his civil rights veto.

3) Congress passed the 14th Amendment in 1868 — Johnson opposed it and the southern states refused to ratify it. Many in the North began to think that a tougher approach was needed in the South.

> The 14th Amendment had a 'Citizenship Clause', which guaranteed citizenship to all males born in the US regardless of race. It also had an 'Equal Protection Clause', which gave black people the same rights to state protection as white people.

If only you could abolish exams...

When you're writing about Reconstruction, think about how the North and the South's different attitudes to slavery might have influenced the way that they wanted the South to be rebuilt.

The Making of America, 1789-1900

The Reconstruction Era

Radical Republicans took charge of Reconstruction, but fell short of their aim to achieve equality.

Radical Republicans took over Reconstruction in 1867

1) The First and Second Reconstruction Acts were passed by Congress in March 1867. These acts placed the South under military rule. Before rebel states could rejoin the Union, they were forced to ratify the 14th Amendment (p.66) and rewrite their constitutions to allow black people to vote.

2) Congress's approach to the South was more forceful than Johnson's — they sent troops to the South to keep the peace and protect freed slaves and their right to vote. Leading rebels were removed from office.

3) Johnson tried to obstruct Radical Reconstruction — he vetoed both Reconstruction Acts, so radicals impeached him (put him on trial). He wasn't convicted, but he lost power and Ulysses Grant was elected President in 1869.

4) The 15th Amendment was passed in 1869 and ratified in 1870 — it ruled that citizens of the USA could not be denied the right to vote based on their 'race, colour, or previous condition of servitude'.

5) By 1870, all states had been re-admitted to the Union. The southern states had Republican governments made up of white southerners who supported Reconstruction, northerners and African Americans.

> Northerners who went to carry out the government's Reconstruction policies in the South were known as 'carpet baggers'. Southerners accused them of being corrupt and exploiting the South. People in the South felt betrayed by southern white Republicans and believed there was a 'black domination' of the South now that black people could vote and hold political power.

6) Three Enforcement Acts were passed between 1870 and 1871. They made it illegal to use terror, force or bribery to stop black people from voting, and they gave the government powers to quickly suppress the Ku Klux Klan.

> The Ku Klux Klan was a white supremacist group that formed in 1865. They murdered, lynched, beat and threatened African Americans, white Republicans and their supporters. They also burned churches, homes and schools. Many Klan members were arrested and put on trial under the Enforcement Acts.

> Radical Reconstruction was a period of hope and idealism for many, in spite of southern grievances. Radicals believed that equality could be achieved.

The Reconstruction Era ended in 1877

> In 1876, the Supreme Court ruled that only states, not the federal government, could prosecute people under the Enforcement Acts — this resulted in many violent crimes going unpunished in the South.

1) By 1873, political support for Reconstruction had weakened in the North. Economic depression in 1874 caused high unemployment, so northerners lost interest in the South.

2) Supreme Court decisions also weakened the power of the 14th Amendment to protect black civil rights.

3) The depression, and corruption and scandal under President Grant, meant that Republicans lost support. The Democrats won control of the lower house of Congress in 1874 for first time since the Civil War.

4) Republican Rutherford B. Hayes was elected president in 1876, but the election results were disputed. In return for recognition of his election, he accepted the Democrats' control of the South and ended federal military involvement there in 1877. The Reconstruction Era was over.

The Reconstruction Era improved rights for African Americans, but many issues were unresolved by 1877:

- More than 700,000 black people were registered to vote and over 1500 were elected to state and national offices. However, while they had representation, it wasn't proportional to their population.
- Some southerners ignored the 15th Amendment by trying to stop black people from voting (see p.75). In 1898, the Supreme Court ruled in defence of this unfair system.
- Many Ku Klux Klan members were fined and let off with a warning. Other violent groups emerged, like the Rifle Clubs and the Red Shirts, who carried on murdering and threatening southern Republicans.

Comment and Analysis

A key barrier to the success of Reconstruction was that the attitude of many southern whites didn't change. African Americans had more independence than under slavery, but in many ways, their rights were still limited.

The Reconstruction Era hit a bit of a brick wall...

Write a summary analysing the different stages of Reconstruction. Give examples to support your answer. (To answer this properly, you'll need to include information from page 66 too.) [9]

Exploitation of the Great Plains

From the 1850s, the USA became more interested in the <u>Great Plains</u> — an area once seen as <u>uninhabitable</u>. The <u>railways</u>, <u>homesteaders</u> and the <u>beef industry</u> kick-started the <u>development</u> of the Plains.

Government and railways Encouraged settlers on the Plains

In the 1850s, people began to see the <u>possibility</u> of settling on the Plains — it wasn't quite the 'Great American Desert' (see p.57) they'd thought. In <u>1854</u>, the government allowed settlement in <u>Kansas</u> and <u>Nebraska</u>, and during the Civil War they did even more to <u>encourage</u> settlement of the Plains:

> Before the war, southerners in Congress <u>opposed</u> Acts encouraging settlers who <u>didn't own</u> slaves to move into new areas. When the South seceded, the North was able to <u>pass</u> these Acts:

The Homestead Act (1862)

1) The <u>Homestead Act</u> gave each settler 160 acres of <u>free land</u>, if they farmed it for 5 years. This opened up <u>2.5 million</u> acres for settlement and was open to <u>everyone</u>, including immigrants, freed slaves and single women. Between <u>1862</u> and <u>1900</u> it has been estimated that <u>600,000</u> people claimed land under the Act.

2) The condition of farming the land for 5 years was meant to discourage <u>speculators</u> — those aiming to make a short-term <u>profit</u> on rising land prices rather than settling and living on the land. However, the Act was still <u>affected</u> by speculators and corruption.

> **Comment and Analysis**
>
> The Act was <u>important</u> because it opened up land ownership to <u>ordinary</u> people. Although there were <u>problems</u>, it helped to <u>establish</u> settlement on the Plains.

The Pacific Railroad Act (1862)

1) The government wanted to build a railway from <u>east to west</u>. They believed it would make <u>migration</u> into unsettled land easier and would create <u>national unity</u> by connecting the West to the East.

2) The <u>Pacific Railroad Act</u> approved the construction of the <u>First Transcontinental Railroad</u>, and work was completed in <u>1869</u>. The railroad <u>encouraged</u> further settlement of the West:

- The government gave the railways <u>land</u>, which the railways <u>sold</u> to settlers cheaply to <u>fund</u> railway building. Promotional <u>posters</u> made <u>exaggerated</u> claims about the good life on the Plains.

- <u>Economic development</u> was made easier because the West was now linked with <u>markets</u> in the East.

- People could be transported more <u>easily</u>, as well as supplies which aided settlement, such as <u>building materials</u> and <u>machinery</u>.

Rich Farming Lands!
For Sale **VERY CHEAP** by the
Union Pacific Railroad Company.
The Best Investment! No Fluctuations!
Always Improving in Value.
The Wealth of the Country is made by the advance in Real Estate.
NOW IS THE TIME!
MILLIONS OF ACRES
Of the finest lands on the Continent, in Eastern Nebraska, now for sale, **Many of them never before in Market**, at prices that **Defy Competition.**
FIVE AND TEN YEARS' CREDIT GIVEN, WITH INTEREST AT SIX PER CENT.
The Land Grant Bonds of the Company *taken at par* for lands. ☞ Full particulars given, new Guide with new Maps mailed free.
THE PIONEER,
A handsome Illustrated paper, containing the Homestead Law, sent free to all parts of the world. Address
O. F. DAVIS,
Land Commissioner U. P. R. R.,
Omaha, Neb.

© The Art Archive / Granger Collection

Union Pacific Railroad advertisement for farming lands in Nebraska.

Life on the Plains was Hard

1) After 1865, thousands of people were <u>willing</u> to move to the Plains.

- Migrants from <u>eastern</u> states who moved because of <u>growing population</u> and <u>high land prices</u>.
- Immigrants who had come to America to escape <u>poverty</u> and religious and political <u>persecution</u>.
- <u>Slaves</u> who had been freed after the Civil War, and ex-Civil War <u>soldiers</u> who wanted a <u>new start</u>.

2) But homesteading was a <u>tough</u> life.

- The soil was <u>fertile</u>, but the thick top layer of earth (known as <u>sod</u>) was too <u>hard</u> for light ploughs. There was little or no <u>wood</u> for building or fuel.
- Lack of <u>water</u> meant crops like maize <u>failed</u> and deep <u>wells</u> had to be dug.
- <u>Wind</u>, extremes of <u>climate</u>, <u>grasshopper</u> plagues and prairie <u>fires</u> often <u>destroyed</u> crops.

The role of the Great Plains was far from settled...

The Homestead Act and the Pacific Railroad Act were both important developments in the settlement of the Great Plains. Make sure you are able to explain why they were so significant.

EXAM TIP

Exploitation of the Great Plains

As more people faced the difficulties of living and farming on the Plains, they found ways to survive.

The Plains were eventually Successfully settled

1) New developments in technology, crops and techniques helped:

- Better machinery — John Deere developed a stronger steel plough in the 1830s which could break through the tough soil. Windpumps increased the supply of water by pumping underground water to the surface. The introduction of barbed wire in 1874 meant that farmers could cheaply fence off their land to keep animals off their crops.
- New crops — Turkey Red Wheat was a hardy crop brought over from Russia in around 1874. It was well-suited to growing on the plains.
- New techniques — Farmers learned techniques to cope with the low rainfall and retain moisture in the soil, e.g. 'dry farming' involved turning the soil after rain.

> The railroads brought machinery to the Plains from the East.

2) Government acts helped. The Timber Culture Act of 1873 and the Desert Land Act of 1877 gave settlers who lived in less fertile areas more land.

> People had started to move onto the even drier High Plains by 1880.

Comment and Analysis

Improved technology and knowledge meant that settlers were now able to cultivate the Great Plains — an area once seen as uninhabitable.

3) People adapted:

- Because of the lack of wood, people made houses out of sod.
- Women were responsible for housework and their children's education. They had to collect buffalo dung for fuel and made a lot of what they needed, such as clothes and soap. They also nursed the sick and helped each other in childbirth.
- Isolation was a constant problem for early settlers, as towns and neighbours were often far away. Women formed church groups and other social networks to combat the loneliness.
- Eventually, as more settlers arrived, communities formed and schools and shops were built.

1) Even though the failure rate for new farms was high, the Great Plains produced huge quantities of wheat and corn. The railways made the boom possible by linking producers to wider markets.

2) There were 10 million immigrants to America during 1865-90 — many of these helped settle the West, such as the Scandinavians in North and South Dakota.

3) The Homestead Act failed to discourage speculators and drain poverty from eastern cities, but it did achieve the settlement of the West. By 1900 there were 500,000 farms on the Plains.

The Beef Bonanza began in Texas

> Texas had been part of Mexico until 1845, when it became a US state. Many Mexicans were driven out, leaving their cattle to American ranchers.

1) The famous Texas Longhorn cattle were the result of interbreeding between Mexican cattle and cattle brought to the USA by Anglo-American settlers.

2) Numbers of Texas Longhorn grew massively during the Civil War. Many Texans left their ranches to fight, and while they were away, their cattle continued to breed. E.g. Charles Goodnight (who would later become a key figure in cattle ranching) left behind 180 cattle, but returned in 1865 to find he owned 5000.

Comment and Analysis

Railroads were very important in the growth of the cattle industry — they connected ranchers with valuable markets. Railroads had become established by the end of the Civil War and continued to expand afterwards.

3) Beef grew in popularity in the 1850s — there was a large demand for it in northern markets. So ranchers drove their cattle to the railroads, which then transported them to these markets.

Life on the Plains was... well... plain difficult...

Make two columns. In the first, make a list of the hardships faced by settlers on the Plains and in the second write down how people tried to overcome them. Use page 68 to help you with this.

Exploitation of the Great Plains

Cowboys drove cattle along cattle trails to reach the markets. The cattle industry continued to develop and thrive with the emergence of cow towns — places where cattle could be bought, sold and transported on.

The great Cattle Trails linked supply with demand

1) The four main cattle trails were the Goodnight-Loving Trail, the Western Trail, the Chisholm Trail and the Shawnee Trail. Trails were between 1200 and 1500 miles long and progress of 15 miles was considered a good day's drive.

> 1871 was the peak year for the cattle drives — 600,000 cattle were driven north.

2) Early cattle drives followed the Shawnee Trail, where they would then be taken east by rail to Chicago.

3) However, Oliver Loving and his partner Charles Goodnight decided to target western markets. They established the Goodnight-Loving Trail in 1866, making it possible to drive cattle from Texas to Wyoming. They sold their beef in New Mexico to the army, to growing numbers of settlers and to the US government to feed Indians on reservations. They then drove the cattle up to Colorado to sell to miners.

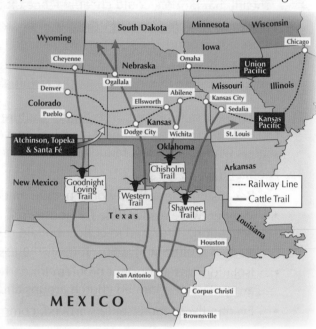

> Some Indian tribes were being put on reservations in the 1860s (see p.71). Goodnight and Loving supplied beef to the Apache and Navajo Indian reservation at Fort Sumter in New Mexico.

4) Instead of driving their herds all the way north from ranches in Texas, some cattlemen decided that it would be more efficient to set up ranches on the Plains.

> Open-range ranching meant there were no fences — cattle were free to graze where they liked.

5) The first man to do this was John Iliff, who set up open-range ranching in Wyoming in 1867. In 1868, Goodnight drove cattle up to Iliff in Wyoming, which Iliff sold on to construction gangs on the Transcontinental Railroad. Iliff also won a government contract in 1868 to supply beef to the Sioux reservation.

> Some ranchers were very successful and became known as cattle barons. John Iliff became a powerful rancher, with 35,000 cattle in Colorado and Wyoming.

The Cattle Trails led to the Cow Towns

> The development of refrigerated rail carriages from 1878 meant that cattle could be slaughtered before transportation.

1) The Shawnee Trail was threatened when homesteaders in Kansas and Missouri objected to ranchers' cattle crossing their land.

2) Joseph McCoy, a livestock trader and entrepreneur, saw the potential of moving beef cattle by rail to the eastern cities and Indian reservations. He decided to create a cow town away from homesteaders' land where cattle could be driven. He chose Abilene to be his cow town — the Kansas Pacific railway had pushed westward to run past Abilene and it was away from settled areas.

3) In sixty days in 1867, McCoy built Abilene up to a fully equipped cow town, with a stockyard, hotel and bank. It was soon connected to Texas via the Chisholm Trail — McCoy persuaded ranchers to drive their cattle to Abilene, where they would be sold and transported to northern markets.

4) In a few years, about 3 million cattle had passed through Abilene. Soon, other cow towns such as Wichita, Ellsworth and Dodge City emerged, as the railway continued to advance westwards.

Beef up your knowledge by making some mind maps...

Create a mind map of how the cattle industry developed. Make sure you have each of the main factors and then add detail to explain each one. You'll need to use the information from p.69 too.

The Making of America, 1789-1900

The Indian Wars 1861-1876

Tension increased between Plains Indians and settlers — this eventually broke out into a series of conflicts.

Railroads, Ranching and Gold angered the Plains Indians

1) Railroad companies often clashed with the Plains Indians. They sold land on the Plains to settlers and frequently built railroads through Native American lands, even if it violated treaties.

2) Railroad companies also encouraged the hunting of buffalo — both to feed the railway construction gangs, and to make money by transporting hunters. The construction of the railroads divided herds and made them easier to hunt.

3) Buffalo were a very important resource for Native Americans (see p.58), so some tribes derailed trains and ambushed workmen. In response, the military built forts to safeguard the railroad.

Sioux raiding a train on the Great Plains.

4) Ranchers also clashed with the Plains Indians. They were attacked because their cattle drives went through Indian land and they built ranches on Indian territories, disrupting buffalo herds. Oliver Loving (see p.70) died in 1867 after a fight with Comanches.

5) When gold was discovered in Montana in 1862, miners arrived in the area and searched for gold on Indian reservation land, breaking the treaties which had promised this land to the Native Americans.

Comment and Analysis

The effects of railroads and increased settlement were long lasting and contributed to the destruction of the Plains Indians' culture after 1877 (see p.73).

Many Plains Indians were Unhappy with the reservation policy

1) More Indians were moved onto reservations as more settlers came to live on the Plains.

2) Life on reservations varied. The Navajos achieved peace and prosperity after 1868 when a treaty with the US allowed them sufficient reservation area in their homeland.

> Many Plains tribes were still able to hunt buffalo, but only within certain areas.

3) Other tribes were moved off their homeland and onto unfamiliar territory. They were encouraged to farm the land, which went against their culture and nomadic lifestyle.

4) Often reservation lands were insufficient and unsuitable for farming — some tribes faced starvation.

5) If the lands were good, they were often grabbed by settlers, despite the promises in the government treaties. Many chiefs also lacked the authority to make their tribes keep to the agreements.

6) Many tribes wanted peace, but the situation had become intolerable. They were forced into conflict during the 1860s in a series of Indian Wars.

> It isn't surprising that the Native Americans went to war. The government had given them the Great Plains (see p.57), but then repeatedly broke its promises and forced tribes onto ever-smaller areas of land.

Little Crow's War was an uprising in Minnesota — 1862

1) The first major Indian War was Little Crow's War. Little Crow was the chief of the Santee Sioux, also known as the Dakota, who lived on a reservation in Minnesota.

2) They were peaceful and accepted reservation life. But they nearly starved as a result of Civil War shortages, a delay in their payment from the government, cheating by traders and a poor harvest.

3) In August 1862, four Dakota returning from an unsuccessful hunt murdered five settlers for a dare. Fearing retaliation on the entire tribe, Little Crow reluctantly led his warriors in an uprising. Hundreds of settlers and about 100 soldiers were killed, and the town of New Ulm was burned.

4) The uprising was ended when the Dakota were defeated at Wood Lake in September. 38 Dakota prisoners were hanged and most of the Dakota were expelled from what was left of their land.

Railroads didn't have a positive impact on everybody...

Explain the impact of railroads on the Plains Indians. Give examples to support your answer. [10]

The Making of America, 1789-1900

The Indian Wars 1861-1876

More Indian Wars followed during the 1860s. The Sioux then won a major battle against the US in 1876.

The Cheyenne Uprising and the Sand Creek Massacre — 1864

1) In 1863, the Cheyenne faced starvation because they couldn't grow enough food on their infertile reservation land at Sand Creek or find any buffalo. They decided to raid settlers' wagon trains for food. There was further violence between Indians and the army during 1864.

2) Chief Black Kettle, who wanted peace, moved his band to a camp where he believed they would be safe. But in November 1864, Colonel John Chivington attacked the camp while most of the band's men were out hunting. Of the 500 people left in the camp, at least 163 were killed — mostly women and children.

3) The Cheyenne, Arapaho and Sioux retaliated by attacking ranches and other settlements, and killing those inside, including women and children. The central Plains erupted into war.

Red Cloud's War and the Bozeman Trail — 1866-1868

1) The Bozeman Trail was established to link the gold fields in Montana with the Oregon Trail. However, this trail passed through the hunting grounds of the Sioux, which had been guaranteed to them by the Fort Laramie Treaty of 1851.

2) The Sioux attacked travellers who used the trail, so the army wanted to build forts to protect them. Talks were held with Red Cloud, a Sioux chief, to negotiate the building of these forts, but they were abandoned when the Sioux saw soldiers marching out to begin building before any deal had been made.

3) The Sioux began to attack the army. In a major incident known as Fetterman's Trap, the Sioux ambushed Captain W.J. Fetterman and his troops — Fetterman and all 80 of his men were killed.

Red Cloud.

4) As a result, the US army surrendered and abandoned the forts. This was a major defeat for the army.

- Red Cloud eventually signed the 1868 Fort Laramie Treaty, which created a large Sioux reservation on an area that included the sacred Black Hills of Dakota. The government also agreed not to rebuild their forts on the Bozeman Trail.
- Red Cloud promised never again to make war on the settlers — and kept his promise. But not all of the Sioux bands agreed with the treaty.

The Great Sioux War — 1876-1877

1) The Great Sioux War was sparked by the discovery of gold in the Black Hills of Dakota in 1874. The US government tried to buy the Black Hills from the Sioux, but they refused — the hills were sacred to them and had been guaranteed to them by the Fort Laramie Treaty of 1868.

2) Despite the Sioux's refusal to sell the Black Hills, miners arrived there to search for gold. In protest, many of the Sioux left the reservation and gathered in Montana in the Bighorn Valley.

3) By the start of 1876, the Sioux chiefs Sitting Bull and Crazy Horse had raised a force of several thousand men, so the US government sent soldiers against them. The Sioux launched a successful attack on the soldiers while they were resting, killing 28 of them. This became known as the Battle of the Rosebud.

4) The government planned another attack on the Sioux 8 days later, led by Lt. Col. George Custer. Custer was ambitious and decided to attack without waiting for the rest of the army. Custer and all 225 of his men were killed. The Battle of Little Bighorn was the greatest Native American victory in battle against the US army. However, this only strengthened the resolve of the army to defeat the Indians.

Little Bighorn was a major Native American victory...

Summarise the main conflicts of the Indian Wars, including the key people and what they did.

The Making of America, 1789-1900

Changes to the Plains Indians' Way of Life

Although the Indians <u>won</u> against the US army at the battle of Little Bighorn (see p.72), it was too <u>little</u> too <u>late</u>.

The Sioux eventually Lost the Great Sioux War

1) After the Battle of Little Bighorn, the army launched a <u>winter campaign</u> against the Sioux in 1876-77. Facing hunger and the loss of their horses, the Sioux <u>surrendered</u> and were forced onto <u>reservations</u>.

2) <u>Crazy Horse</u> surrendered in <u>May 1877</u> and was later <u>killed</u> by a US soldier while resisting arrest. <u>Sitting Bull</u> retreated to Canada, but returned and surrendered in <u>1881</u>.

3) Sioux reservations were put under <u>military control</u> and, in 1877, the Black Hills were <u>opened</u> to white settlement.

> **Comment and Analysis**
>
> Little Bighorn was only a <u>short term victory</u> for the Native Americans. It <u>wasn't</u> enough to turn their fortunes around.

Buffalo Slaughter forced Native Americans to accept Reservations

1) <u>Millions</u> of buffalo had once roamed the Plains. They were <u>vital</u> to many Plains Indians' survival (see p.58) and were <u>sacred</u> to them.

2) Buffalo were <u>slaughtered</u> in large numbers by white settlers (see p.71). They were killed to <u>feed</u> soldiers and railroad construction workers. People also killed them for their <u>skins</u> and others just killed them for <u>sport</u> — men would shoot the animals from the windows of trains.

3) As a result of this, buffalo numbers <u>decreased</u> rapidly — there roughly were <u>13 million</u> buffalo on the plains in <u>1865</u>, but by the <u>end</u> of the century they were almost <u>extinct</u>.

4) The effect on the Plains Indians was <u>devastating</u> — their main source of <u>food</u> was gone, as well as a major part of their <u>culture</u>. This caused many Indians to accept life on the <u>reservations</u> — they feared <u>starvation</u>.

5) It's <u>unclear</u> whether there was an official <u>policy</u> to exterminate the buffalo, but many people recognised that destroying them would help <u>defeat</u> the Indians.

> General Sheridan is quoted as saying, 'let them kill, skin and sell until the buffalo is <u>exterminated</u>, as it is the only way to bring lasting <u>peace</u> and allow <u>civilisation</u> to advance'.

A buffalo skinner. Buffalo skins were much in demand. The rest of the animal would be left to decay on the Plains.

Reservations destroyed their Culture

1) The formerly nomadic Plains Indians, now confined to smaller areas, could no longer feed or clothe themselves without government aid. Living on <u>hand-outs</u>, they became demoralised and there were high rates of <u>alcoholism</u>.

2) Many tribes were moved off their culturally significant <u>ancestral lands</u> and onto reservations elsewhere. The influence of <u>chiefs</u> declined because reservations were run by Indian agents, <u>undermining</u> tribal structure. <u>Hostile</u> tribes were sometimes put on reservations in close <u>proximity</u>.

3) Many children were taken away to be <u>educated</u>, for example at the Carlisle Indian School in Pennsylvania (founded in 1879). <u>Polygamy</u> (having more than one wife) and <u>religious practices</u> such as the Sun Dance were banned. The threat of <u>withholding rations</u> was used to enforce cooperation.

> **Comment and Analysis**
>
> The government had always wanted the Indians to <u>assimilate</u>. As Indians living on the reservations were now <u>dependent</u> on the state, there was a way to force them to abandon their own <u>culture</u>.

> It is debatable whether the Plains Indians could have protected their way of life. There were many factors at work against them. The US army usually had better <u>weapons</u> than the Native Americans — repeating rifles, machine guns and cannons. The system of <u>forts</u> gave the US army control on the Plains. The <u>railroads</u> and <u>telegraph</u> system provided fast transport and communication. <u>Divisions</u> between Native American nations meant that they had no <u>organised</u> resistance. Reservation life also made it more <u>difficult</u> for them to resist.

The Native Americans couldn't bring the buffalo back...

If you're writing about how the Native Americans were defeated, make sure you mention the impact of the destruction of the buffalo — the buffalo were crucial to their survival.

Assimilation of the Native Americans

America's population was growing — increasing the pressure on reservation land.

The Dawes Act (1887) Parcelled Out tribal lands

1) The aim of the Dawes Act was to convert tribesmen into independent farmers. It was hoped this would help destroy tribal bonds and lead to the assimilation of Native Americans into white society.

> Some reformers supported the Act because they wanted to stop Indian suffering on reservations. Some believed that reservation life encouraged idleness and reliance on government hand-outs. Others just wanted to open up reservation lands to settlers.

2) The Dawes Act broke reservations up into allotments. Each head of family was assigned 160 acres, each single adult 80 acres, and each child 40 acres. US citizenship was also part of the deal.

3) When all the inhabitants of a reservation had been assigned their holdings, the remaining land was thrown open to white settlement. Indian schools were established from the sale of this surplus land.

4) The Act was a disaster for the Native Americans:

> Men found it difficult to adapt to farming — this had traditionally been seen as a woman's role. In Indian schools, children had to dress like white Americans and weren't allowed to speak tribal languages.

- Their tribal communities were broken up and their culture almost destroyed — the idea of land ownership went against Native American tradition.

- The creation of allotments led to Indians losing their land — down from 138 million acres in 1887 to 78 million acres in 1900. They also lost land granted to them under the Act (nearly two thirds of it between 1887 and 1934) as a result of being cheated by land speculators.

Comment and Analysis

While many reformers may have believed they had good intentions, their actions were based on their prejudiced belief that Native Americans needed to be introduced to Christianity and western civilisation to improve themselves.

- Lands belonging to the five eastern tribes that had been moved on to the Plains in the 1830s (see p.57) were exempt from the Dawes Act, yet through forced sales they too were eventually lost.

- In 1934, the government repealed the Dawes Act and encouraged tribal identities. But by that time, Native Americans had lost over 60 per cent of their original reservation lands and were suffering from high rates of poverty, alcoholism, illiteracy and suicide.

The Wounded Knee Massacre was the End of Indian resistance

The Wounded Knee Massacre was the last confrontation between Native Americans and the US army.

- The spiritual leader Wovoka taught that a special Ghost Dance could raise the dead and bring a new world free from settlers. He was against violence, but ghost dances built the dancers up into a frenzy — this unsettled white Americans, who feared that the dance would lead to rebellion.

- Tensions peaked at the Pine Ridge Reservation in Wounded Knee Creek, South Dakota. Fighting broke out between a band of Sioux and the US army — 150 Sioux and 25 soldiers died.

> Some of the ghost dancers believed that special shirts would protect them from bullets. The sight of the shirts pierced by bullets after the battle destroyed their faith in a magical restoration of the old way of life. The reservation was reluctantly accepted as home.

Americans became aware of the End of the Frontier

1) In 1890, census results revealed that, unlike in 1880, there was no longer a definable western frontier of settlement. The frontier was declared officially closed.

2) This didn't mean that there was no more land available for settlers, but what remained was in isolated pockets and the best areas had been taken.

> The Native Americans were no longer a barrier to settlement — they'd been subdued and were in the process of being assimilated into white society.

The frontier closed — and the West is history...

To sum up — settlers in, Indians out. It's all very well knowing all the little facts about this period of American history, but to write a good answer you've got to know how they fit together too.

Changes to the Lives of African Americans

After 1877, African Americans lost many of the gains they had made during Reconstruction (see p.66-67).

African Americans lost their Civil Rights

African Americans had an inferior status in society as a result of segregation. This meant that they were separated from white people, for example in schools, shops, hotels, theatres and on public transport.

1) Southern states passed 'Jim Crow' laws which legalised segregation. Intermarriage also became illegal.

2) In 1883, the Supreme Court ruled that the 1875 Civil Rights Act, which had outlawed discrimination in public places, was unconstitutional (against the constitution).

3) The Supreme Court also supported segregation. In the Plessy v. Ferguson case of 1896, it ruled that a Louisiana law requiring separate railway coaches for African Americans was constitutional.

> There was an increase in violence against African Americans in the 1890s. Lynchings became more common — lynchings are killings without trial, often by hanging.

They faced Economic Repression

Many African Americans lived in poverty and were prevented from making money.

1) Many worked as sharecroppers, harvesting cotton and tobacco, or in low paid jobs in the coal and iron industries. Sharecroppers were often exploited by landowners and became trapped in a cycle of poverty and debt.

2) They had few chances to improve their lives — legal restrictions and violence often prevented them from working in skilled professions. Education for African Americans was poor — African American schools were given less funding than white schools by state governments.

> White southerners felt threatened by African Americans and wanted to maintain white superiority. Many in the South were still bitter about the outcome of the Civil War.

3) States passed laws which punished small crimes with harsh sentences, e.g. the Pig Laws, which punished people for stealing farm animals, and vagrancy statutes, which made it a crime to be unemployed. These laws targeted African Americans as they were more likely to be poor and unemployed.

They were Denied their Political Rights

Democrats regained control of the South in 1877. They tried to remove African American voting rights — rights which they had been guaranteed under the 15th Amendment (see p.67).

1) States passed new state constitutions which introduced voting restrictions, such as poll taxes and literacy tests. This mostly affected African Americans because they were more likely to be poor or unable to read and write — the voting restrictions made it difficult or impossible for many of them to vote.

> People who couldn't vote weren't able to run for office or serve on juries — reducing African American participation in politics even further.

2) The Supreme Court upheld these new constitutions. It ruled that Mississippi's 1890 constitution wasn't discriminatory and other southern states adopted similar constitutions between 1890 and 1908.

Many African Americans Moved out of the South

1) Many African Americans moved to the West. For example, around 20,000 'Exodusters' moved to Kansas in 1879, creating all-black communities such as Nicodemus. Others moved to the North.

2) Even though there were no discriminatory laws in these areas, African Americans still faced racism. 'Sundown towns' were white communities which excluded African Americans — these towns existed all across America. In the North, African Americans and whites lived separately, and African Americans experienced racism from European immigrants who they competed with for housing and jobs.

Sadly, the battle for equality wasn't over...

Summarise the ways the lives of African Americans changed after 1877.
Explain how these changes went against acts passed during Reconstruction.

The Making of America, 1789-1900

Big Business, Cities and Mass Migration

The USA underwent huge <u>economic growth</u> between 1870 and 1900 — a few people became very <u>wealthy</u>. But this period is known as the '<u>Gilded Age</u>' — <u>beneath</u> the appearance of wealth, there were <u>problems</u>.

America Industrialised and Big Business emerged

1) The period between <u>1870</u> and <u>1914</u> is known as the <u>Second Industrial Revolution</u>. It was a time of rapid industrial <u>growth</u> and technological <u>change</u>. America's economy changed from being mainly <u>agricultural</u> to <u>industrial</u>.

> The nature of industry changed from <u>small</u> businesses employing <u>skilled</u> craftsmen to <u>big</u> businesses using <u>mass production</u> techniques and employing <u>unskilled</u> workers.

2) Industries were developed such as <u>steel</u> and <u>oil</u>. New technologies like <u>electricity</u> emerged. Factories <u>multiplied</u> — they began to use <u>machinery</u> and production <u>increased</u>.

3) <u>Successful</u> businesses were created in these industries. Big businesses appeared when several businesses were <u>merged</u> to form one <u>large</u> corporation — these corporations <u>forced out</u> competition and took <u>control</u> of the market. The businessmen who owned these corporations became very <u>wealthy</u>.

> <u>John Rockefeller</u> founded the <u>Standard Oil Company</u>. He introduced new <u>techniques</u> which transformed the oil industry. He was the first American <u>billionaire</u>.

> <u>Andrew Carnegie</u> created the <u>Carnegie Steel Company</u>. He used improved technology and methods to <u>quickly</u> and <u>efficiently</u> mass produce steel.

> These figures were seen as contributing to the <u>prosperity</u> of America. They were also <u>philanthropists</u> — they gave away much of their wealth to good causes such as schools and libraries.

Industrialisation and mass Migration led to the Growth of Cities

1) Industrialisation was centred on the <u>cities</u> where <u>factories</u> were built. <u>Growing</u> numbers of factories created a demand for <u>labour</u>, attracting people to <u>move</u> to cities for jobs — <u>migrants</u> from rural areas in America and <u>immigrants</u> from Europe. Nearly <u>11 million</u> immigrants arrived between <u>1870</u> and <u>1900</u>.

2) The US population nearly <u>doubled</u> between 1870 and 1900. It has been estimated that in 1870 <u>25.7%</u> of the population lived in cities, but this increased to almost <u>40%</u> by 1900.

> Initially, most immigrants came from <u>north-west</u> Europe, but after <u>1890</u>, most came from <u>southern</u> and <u>eastern</u> Europe, e.g. <u>Italy</u> and <u>Russia</u>.

3) Cities like <u>New York</u> and <u>Chicago</u> grew and developed as more people moved to them. America began to build its first skyscraper in Chicago in <u>1884</u> — the first tall building to use <u>steel</u> in its frame.

> New electric transport was introduced, such as <u>electric streetcars</u> (trams). This resulted in the growth of <u>suburbs</u> — people could now travel into cities <u>quickly</u>, which meant that those who could afford to didn't have to live <u>in</u> the cities themselves.

There was Corruption, Poverty and Inequality

1) While some businessmen grew very <u>wealthy</u>, many other people struggled in <u>poverty</u>. Some people called the wealthy '<u>robber barons</u>' — accusing them of using unfair methods to gain their wealth.
   - They put smaller competitors <u>out</u> of business, could <u>control</u> markets and had <u>political</u> influence.
   - Workers were paid <u>low wages</u> and worked <u>long hours</u>, often in <u>dangerous</u> conditions.

2) The rich <u>showed off</u> their wealth while many others struggled with life in <u>crowded</u> and <u>unsanitary</u> cities — <u>crime</u> was common and there was a lot of <u>racial conflict</u>.

> Men at the Carnegie steelworks worked <u>12 hours</u> a day, <u>seven days</u> a week with only <u>one day</u> off a year. <u>Accidents</u> and <u>deaths</u> were common.

3) <u>Discontent</u> among workers led to the rise of <u>trade unions</u> — organisations formed by workers which aim to improve their <u>rights</u>. Workers also went on <u>strikes</u>.

> Many of the elite believed in <u>survival of the fittest</u> — that people with the right <u>skills</u> would be successful in life. As a result, they didn't <u>support</u> measures to help the poor, such as improving working conditions.

Comment and Analysis

While the wealth of the <u>country</u> increased, there was a <u>growing gap</u> between the <u>wealthy</u> and the <u>poor</u>.

From a few farms to a powerful industrial nation...

Name one of the main industries which developed during the 'Gilded Age'. [1]

Revision Summary

Well, that was the Making of America — now you need to see how well you've taken it all in.
- Try these questions and <u>tick off each one</u> when you <u>get it right</u>.
- When you've done <u>all the questions</u> for a topic and are <u>completely happy</u> with it, tick off the topic.

America's Expansion, 1789-1838 (p.54-57) ☑

1) Name two of the original 13 states. ☑
2) Give two reasons why the Louisiana Purchase was important for the expansion of the USA. ☑
3) How did the war of 1812 affect Native Americans? ☑
4) Which part of the USA became reliant on slavery? ☑
5) How did settlers view the Great Plains before the 1860s? ☑
6) What was the Permanent Indian Frontier? What was its purpose? ☑

The West, 1839-1860 (p.58-62) ☑

7) Why were buffalo important to the Plains Indians? ☑
8) Summarise the Plains Indians' beliefs about land and nature. ☑
9) Give 3 reasons why settlers went to the west coast. ☑
10) What difficulties did the Mormons face on their journey to Salt Lake Valley? ☑
11) How did the expectations of miners compare with the reality of life in California? ☑
12) Why was the Permanent Indian Frontier abandoned? ☑

Civil War and Reconstruction, 1861-1877 (p.63-67) ☑

13) Explain why westward expansion increased tension over slavery. ☑
14) What was the impact of Lincoln's election as President?
15) How and why did African Americans help the Union war effort? ☑
16) How were African Americans treated in the Union Army? ☑
17) a) Give two examples of Andrew Johnson's lenient approach during Reconstruction.
    b) Why did some Republicans disapprove of this approach? ☑
18) Explain how Reconstruction fell short of the ideals of Radical Republicans. ☑

Settlement and Conflict on the Plains, 1861-1877 (p.68-72) ☑

19) What was the 1862 Homestead Act? ☑
20) List 3 developments which helped settlers live and farm on the Plains. ☑
21) What was the role of Joseph McCoy in the growth of the cattle industry? ☑
22) Why did many Native Americans dislike life on the reservations? ☑
23) Describe the events of the Cheyenne Uprising and the Sand Creek Massacre. ☑
24) Why did the Great Sioux War break out in 1876? ☑

American Cultures, 1877-1900 (p.73-76) ☑

25) What impact did the destruction of the buffalo have on the Native Americans? ☑
26) What was the aim of the Dawes Act? ☑
27) Why did the African Americans lose their civil rights after 1877? ☑
28) Who were the 'Exodusters'? ☑
29) Why did cities grow between 1870 and 1900? ☑
30) What problems were there during the 'Gilded Age'? ☑

Exam Skills for the Depth Studies

These pages are about the <u>wider world depth study</u> and the <u>British depth study</u> sections of your exam.

Depth studies are about knowing a *Short Period* in Detail

1) The depth studies cover a <u>short</u> period of history (less than 25 years) in <u>detail</u>.

2) You'll need to have a detailed <u>knowledge</u> of the period — this means knowing the <u>main developments</u> and <u>important events</u> that took place, but also people's experiences.

3) You'll need to understand <u>how</u> and <u>why</u> historical sources or events can be interpreted in <u>different ways</u> by <u>different people</u> at <u>different times</u>.

> To help with this, <u>practise</u> analysing visual and written sources.

There are *Two* different *Depth Studies*

The *World Depth Study* has *Three* basic types of exam questions

1) One question will ask you to <u>evaluate</u> what a <u>visual</u> or <u>written</u> source is saying. You'll need to use your <u>own knowledge</u> of the period to answer this question.

> What can Source A tell us about Nazi education policies? [7 marks]

2) The next question will ask you to analyse a <u>group</u> of visual or written sources. You'll have to decide how <u>useful</u> they are using the sources and what you know about the period.

> How useful are Interpretation B and Sources C and D for a historian studying the growth of opposition to the Nazi Party during World War Two? [15 marks]

3) Then you will get a <u>choice</u> of <u>two</u> questions. You have to answer one — choose the one you're most <u>comfortable</u> with. Both questions will ask you <u>how far you agree</u> with a view.

> 'The Nazis rose to power in the 1930s because of the economic depression in Germany.' How far do you agree with this view? [18 marks]

The *British Depth Study* has *Four* basic types of exam questions

1) The first question is in <u>two parts</u>. The first part identifies a <u>feature</u> of your period and asks you to explain <u>how</u> an interpretation shows that feature.

The <u>second</u> part will ask you to identify something about the interpretation you'd like to <u>find out more</u> about.

> **a)** In Interpretation A, the illustrator portrays the hierarchical nature of Anglo-Saxon society. Identify and explain one way in which the illustrator does this. [3 marks]
>
> **b)** If you were asked to do further research on one aspect of Interpretation A, what would you choose to investigate? Explain how this would help us to analyse and understand Anglo-Saxon society. [5 marks]

2) The third question will ask you to explain <u>how far</u> two interpretations differ and <u>why</u>.

> Interpretations B and C both focus on poverty in Elizabethan England. How far do they differ and what might explain any differences? [12 marks]

3) You'll then be given a <u>choice</u> of two questions — both will give you an <u>interpretation</u> and ask <u>how far you agree</u> with it.

> In his 2014 book *Elizabeth I*, Christopher Haigh argued that Elizabeth 'was not... a political genius who got everything right.' How far do you agree with this view? [20 marks]

Exam Skills for the Depth Studies

Here's a bit more advice and a sample answer to a question from the depth study sections of your exams.

You'll need these Skills to answer the questions

1) When you're working with sources, it's not just a case of describing what you see or read. You need to analyse the source and draw conclusions from it — ask yourself what it's trying to tell you.

2) To evaluate interpretations, you need to figure out what the author's saying by looking at the information they give. Think about why the interpretations are different — for example, they could have been written at different times, or one author might have a biased view.

3) When you're asked how far you agree with something, decide your opinion before you start writing and state it clearly at the beginning and end of your answer. Include different sides of the argument to show that you've considered all of the evidence.

For some more general advice on answering exam questions, see p.136.

Here's a Sample Answer to help you

Questions on the British depth study ask about interpretations instead. You'll still need to work out what the interpretations are saying though.

This sample answer will give you an idea of how to interpret a source. For all source questions, you need to be able to analyse what sources are saying.

Source A

> The government has ordered that the Hitler Greeting is to be used in conversation between teachers and pupils. Every day at the beginning of the first lesson, the pupils will get up from their places as soon as the teacher enters the class, stand to attention and each raise their outstretched arm level with their eyes. The teacher will go to the front of the class and offer the same greeting accompanied by the words 'Heil Hitler!' The pupils will reply 'Heil Hitler!'

A translated extract from a German newspaper published in the mid-1930s.

What can Source A tell us about Nazi education policies?
Use the source and your own knowledge to support your answer. [7 marks]

Source A tells us that education policies were used by the Nazi Party to control the actions of pupils and teachers. It discusses the requirement for teachers and pupils to greet one another using the 'Hitler Greeting'. This suggests that education policies exposed schoolchildren to Nazi propaganda, in an attempt to build Nazi beliefs and values in children from a young age. The Nazis also did this through curriculum changes, for example science courses taught that Jews were biologically 'inferior' to Aryans. Youth organisations, like the Hitler Youth and the League of German Maidens, helped to build on the loyalty and idolisation of Hitler that was encouraged in the classroom.

Source A says that teachers also had to use the greeting, which demonstrates that Nazi policies in education were far-reaching — the Nazis wanted the whole education system (not just schoolchildren) to follow National Socialist principles. The establishment of Nazi organisations like the National Teachers' Association also supports this view. Hitler wanted every aspect of education to be under Nazi control.

This gives a direct answer to the question straight away.

The answer doesn't just repeat what the source says — it explains what it reveals about the Nazis' education policies.

Your own knowledge can also be used to back up a point you've made and will show a good understanding of the topic.

This is a shortened example — in the exam, you'd need to make another point.

These depth studies really get to the bottom of things...

The wider world depth study and British depth study are examined on separate papers, so make sure you revise the right one for the right exam. Don't forget about History Around Us, too — see p.133-135.

Anglo-Saxon Society

To understand the <u>impact</u> of the <u>Norman conquest</u>, you need to know what England was like <u>before 1066</u>. The next few pages will tell you all about Anglo-Saxon <u>society</u>, <u>religion</u> and <u>culture</u>.

Anglo-Saxon society was Unequal and Hierarchical

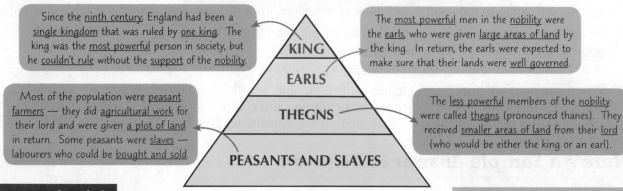

Since the <u>ninth century</u>, England had been a <u>single kingdom</u> that was ruled by <u>one king</u>. The king was the <u>most powerful</u> person in society, but he <u>couldn't rule</u> without the <u>support</u> of the <u>nobility</u>.

The <u>most powerful</u> men in the <u>nobility</u> were the <u>earls</u>, who were given <u>large areas of land</u> by the king. In return, the earls were expected to make sure that their lands were <u>well governed</u>.

Most of the population were <u>peasant farmers</u> — they did <u>agricultural work</u> for their lord and were given <u>a plot of land</u> in return. Some peasants were <u>slaves</u> — labourers who could be <u>bought and sold</u>.

The <u>less powerful</u> members of the <u>nobility</u> were called <u>thegns</u> (pronounced thanes). They received <u>smaller areas of land</u> from their <u>lord</u> (who would be either the king or an earl).

KING
EARLS
THEGNS
PEASANTS AND SLAVES

Comment and Analysis

People's <u>lives</u> and <u>experiences</u> were <u>shaped</u> by their <u>social status</u>. People at the <u>top</u> of the hierarchy were pretty <u>wealthy</u> and <u>powerful</u>. Those at the <u>bottom</u> were often <u>poor</u> and didn't have much <u>power</u> or <u>control</u> over their lives (especially <u>slaves</u>). People could <u>gain</u> or <u>lose</u> status (e.g. a slave might be freed), but <u>most</u> died with the <u>same status</u> that they had at birth.

A <u>lord</u> was anyone who had others <u>relying</u> on them for <u>food</u>, <u>land</u> and <u>protection</u> (dependents). Lots of <u>free men</u> were lords, not just those <u>high up</u> in the hierarchy. Dependents often had to <u>fight</u> or <u>work</u> for their lords.

The system of Government was Sophisticated and Well Organised

1) England was divided into <u>shires</u> (these were a bit like modern counties). A <u>shire-reeve,</u> or <u>sheriff,</u> (usually a thegn) controlled the government within each <u>shire</u>, while an <u>earl</u> oversaw the government of <u>several shires</u>.

2) Earls and their sheriffs enforced <u>law</u> and <u>order</u>. They did this using the <u>shire courts</u> — these <u>resolved disputes</u> (e.g. over property) and tried <u>criminal cases</u>.

3) Earls and sheriffs also made sure that <u>taxes</u> were <u>collected</u>. The Anglo-Saxon <u>tax system</u> was very <u>organised</u>. The amount of <u>tax</u> owed by each shire was based on the <u>value</u> of its <u>land</u>, and taxes were paid in <u>cash</u>.

4) The <u>value</u> and <u>quality</u> of the <u>currency</u> was controlled by the <u>king</u>. He used a network of local mints (where money is made) to create <u>standardised coins</u> (these had a set <u>design</u> and were <u>worth the same</u> throughout the kingdom). This financial system was the most <u>sophisticated</u> in Europe at the time.

5) When the king summoned a region's <u>fighting forces</u> (the <u>fyrd</u>, see p.85), it was the job of <u>earls</u> and the nobility to <u>organise</u> the troops and <u>lead</u> them into <u>battle</u>.

The <u>king's council</u> (sometimes called the <u>Witenagemot</u>) was a group of the most powerful <u>nobles</u> and <u>churchmen</u> in the country. It <u>advised</u> the king and helped him to <u>govern</u>. When the king <u>died</u>, the council could play a role in <u>choosing</u> the next king, especially if there was a <u>dispute</u> over who should <u>rule</u>.

Life in Anglo-Saxon England could be <u>dangerous</u>. There were several Viking invasions between the <u>late 7th</u> and <u>early 11th</u> century. <u>Rival kingdoms</u> were often at <u>war</u> with each other too.

There were Laws protecting Women's Rights

1) Under Anglo-Saxon law, women could <u>own</u>, <u>inherit</u> and <u>sell property</u>. There were laws <u>protecting</u> women from being <u>forced</u> to get <u>married</u>. If a couple got <u>divorced</u>, the woman would receive half of the <u>property</u> and get custody of the <u>children</u>.

2) However, Anglo-Saxon <u>women</u> still had <u>fewer rights</u> and freedoms than <u>men</u>. Many parts of their lives were <u>controlled</u> by their <u>male relatives</u> or, if they were <u>married</u>, their <u>husbands</u>.

Comment and Analysis

It's <u>hard</u> to find out what <u>life</u> was like for <u>medieval women</u>, because nearly all of the <u>sources</u> were written by <u>men</u>. Sources often focus on the most <u>powerful</u> people in society too, and these were <u>usually men</u>.

It wasn't pleasant to be a peasant...

Scribble down a quick explanation of how society was organised in Anglo-Saxon England. Make sure to talk about the king, earls, thegns, peasants and slaves.

REVISION TASK

Anglo-Saxon Religion

By 1066, Christianity was the main religion in England, and the church was a very powerful force.

The Anglo-Saxon Church was Wealthy and Powerful

1) The Anglo-Saxon church had suffered during Viking raids in the 9th century — many monasteries had been attacked. The church recovered slowly in the 10th century and became increasingly rich and powerful.

2) In the second half of the 10th century, monasteries that had been destroyed by the Vikings were rebuilt. These new monasteries were supported by the kings of England and the nobility, who gave them valuable gifts and land. This was seen as a monastic revival.

3) Churchmen played a key role in government. They were able to read and write, so the king relied on them to create all of the written records that were needed to govern the country.

> Literacy was important for churchmen (monks and the clergy) — they needed to be able to read the Bible and other Christian texts. However, most people thought that laymen (people who weren't part of the clergy) didn't need to be literate, so very few people outside the church learned to read or write. As a result, almost all of the written sources that we have from this period were created by churchmen.

The Church and the Nobility had an Important relationship

1) Kings and nobles gave churches gifts of land and precious objects, and helped to protect them from violence and robbery. This is called patronage.

2) The nobility sent their second-born sons to train as priests, which helped the church to grow. This also reduced competition for land within the nobility by giving some men a job within the church.

3) Nobles tried to control the appointment of bishops, abbots and parish priests so that they could give these valuable, influential posts to their relatives and followers.

> The church and the nobility both benefited from their relationship.

4) In return, churchmen prayed for their patrons. Prayer was important to the nobility, because they believed it would give them success on earth and help them get into heaven.

5) The church could also help to legitimise a king or lord's claim to power — people believed that a ruler needed God's support to be successful. If the church supported him, this was seen as a sign that God was on his side.

Comment and Analysis

The sources produced by churchmen were often influenced by the relationship between the church and the nobility. For example, this image shows King Cnut (a Danish king who ruled England in the early 11th century) being crowned by an angel. It was created by the monks of Winchester, who were close to the king. It makes his claim to the English throne more legitimate (valid), as it suggests that God wants him to be king.

The Church's Influence over Ordinary People was Growing

1) The Anglo-Saxon church was organised into sixteen large areas called dioceses. By 1066, these regions were being divided into smaller areas called parishes. Each parish was based around a local community, so the church became more involved in the lives of ordinary people.

2) Parish churches were built in towns and villages. Each church had its own priest who looked after people in the parish. The priest said mass regularly and performed key Christian rites like baptism and burial. He also got people to confess their sins and do penance (show that they're sorry for their sins).

The Church was very important in Anglo-Saxon society...

Explain one way the illustrator shows the power and legitimacy of King Cnut in the manuscript image above. [3]

Anglo-Saxon Culture

Anglo-Saxon England was <u>rich</u> in <u>precious metals</u>, especially gold. In fact, there was so much <u>gold</u> sloshing around that some people call the century before 1066 a '<u>golden age</u>' for <u>Anglo-Saxon culture</u>.

The Anglo-Saxons wrote Literature in Latin and Old English

1) In medieval Europe, most <u>books</u> were written in <u>Latin</u>, but <u>few people</u> outside the church <u>understood</u> this language. England was <u>unusual</u>, as it didn't just produce books in Latin — it also had a <u>long tradition</u> of writing in <u>Old English</u>, which was the language spoken by <u>most</u> of the population.

2) The <u>earliest</u> Old English texts we have date from about <u>700</u>. Most of the surviving texts were <u>written by churchmen</u> and focus on <u>religion</u>. However, Old English literature also includes <u>secular</u> (non-religious) texts, some of which were <u>written by laymen</u>. These include <u>riddles</u> and <u>poems</u>.

Comment and Analysis

The use of <u>Old English</u> in books made it <u>easier</u> for <u>laymen</u> in England to learn to <u>read</u> and <u>write</u> (compared to other places in Europe). Even so, <u>churchmen</u> still wrote most of the books.

One of the <u>most important</u> examples of Old English literature is the <u>epic poem</u> 'Beowulf'. It was passed down <u>orally</u> (it was spoken) for <u>many generations</u> before it was <u>written down</u> at some point before <u>1066</u>.

England was Famous for producing Beautiful works of Art

Anglo-Saxon <u>goldsmiths</u> were known for making <u>beautiful jewellery</u> and other precious things (like the <u>Alfred Jewel</u> from the late 9th century). <u>Written sources</u> show that England still had <u>famous goldsmiths</u> in the <u>11th century</u>.

© Ashmolean Museum / Mary Evans

Anglo-Saxon monasteries had a long tradition of producing <u>beautifully decorated books</u>. In the <u>11th century</u>, the main centre of book production in England was <u>Canterbury</u>. The monks of Canterbury produced <u>extravagant books</u> like the <u>Arundel Psalter</u> (a book of Psalms) that included lots of <u>gold decoration</u>. This style of decoration was <u>linked</u> with other places in <u>Europe</u>, including <u>Normandy</u>.

The Anglo-Saxons were famous for their <u>textiles</u> — these included <u>tapestries</u> that could be hung in homes and churches, and <u>vestments</u> that were worn by <u>priests</u>. Hardly any Anglo-Saxon textiles have <u>survived</u>, but one famous example that has survived is the <u>Bayeux tapestry</u>. While it was produced <u>after 1066</u>, it was made using Anglo-Saxon <u>traditions</u>.

There is Little Evidence about Anglo-Saxon Buildings

1) <u>Houses</u> and most other buildings would have been <u>simple structures</u> with a <u>wooden frame</u> and walls made from <u>wattle and daub</u> (sticks covered with mud or clay). Because of the <u>materials</u> used to make them, these buildings have <u>not survived</u>.

2) Most <u>English churches</u> were <u>rebuilt</u> by the <u>Normans</u>, so we don't have much <u>evidence</u> of how they looked.

3) The <u>evidence</u> that we <u>do</u> have suggests that Anglo-Saxon churches might have been built from <u>brick</u> or <u>stone</u>. They often had a <u>very tall tower</u>, too. There is some evidence that churches had <u>stone carvings</u>, but most English churches don't seem to have been <u>elaborately decorated</u>.

Anglo-Saxon art — golden oldies...

If you're asked about whether the Anglo-Saxon period was a golden age, then it's a good idea to think about the arguments both for and against this idea. Talk about society as well as culture.

EXAM TIP

Norman Society, Warfare and Culture

Warfare was an important part of Norman culture, but 11th century Normandy wasn't all swords and shields. The Normans also supported changes in the church and encouraged people to record history...

Norman society was Dominated by a Warrior Aristocracy

1) The Normans were originally Vikings from Scandinavia. In the early 10th century, they settled in northern France and established the duchy of Normandy around the mouth of the river Seine.

2) Norman society was dominated by a small elite of fighting men. This warrior upper class was bound together by vassalic bonds — lords gave their subjects (vassals) land and promised to protect them and treat them fairly. In exchange, vassals promised to be loyal to their lord and provide him with military service. The Duke of Normandy was the most powerful lord, because he could control who received the biggest and most valuable estates.

3) The Norman elite was closely connected by marriage alliances and family relationships. These ties could be a source of loyalty, but they could also create tension and conflict, especially when resources (e.g. land) had to be shared between members of the same family.

Comment and Analysis

The Norman elite was very powerful, but it only made up a tiny proportion of the Norman population — most of the people who lived in Normandy were peasant farmers. We know very little about the lives of Norman peasants because medieval sources usually focus on members of the elite.

Warfare played an Important Role in Norman society

1) The Normans were extremely successful warriors. They were constantly fighting to defend the borders of Normandy and to increase the size of the duchy. The conquest of England in 1066 was part of the Normans' constant efforts to expand the region under their control.

2) The Norman army included archers, and Norman knights fought on horseback. This gave the Normans a military advantage over armies like the Anglo-Saxons who didn't use archers and fought on foot.

3) Warfare was a way of life for male members of the Norman elite, and Norman knights were highly trained and extremely disciplined. At a young age, the sons of Norman lords were sent to other noble households to learn how to fight. They were trained to ride horses and use weapons, including bows and arrows, javelins, lances and swords.

Comment and Analysis

Warfare was important for the stability of Norman society. To make sure his relatives and followers were loyal, the Duke of Normandy needed to be able to offer them valuable rewards, especially land. It was only by conquering new territory that the duke could gain more land to give to his followers.

The Normans supported Historical Writing and the Church

1) When they settled in Normandy, the Normans intermarried with the native population and adopted many aspects of the local culture. This process is called assimilation.

2) The Normans didn't completely forget their Scandinavian heritage. Churchmen like Dudo of St Quentin and William of Jumièges were encouraged to write about Norman history. These writings described the Viking origins of the Normans and celebrated their success as rulers of Normandy.

3) The Normans had converted from paganism to Christianity, and they became generous supporters of the church. Norman dukes and lords set up monasteries and gave valuable gifts to churches. This contributed to the changes in English monasteries after the conquest (p.95).

The Normans didn't horse around when it came to warfare...

Write down as many similarities and differences between Norman and Anglo-Saxon culture as you can think of. Why might their cultures have been similar/different?

Claimants to the Throne in 1066

When the <u>king</u> of England <u>died</u> in <u>1066</u>, there were <u>three</u> powerful men who all had a claim to the <u>throne</u>...

England faced a Succession Crisis in 1066

1) <u>King Edward</u> died in <u>January 1066</u>. Edward <u>didn't have any children</u>, so there was <u>no direct heir</u> to the throne.

- <u>Edward</u> had been king of England since <u>1042</u>. Edward's father was the <u>Anglo-Saxon</u> king, <u>Aethelred II</u>. His mother was a daughter of the <u>Duke of Normandy</u>, and Edward had been <u>raised</u> in <u>Normandy</u>.
- Between 1013 and 1042, England's kings included three <u>Scandinavians</u> — <u>Swein</u>, <u>Cnut</u> and <u>Harthacnut</u>.

2) Because of the <u>close connections</u> between <u>England</u>, <u>Normandy</u> and <u>Scandinavia</u>, there were people in <u>all three regions</u> who thought they had a <u>strong claim</u> to the English throne.

There were Three main Claimants to the throne

Harold Godwinson, Earl of Wessex

1) Harold was the <u>most powerful nobleman</u> in England and he had experience of <u>leading an army</u>.

2) He was close to the royal family — his <u>father</u> had helped <u>Edward</u> become king, and his <u>sister</u> was <u>Edward's wife</u>.

3) Harold claimed that, on his <u>deathbed</u>, Edward <u>asked him</u> to become <u>king</u>. His claim to the throne was <u>supported</u> by the <u>Witenagemot</u>, a council of powerful English nobles.

Comment and Analysis

At the time, there were <u>no fixed rules</u> about the <u>order of succession</u>, although being <u>closely related</u> to the king could <u>strengthen</u> your claim to the throne. However, even those with a strong claim also had to be able to use <u>military force</u> to <u>take control</u> of the country and show that they would be an <u>effective ruler</u>.

William, Duke of Normandy

1) William was a powerful and successful <u>military leader</u>. He had already brought <u>stability</u> to Normandy, successfully defeating several challenges to his rule.

2) William was a distant <u>relative</u> of Edward. According to some sources, Edward had <u>promised</u> the throne to William in <u>1051</u>. William said that, in <u>1064</u>, Harold Godwinson had <u>repeated</u> this offer and promised to <u>support his claim</u> to the throne.

3) William's claim was <u>supported</u> by the <u>Pope</u>, which <u>strengthened</u> it by suggesting that <u>God</u> was on <u>his side</u>.

Comment and Analysis

Many of the <u>sources</u> are <u>biased</u> — they were written to <u>support one claimant</u> and weaken the others. This makes it <u>difficult</u> to tell who really had the <u>strongest claim</u> to the throne.

King Harald Hardrada of Norway

1) Harald was an <u>experienced ruler</u> and a successful <u>military leader</u>. He claimed that he was the <u>rightful heir</u> to the <u>Scandinavian kings</u> who had ruled England between 1013 and 1042.

2) His claim was supported by Harold Godwinson's brother <u>Tostig, Earl of Northumbria</u>. Harold played a part in having Tostig <u>exiled</u> in 1065. By supporting Harald Hardrada, Tostig hoped to <u>reclaim Northumbria</u> and get <u>revenge</u> on his brother.

Don't get your Harolds mixed up...

There are loads of names here, but things make more sense once you've got your head around who's who. Write a list of everyone who had a claim to the throne in 1066 and explain why.

The Struggle for the Throne

After Edward's death in January 1066, <u>Harold Godwinson</u> was crowned <u>king</u> of England. Unfortunately for Harold, his <u>competitors</u> weren't willing to give up on their claims to the throne without a <u>fight</u>...

Harold was Prepared for an invasion in Mid-1066

1) Once Harold had been <u>crowned king</u>, he gathered his forces and prepared to <u>defend</u> the <u>south coast</u> in case the <u>Normans invaded</u>. Harold's army consisted of <u>housecarls</u>, who were highly trained <u>professional warriors</u>, and the <u>fyrd</u>, a <u>part-time</u> defensive force.

2) The English army <u>waited</u> on the south coast throughout <u>mid-1066</u>, but <u>nothing happened</u>. By <u>September</u>, <u>supplies</u> were running low and Harold's men needed to <u>return to their land</u> for the harvest, so he <u>dismissed the fyrd</u> and returned to London.

> The <u>fyrd</u> was made up of <u>ordinary men</u> who had to <u>leave their normal work</u> and provide <u>military service</u> when the king summoned them. Members of the fyrd were <u>not professional fighters</u> and they usually only served for <u>two months</u> at a time.

Harold won the battles of Fulford and Stamford Bridge

1) Soon after Harold dismissed the fyrd, a <u>Scandinavian army</u> led by Harald Hardrada and supported by Harold's brother Tostig, invaded <u>northern England</u>.

2) On <u>20th September</u>, they <u>defeated</u> Harold's northern allies, <u>Earl Edwin of Mercia</u> and <u>Earl Morcar of Northumbria</u>, at the <u>battle of Fulford</u>.

3) Harold <u>raced north</u> to face the Scandinavian invaders. Because he had <u>dismissed the fyrd</u>, he had to <u>gather troops</u> on the way. Harold moved <u>quickly</u> and was able to take Harald Hardrada by <u>surprise</u>.

4) This gave Harold an <u>advantage</u>, and he <u>defeated the invaders</u> at the battle of <u>Stamford Bridge</u> on <u>25th September</u>. <u>Harald Hardrada</u> and his ally <u>Tostig</u> were both <u>killed</u>, and the Scandinavian army <u>withdrew from England</u>.

... but he was Defeated by the Normans at the Battle of Hastings

1) The Normans landed at <u>Pevensey</u> on <u>28th September</u> and began <u>pillaging</u> (raiding and stealing from) Harold's lands. This forced Harold to <u>hurry south</u> to <u>defend</u> his people and try to <u>drive the Normans out</u>.

2) He didn't have time to <u>gather all his troops</u>, or to <u>recover</u> from the long journey and the battle of Stamford Bridge.

3) On <u>14th October 1066</u>, the Anglo-Saxon and Norman forces faced one another in the <u>battle of Hastings</u>.

> Harold chose a <u>strong defensive position</u> for the battle — the top of a ridge. This favoured the Anglo-Saxon tactic of using the <u>housecarls' shields</u> to create a <u>defensive wall</u> in front of the army. At first, this tactic was very <u>successful</u> and the Normans were <u>unable</u> to break through.

Comment and Analysis

William's forces were <u>ready</u> in <u>August</u>, but he didn't <u>invade</u> until <u>late September</u>. His ships could only cross the <u>Channel</u> on dry, windy days, so <u>chance</u> played a role in this <u>delay</u>. However, the timing was also a <u>strategic choice</u> — one historian has argued that William probably knew about <u>Harald Hardrada's invasion</u>, so he didn't set sail until Harold had <u>moved north</u>, leaving the <u>south coast undefended</u>.

4) Eventually, part of the Norman army <u>pretended to flee</u>, and some Anglo-Saxon fighters left their positions to <u>follow them</u>. This <u>weakened</u> the Anglo-Saxon shield wall, allowing the Normans to <u>break through</u> and make good use of their <u>archers</u> and <u>cavalry</u>. <u>Harold</u> was <u>killed</u> (possibly by a Norman arrow) and the <u>Anglo-Saxon army</u> was <u>defeated</u>. <u>William</u> was now one step closer to becoming <u>king</u>.

The 'pretend to run away' trick — sneaky, but effective...

Don't assume that William's victory was inevitable. He got the upper hand through a combination of luck and skill, e.g. he took advantage of the timing of Harald Hardrada's invasion.

William Becomes King of England

William of Normandy defeated his main rival, Harold Godwinson, at the battle of Hastings, but William wasn't king yet. There were plenty of people who wanted to stop him taking control of England.

William was crowned King in December 1066

1) Even though William had won the battle of Hastings, the English didn't recognise him as king. A group of powerful English nobles, including Harold's former allies, Edwin and Morcar, proclaimed Edgar Atheling king. They tried to keep William out of London.

2) Over the next two months, William took control of south-eastern England and prepared to attack London. The Anglo-Saxon rebels were unable to gather a strong army, and they surrendered to William in December without a fight.

3) On 25th December 1066, William was crowned king at Westminster Abbey in London.

> Edgar Atheling had a claim to the throne because he was related to King Edward (p.84). When Harold Godwinson died, Edgar became the focus of English resistance. However, Edgar was only in his teens and he wasn't a strong leader — some English nobles abandoned him and submitted to William. In the end, Edgar gave up his claim to the throne, but he carried on interfering in politics for many years.

Anglo-Saxon resistance wasn't the only threat to William's rule — he was surrounded by hostile forces:
- The Welsh and the Scottish gave refuge and support to Anglo-Saxon rebels.
- Harold Godwinson's sons were in exile in Ireland and launched attacks from there.
- The Danish kings still believed that they had a claim to the English throne (though they were too busy trying to keep Denmark under control to launch a bid for the throne).

William tried to Satisfy both the Normans and the Anglo-Saxons

When he first became king, William tried to create a mixed Anglo-Norman nobility, which would include both Norman settlers and surviving members of the Anglo-Saxon elite.

He let most Anglo-Saxon nobles Keep their Lands...

William seized the lands of Anglo-Saxon nobles who had died at Hastings or refused to accept him as king, but he let those of the Anglo-Saxon elite who accepted his rule keep their lands. William was also lenient towards rebels — he forgave the men who had proclaimed Edgar king.

Comment and Analysis

William hoped to carry on in the style of Edward's reign, so that he was seen as Edward's successor. At the start of his reign, he kept as many of the Anglo-Saxon nobles in power as possible.

...and gave Land to his Norman Followers...

William had promised his followers that, if they helped him to become king, they would receive land in England. Immediately after the battle of Hastings, he began to give out the lands he had seized from the Anglo-Saxons to his Norman supporters.

> Norman settlement in England was really important in helping William to establish his rule, because it made sure that he would always have loyal fighters on hand when he needed them.

...but he Couldn't Please Everyone

While William had seized the land of dead and disloyal English nobles, there wasn't enough of this unoccupied land for him to satisfy all of his followers. Some Norman settlers took things into their own hands and seized lands that belonged to surviving Anglo-Saxon nobles. This created resentment among the Anglo-Saxon nobles. It also motivated many of the revolts that broke out in the late 1060s (p.87).

Dividing up the land was a royal mess...

You need to know how William became the king of England. Make a timeline that includes all of the key events that led up to William being crowned in December 1066.

Resistance to Norman Rule, 1067-1069

The <u>Anglo-Saxons</u> were <u>revolting</u>... They wanted their <u>land</u> back after the <u>Normans</u> had seized it.

There were Constant Rebellions, especially in the West and Mercia

1067
- Anglo-Saxon rebels in Kent launched an <u>unsuccessful attack</u> on <u>Dover castle</u>. They were supported by the Norman noble, <u>Eustace II of Boulogne</u>, who wanted to gain <u>control</u> of Dover for himself.
- The Anglo-Saxon thegn <u>Eadric the Wild</u>, whose lands had been <u>taken over</u> by the Normans, attacked <u>Hereford castle</u>.

1068
- There was a revolt in <u>Exeter</u>, probably in response to <u>tax increases</u>. At the same time, <u>Harold Godwinson's sons</u> raided the <u>south west</u> by sea.
- <u>Edwin</u> and <u>Morcar</u> launched a rebellion in <u>Mercia</u> with support from the <u>Welsh</u>. There was also unrest in <u>Northumbria</u>.

William and his supporters successfully <u>put down</u> these rebellions using <u>military force</u> and the construction of <u>castles</u> (see p.89). William treated the rebels who <u>surrendered</u> to him pretty <u>leniently</u>. He let <u>Edwin</u> and <u>Morcar</u> go back to their lands after the Mercian rebellion. When <u>Exeter</u> surrendered, William promised to <u>protect</u> the town's inhabitants.

> In <u>1068</u>, quite a few of the men that William had given <u>land</u> to <u>deserted him</u> — they went back to <u>Normandy</u> with their <u>followers</u>, even though parts of England were in <u>revolt</u>.

In 1069 there was a Major Revolt in Northern England

1) In <u>1069</u>, the nobles of <u>Northumbria</u> joined forces with <u>Edgar Atheling</u>, <u>King Malcolm III of Scotland</u> and <u>King Swein of Denmark</u> in a major <u>rebellion</u>, which posed a serious <u>threat</u> to William's rule.

2) Early in 1069, the rebels <u>massacred</u> the newly-appointed <u>Norman earl of Northumbria</u> and several hundred of his knights at <u>Durham</u>. They then moved south to <u>besiege York</u>.

3) <u>William</u> hurried to the North and <u>put down</u> the rebellion. He built a second castle at <u>York</u> and strengthened the Norman forces in <u>Northumbria</u>.

> For more on the Harrying of the North, see p.88.

4) In September, a <u>Danish fleet</u> sent by King Swein arrived and <u>joined forces</u> with the northern rebels. Together, they took <u>York</u>, seized both of its <u>Norman castles</u> and took control of <u>Northumbria</u>.

> There was also <u>unrest</u> in other places — Eadric the Wild and his Welsh allies attacked <u>Shrewsbury</u>, there were risings in the <u>west country</u>, and Edwin and Morcar led another rebellion in <u>Mercia</u>. William's local forces dealt with the unrest in the <u>South</u> and <u>West</u>, while William marched to the <u>North</u>.

The Anglo-Saxon Resistance was Widespread but Inconsistent

Lots of things <u>weakened</u> the <u>Anglo-Saxon resistance</u> to the Normans:

- The Anglo-Saxon rebels in different parts of the country were motivated by their own <u>local concerns</u>, so they didn't form a <u>national movement</u> with common goals.
- There was no single, <u>strong leader</u> who all of the rebels supported.
- The rebels <u>didn't</u> have a <u>shared strategy</u> and they failed to <u>coordinate</u> their attacks.
- Many English nobles actually <u>supported</u> William and some even helped him to <u>fight</u> the <u>rebels</u>. Others just didn't <u>take sides</u> against him.

> The <u>Danes</u> had promised <u>military support</u> to the rebels in 1069, but William <u>paid them off</u> and they quickly <u>abandoned</u> the Anglo-Saxon rebels.

William made more enemies after he became king...

If you're asked about how William managed to establish power over England and secure his crown, then it's a good idea to talk about the way that he responded to English rebellions.

The End of English Resistance, 1069-1071

William's <u>response</u> to the revolt of 1069 was <u>brutal</u>, but <u>effective</u>. It put an <u>end</u> to Anglo-Saxon rebellions.

William Responded to the 1069 revolt with the Harrying of the North

1) During the winter of <u>1069-1070</u>, William and his troops marched through <u>Northumbria</u>, <u>burning</u> <u>villages</u> and <u>slaughtering</u> their inhabitants.

2) They also caused a <u>famine</u> by deliberately <u>destroying</u> all <u>food supplies</u> and livestock. This brutal campaign became known as the '<u>Harrying of the North</u>'.

Comment and Analysis

William's goal was to <u>prevent</u> any <u>future rebellion</u> in the north by <u>destroying</u> the rebels' <u>supplies</u> and <u>support</u>. The Harrying also sent a powerful <u>message</u> to other parts of the country about what to expect if they <u>rebelled</u>.

The Harrying of the North was a big <u>turning point</u> in relations between the <u>Normans</u> and the <u>Anglo-Saxons</u>. After this, William stopped trying to integrate the Anglo-Saxons into an <u>Anglo-Norman nobility</u>. Instead, he started to <u>replace</u> Anglo-Saxon nobles by <u>confiscating</u> (taking away) their lands and <u>giving</u> them to <u>Normans</u>.

Historians Disagree about the Extent and Impact of the Harrying

1) It's clear from the sources that the <u>Harrying of the North</u> was a <u>brutal</u> campaign that caused lots of <u>suffering</u> for those who were caught up in it.

2) In <u>Domesday Book</u> (see p.92), which was completed in 1086, many <u>northern villages</u> are described as '<u>waste</u>'. Some <u>historians</u> see this as evidence that lots of villages were completely <u>destroyed</u> during the Harrying.

3) But others think that using Domesday Book like this <u>exaggerates</u> the <u>impact</u> of the Harrying. There were lots of reasons why a village might have been described as '<u>waste</u>' (e.g. if it didn't pay taxes).

People at the time <u>criticised</u> William for the Harrying of the North. The 12th century historian <u>Orderic Vitalis</u> wrote that 'I have often praised William in this book, but I can say <u>nothing good</u> about this <u>brutal slaughter</u>. God will <u>punish</u> him.'

4) The <u>Harrying of the North</u> has been described as an act of '<u>genocide</u>' by some <u>modern historians</u>. Others argue that laying waste to enemy territory was a pretty common <u>military tactic</u> in the middle ages — they say that we shouldn't <u>judge</u> William's actions by <u>modern moral standards</u>.

Comment and Analysis

The Harrying has been seen as evidence of the '<u>Norman Yoke</u>' — the idea that the Anglo-Saxons were <u>brutally oppressed</u> by the Normans. However, some historians have argued that, while the Harrying had a big <u>short-term impact</u>, it <u>didn't</u> cause <u>long-term damage</u> to the <u>economy</u> of the North.

The Last Anglo-Saxon Rebellion was led by Hereward the Wake

1) William's new policy of <u>confiscating</u> Anglo-Saxon lands created more <u>unrest</u>. In <u>1070</u>, there was an <u>uprising</u> in East Anglia led by an Anglo-Saxon thegn called <u>Hereward the Wake</u> whose lands had been confiscated.

2) At first, Hereward was <u>supported</u> by <u>Danish forces</u>. However, William paid them off and they <u>abandoned Hereward</u>. This tactic had worked for William in <u>1069</u> too (p.87).

3) In <u>1071</u>, Hereward was joined by other Anglo-Saxon rebels, including <u>Morcar</u>. They tried to hold the <u>Isle of Ely</u> against William, but the Normans besieged the island and eventually <u>defeated the rebels</u>.

Comment and Analysis

By 1071, <u>resisting</u> the Normans was starting to seem <u>pointless</u>. Many Anglo-Saxon <u>rebels</u> had been <u>killed</u> or forced into <u>exile</u>. The survivors realised that they were had to <u>come to terms</u> with their new <u>Norman rulers</u>.

4) <u>Morcar</u> was <u>captured</u> and imprisoned. <u>Hereward surrendered</u> to William, who pardoned him and let him <u>keep his lands</u>. This was the <u>last</u> major <u>Anglo-Saxon rebellion</u> against Norman rule.

William used lots of different tactics to get what he wanted...

'William wasn't fully in control of England until after Hereward the Wake surrendered in 1071.'
To what extent do you agree with this statement? [20]

Early Norman Castles

The Anglo-Saxons weren't very keen on castles before the Norman conquest — they preferred to build forts. They probably liked castles even less once the Normans started building them all over the place.

Anglo-Saxons Didn't build Motte and Bailey Castles before 1066

1) In the 11th century, castles were becoming more and more common in parts of northern France, including Normandy. This included motte and bailey castles (see p.90). However, the Anglo-Saxons didn't build castles before the Norman conquest.

2) The Anglo-Saxons did build some other types of fortification:

   - Burhs were large fortifications, often built around a town or village. They were designed to defend the whole community that lived in and around that town or village.

   - The homes of earls and thegns may sometimes have had simple fortifications, like ditches, earth banks or timber palisades (high wooden fences). For example, archaeologists have uncovered a thegn's residence in Lincolnshire called Goltho manor that had fortifications like this.

3) There were a few motte and bailey castles in England before 1066, but these were all built by Norman immigrants who came to England during the reign of King Edward.

The Normans built Lots of Castles throughout England

1) When the Normans landed at Pevensey in September 1066, they immediately began building a castle there. They also built a castle in Hastings before fighting the battle of Hastings. This meant that William could fight for the English throne from a strong base.

2) After William won at Hastings, he built castles all over England as he marched around the country. He put down rebellions and established his rule as he went.

3) There are just under fifty Norman castles recorded in Domesday Book — all but one were built between 1066 and 1086. However, many castles and fortified sites were built in this period which just weren't recorded in Domesday Book.

> **Comment and Analysis**
>
> The castle at Pevensey was built using timber that was prepared and then brought from Normandy. This shows that a lot of planning and preparation went into the Norman invasion.

Several Factors influenced the Distribution of Norman Castles

1) Castles were often built in response to Anglo-Saxon rebellions. They were used as bases — the Normans could fight back against any future unrest in the area quickly. They were also a symbol of Norman power. For example, William built a castle in Exeter after the uprising in the town in 1068 (p.87).

2) Some castles were built to prevent invasion. Castles along the south coast (e.g. Dover, Arundel, Corfe) helped to protect England from invasion by sea. There were also castles along the border with Wales (e.g. Chepstow, Hereford, Shrewsbury), which prevented Welsh invasion.

3) More than two-thirds of Norman castles were built in towns and cities, including London, Lincoln, Cambridge and Warwick. This helped the Normans to control the urban population. Urban locations were also important for the castles' economic functions (see p.91).

4) Norman castles were sometimes built on the sites of Anglo-Saxon thegns' residences. This way, the Normans could reuse any fortifications that these buildings might have had already.

> **Comment and Analysis**
>
> The decision to use sites that had belonged to the Anglo-Saxon elite was symbolic as well as practical — the Normans were showing that they had replaced the Anglo-Saxons as rulers of the country.

Maybe William just appreciated a nice castle...

You need to know how William's castles were distributed. Think about why he chose each place. For example, lots of his castles were used to counter threats from certain rivals and English rebels.

The Design of Norman Castles

Norman castles were designed to combine <u>military strength</u> with <u>living accommodation</u>.

Most Norman Castles in England were Motte and Bailey castles

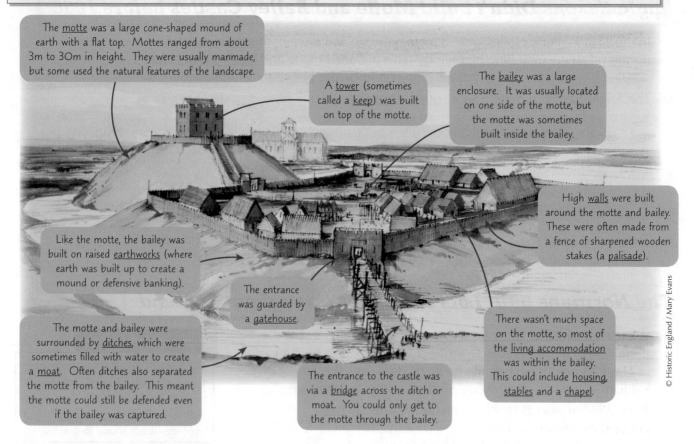

The <u>motte</u> was a large cone-shaped mound of earth with a flat top. Mottes ranged from about 3m to 30m in height. They were usually manmade, but some used the natural features of the landscape.

A <u>tower</u> (sometimes called a <u>keep</u>) was built on top of the motte.

The <u>bailey</u> was a large enclosure. It was usually located on one side of the motte, but the motte was sometimes built inside the bailey.

High <u>walls</u> were built around the motte and bailey. These were often made from a fence of sharpened wooden stakes (a <u>palisade</u>).

Like the motte, the bailey was built on raised <u>earthworks</u> (where earth was built up to create a mound or defensive banking).

The entrance was guarded by a <u>gatehouse</u>.

The motte and bailey were surrounded by <u>ditches</u>, which were sometimes filled with water to create a <u>moat</u>. Often ditches also separated the motte from the bailey. This meant the motte could still be defended even if the bailey was captured.

The entrance to the castle was via a <u>bridge</u> across the ditch or moat. You could only get to the motte through the bailey.

There wasn't much space on the motte, so most of the <u>living accommodation</u> was within the bailey. This could include <u>housing</u>, <u>stables</u> and a <u>chapel</u>.

© Historic England / Mary Evans

Norman castles Weren't all the Same

Although the motte and bailey design was very common, Norman castles <u>varied</u> in <u>size</u>, <u>structure</u>, <u>building materials</u> and <u>location</u>.

Size

Some Norman castles were <u>large</u> and <u>complex</u>. However, many others were <u>small</u> and <u>simple</u> — they just had a low motte that was topped with a simple wooden structure.

Structure

Norman castles <u>didn't all</u> use the <u>motte and bailey</u> design. For example, <u>Exeter</u> castle didn't have a <u>motte</u> or <u>keep</u> — it just had a fortified enclosure.

Building Materials

The earliest Norman castles were almost all built from <u>wood</u> and <u>earth</u>. This meant they could be <u>built very quickly</u> and without skilled labour. Lots of wooden castles were <u>replaced</u> with <u>stone</u> ones later on. For example, in <u>1070</u>, William ordered that <u>Hastings</u> castle should be rebuilt in stone.

Location

Sometimes, the Normans used natural parts of the landscape to defend their castles. For example, <u>Richmond</u> castle in Yorkshire is protected on one side by a <u>steep drop</u> down into the River Swale. They also reused existing <u>Anglo-Saxon structures</u>. The castles of <u>Pevensey</u> and <u>Exeter</u> were built inside <u>fortifications</u> that existed <u>before</u> the conquest.

Make sure you know your motte from your moat...

Imagine you have been asked to research an aspect of the image above. What would you choose to research? How would this help us to understand the purpose of Norman castles? [5]

EXAM QUESTION

The Norman Conquest, 1065-1087

The Purpose of Norman Castles

While Norman castles were designed with military matters in mind, they also played an important role in Anglo-Saxon society after the conquest. However, not everyone liked the castles...

Castles were a Key Part of the Normans' Military Strategy

Castles were vital in the early stages of the Norman conquest — their defensive and military features were really useful when William was struggling to put down Anglo-Saxon resistance and establish himself as king.

1) Castles gave the Normans good defensive positions, so that they could hold their ground against Anglo-Saxon attacks.

2) The Normans used castles to control strategically important places (like towns, major roads and rivers), so that Normans around the country wouldn't get cut off from each other. This also made it harder for Anglo-Saxon rebels to move around the country freely.

3) The network of castles throughout England meant that William could station Norman troops all over the country. This meant that troops could be sent quickly to deal with local unrest — this happened in the South and West in 1069, when William was busy putting down the revolt in northern England (see p.87).

4) Castles weren't just defensive — they were also used as bases so Norman troops could launch attacks on the surrounding territory. This helped the Normans to bring more land under their control.

> 'The fortifications called castles by the Normans were scarcely known in the English provinces, and so the English — in spite of their courage and love of fighting — could put up only a weak resistance to their enemies.'
> *Orderic Vitalis, a 12th century historian*

Comment and Analysis

The Anglo-Saxons didn't have much experience of warfare involving castles and they didn't have many strong fortifications that they could hold against the Normans. This gave the Normans a big military advantage over the Anglo-Saxons.

Castles had Social, Administrative and Economic functions

Even after William was established as king, castles carried on playing an important role in Norman rule. They became a key part of society and acted as centres of settlement, administration and economic activity.

- Norman castles were residential — the castellan (the lord in charge of the castle) lived there with his household. Groups of troops (garrisons) sometimes lived there too. Some castles became the centre of big settlements — people moved to the area to take advantage of the economic opportunities and safety that castles offered.

- As well as holding the castle itself, it was the castellan's job to govern the area around his castle. As a result, many castles became centres of local government, where taxes were collected and law and order was enforced.

- Castles often became the focus of local economic activity. The castle offered a secure place for trade and markets sometimes moved from the local town centre into the castle. The garrison living there created a demand for goods and services, which was good for the area's economy.

Castles were often seen as Symbols of Norman Domination

1) A big proportion of the Anglo-Saxon population came into contact with Norman castles, since they played a central part in the Normans' conquest and control of England. They often occupied highly visible locations too.

2) As a result, many Anglo-Saxons resented the castles. They saw them as evidence of the 'Norman Yoke' — Norman domination and oppression of the Anglo-Saxons (p.94).

If you wanted it then you should've stuck a castle on it...

To what extent do you agree with the argument that castles weren't really important to William's conquest of England? [20]

EXAM QUESTION

The Norman Conquest, 1065-1087

Domesday Book

Domesday Book (not 'the Domesday Book' — weird, I know) is a detailed <u>survey</u> and <u>valuation</u> of England's <u>land</u> and <u>resources</u>. No other public record on a similar scale was made in England until the <u>19th century</u>.

Domesday Book records Who owned What

1) The Domesday survey was commissioned by <u>King William I</u> in <u>December 1085</u> and carried out in <u>1086</u>.

2) It recorded the amount of <u>land</u> held by the <u>King</u>, his <u>tenants-in-chief</u> (men who were given land to manage by the King) and their <u>vassals</u> (p.83). It covered every shire (p.80) south of the Ribble and Tees rivers. It also recorded who held the land in <u>1066</u> (before the Norman conquest) how much it was worth then, and its <u>value</u> in 1086.

3) The survey was written down in <u>Domesday Book</u>. Because it contains information from <u>before and after</u> the Norman conquest, this is a very important source for studying the <u>impact of the conquest</u>.

© Mary Evans / The National Archives, London. England.

Comment and Analysis

The Domesday survey was only possible thanks to the <u>Anglo-Saxons'</u> taxation <u>records</u> and <u>government</u> system, as well as their system for <u>dividing</u> the country into shires and smaller areas called 'hundreds'.

There were Four Stages in the Creation of Domesday Book

1) The country was divided into seven regions (known as <u>circuits</u>), and several <u>commissioners</u> were assigned to each circuit.

2) The tenants-in-chief and government officials in each shire made <u>lists</u> of who owned the land, and the commissioners compared these lists with <u>existing records</u>.

3) The commissioners travelled around their circuit to <u>check</u> the information. <u>Juries</u> from each hundred were called to special meetings of the <u>shire courts</u>, where they were asked about the <u>ownership</u> and <u>value</u> of the local land.

4) The information collected by the commissioners was written down in <u>circuit summaries</u>. These were then compiled into Great Domesday Book (usually just called <u>Domesday Book</u>).

Comment and Analysis

The Domesday <u>juries</u> consisted of <u>equal</u> numbers of <u>Anglo-Saxon</u> and <u>Norman</u> men. This allowed the commissioners to collect information about land ownership both <u>before and after</u> the conquest.

The circuit summary for <u>Essex</u>, <u>Norfolk</u> and <u>Suffolk</u> was <u>never added</u> to Great Domesday Book — it is unclear why. Instead it can be found in <u>Little Domesday Book</u>.

The survey had Financial, Military and Legal purposes

It's <u>not</u> very clear <u>why</u> the survey was <u>carried out</u>, but historians have suggested <u>three purposes</u>:

Financial

William wanted to make sure that he received all the <u>taxes</u> and other payments that his subjects owed him. In order to do this, he needed a <u>detailed record</u> of who owned what and how much their lands were worth.

Military

In 1085, England was facing the threat of an <u>invasion</u> by King Cnut IV of Denmark and his Norwegian allies. In order to <u>defend</u> the country, William needed to know what <u>military and financial resources</u> were available to him.

Legal

Between 1066 and 1086, there had been constant <u>disputes</u> between Normans and Anglo-Saxons about land ownership. By creating a <u>clear</u>, <u>written record</u> of who owned what, William hoped to put an end to these disputes and <u>legalise</u> Norman land ownership.

Domesday Book — not as scary as it sounds...

Write a short paragraph on each of the three possible purposes of Domesday Book.

REVISION TASK

The Norman Conquest, 1065-1087

The Social Structure of Norman England

Domesday Book gives us lots of information about how the social structure of England changed after 1066.

The Anglo-Saxon Elite was Replaced with Normans

1) At first, William tried to work with the Anglo-Saxon elite, but he abandoned this policy after the rebellions of the late 1060s (see p.87-88).

2) From 1070, William began to systematically replace English earls and thegns with Norman nobles. Domesday Book shows that, by 1086, the Anglo-Saxon elite had been almost entirely replaced with Normans.

3) William rewarded his most important supporters with land, making them tenants-in-chief (see p.92). The tenants-in-chief kept some of this land for themselves and passed the rest on to their vassals.

4) The new Norman elite was smaller than the Anglo-Saxon elite had been — Domesday Book records fewer than 200 tenants-in-chief in 1086.

Comment and Analysis

The Normans only ever made up a small minority of the English population. Although they forced out almost every member of the Anglo-Saxon elite, they didn't replace the Anglo-Saxon peasants and slaves who made up the vast majority of the population.

William Changed patterns of Landholding in England

1) William increased the proportion of English land held by the king and limited the amount of land any single noble family could hold.

2) He also changed the size and shape of English estates. In Anglo-Saxon England, some lords (e.g. the Earls of Wessex, Mercia and Northumbria) had held vast areas of land, while others held lands that were scattered across several different shires. William broke up the large areas of land owned by earls and gave his followers smaller, compact areas of land that were often limited to a single shire or region.

3) There were military and political reasons why William did this:

- **Military** — Compact estates were easier to defend and control. This was particularly important in regions where there was a risk of invasion or serious unrest, like the Welsh border, the south coast and the north.
- **Political** — By limiting the amount of land his followers could hold, William hoped to restrict their power and ensure that none of them could become strong enough to threaten his position as king.

The conquest had a Limited Impact on Peasants and Slaves

Anglo-Saxons with low social status saw the land they lived on given to the Normans, but they mostly continued to farm the land as they had before 1066. Even so, the Norman conquest had an impact on them:

Peasants

Conditions got worse for most Anglo-Saxon peasants after 1066. Some were badly affected by the pillaging and destruction that the Normans caused after the conquest. In the longer term, peasants were also affected by increased rents and taxes as Norman lords tried to make more money from their new English lands.

Slaves

The Normans helped to get rid of slavery. Slavery was already declining in England before 1066, but the Normans sped the process up. Domesday Book shows that fewer people were slaves in England in 1086 than in 1066.

There was a new elite in town...

When talking about society, it might help to think about the pyramid on p.80. It's important that you can talk about all classes of society and how they were affected by the conquest.

EXAM TIP

The Norman Conquest, 1065-1087

Changes and Continuities

It wasn't just England's social structure that was altered by the conquest. The Normans also had an impact on English language, laws and the church. It wasn't all change though, some things stayed the same.

The conquest affected Spoken and Written language Differently

Before the conquest, Old English was the dominant spoken and written language in England. The Normans spoke a dialect of Old French and used Latin for most written documents.

Spoken Language

After the conquest, Old English was still spoken by the majority of the population. However, the Normans changed Old English significantly because they used a large number of French loanwords (a word that comes from one language into another).

Written Language

The main language for government documents and religious writing changed from Old English to Latin. At first, William issued many documents in Old English, as well as some bilingual documents in Old English and Latin. From 1070, however, government documents were increasingly written only in Latin.

The Normans Did Not make major Changes to English Law

1) When he became king, William promised that he would not change the laws that had existed during King Edward's reign. As a result, English law was almost the same before and after 1066.

2) However, William did make some changes:

Comment and Analysis

Maintaining pre-conquest law was another way that William tried to create continuity with King Edward's reign and show that he was Edward's legitimate successor.

- He introduced forest law, which set aside large areas of the country as royal forest for the king to hunt in. Ordinary people weren't allowed to use these forests, and they faced serious punishment if they broke the law. Forest law was very unpopular and contributed to the myth of the 'Norman Yoke'.

- He introduced the 'murdrum fine' to protect Norman settlers from violent attacks. If a Norman was murdered and his killer wasn't caught, then the whole village where he was killed had to pay a large fine.

The 'Norman Yoke' myth is the idea that Norman rule was an oppressive burden for Anglo-Saxon people. Many medieval sources describe Norman rule in this way. However, modern historians disagree about how far the 'Norman Yoke' myth reflects the reality of England after the conquest.

William Replaced Anglo-Saxon Church Leaders with Normans

1) William gradually replaced the most powerful figures in the English church (archbishops, bishops and abbots) with his supporters from Normandy. Some Anglo-Saxon church leaders were forced to leave their posts, but sometimes William waited until an Anglo-Saxon bishop or abbot stepped down and then replaced him. By 1087, only one of England's fifteen bishops was Anglo-Saxon.

2) William did not replace Anglo-Saxon churchmen at lower levels. There were still many Anglo-Saxon monks in 1087, and the majority of parish priests were also Anglo-Saxon.

Comment and Analysis

William needed the support of church leaders because they were powerful figures in Anglo-Saxon society. They controlled large areas of land, played a vital role in government, and could influence people's opinions about the conquest and their attitudes towards the Normans.

Out with the old, in with the new...

Get a blank piece of paper, divide it into three and write the headings 'Language', 'Law' and 'Church'. Jot down what changed and what stayed the same for each one.

Changes and Continuities

The Normans made some pretty <u>major changes</u> in England after 1066, but they didn't alter everything — there was also a fair bit of <u>continuity</u> with things that had gone before.

The Normans had a Negative Effect on the Church at first...

The English church was very <u>wealthy</u>, and this made it an attractive target for <u>greedy Norman settlers</u>. When they first came to England, some Normans stole <u>precious objects</u> from churches or seized <u>church lands</u>.

...but they also made some Positive Changes

1) Norman settlers soon became more <u>generous</u> towards the English church. They gave <u>gifts</u> of land to churches and founded <u>new monasteries</u>. For example, <u>Shrewsbury Abbey</u> in Shropshire was founded in <u>1083</u> by the Norman Earl of Shrewsbury, <u>Roger of Montgomery</u>.

2) The Normans changed where some <u>bishops</u> were based, moving them from remote rural sites into <u>towns</u>.

3) They started a huge <u>church-building</u> programme — within fifty years of the invasion, work had started on rebuilding <u>almost all major churches</u> in England, and many <u>parish churches</u> were also rebuilt.

4) The Normans helped to <u>reform</u> the Anglo-Saxon church. Since the early 11th century, Norman church leaders had been working to reform the church in Normandy by imposing <u>stricter rules</u> about how churchmen should behave. Norman churchmen brought this <u>reform movement</u> to England when they took over as leaders of the <u>English church</u>.

<u>Durham Cathedral</u> is an example of an English church that was <u>rebuilt</u> by the Normans. It was rebuilt in the <u>Romanesque</u> style (inspired by Roman buildings). This style of architecture had been introduced to England during the reign of <u>King Edward</u>, but it only became <u>widespread</u> after the <u>conquest</u>.

Comment and Analysis

In the 11th century, there was a widespread movement for <u>church reform</u> throughout <u>Europe</u>. This movement had just started to affect England <u>before 1066</u>. The Norman conquest may have <u>sped up</u> the pace of change by introducing <u>new churchmen</u> who were particularly keen on reform.

There was Continuity as well as Change after the Conquest

1) The Norman conquest <u>affected</u> different parts of Anglo-Saxon <u>society</u> and <u>culture</u> differently.

2) The conquest was a <u>major turning point</u> in English history:
   - It had a huge impact on the <u>elite</u> — the <u>Anglo-Saxon</u> elite and church leadership was almost entirely removed and <u>replaced</u> with <u>Normans</u>.
   - It led to major <u>changes</u> in patterns of <u>land ownership</u>.
   - There were significant changes to the <u>written</u> and <u>spoken language</u> used in England.

3) However, the impact of the conquest was more <u>limited</u> in some areas:
   - There were only <u>minor changes</u> to the <u>law</u>.
   - Changes to the <u>church</u> were <u>small</u>, and some of these (especially church reform) probably would have happened even without the Normans.

Comment and Analysis

Anglo-Saxon <u>experiences</u> of the conquest <u>varied</u> hugely depending on individuals' <u>personal circumstances</u>, including their social status, their gender and where in the country they lived. For example, the experience of a leading member of the Anglo-Saxon <u>elite</u> would have been very <u>different</u> to that of one of his <u>peasant farmers</u>.

All this change — it's hard to keep up with the Normans...

'The Normans made significant changes in many areas of Anglo-Saxon society'.
To what extent do you agree with this statement? [20]

The Norman Conquest, 1065-1087

Revision Summary

That's the Norman conquest all done and dusted. Now let's see what you can remember.
- Try these questions and <u>tick off each one</u> when you <u>get it right</u>.
- When you've done <u>all the questions</u> for a topic and are <u>completely happy</u> with it, tick off the topic.

England on the Eve of the Conquest (p.80-82) ☑

1) a) What were the four tiers of Anglo-Saxon society?

   b) Give a brief description of each social class. ☑

2) Explain two ways the nobility was connected to the Anglo-Saxon church. ☑

3) Which languages did the Anglo-Saxons write books in? ☑

4) Name two art forms that Anglo-Saxon England was famous for. ☑

Invasion and Victory (p.83-85) ☑

5) Describe the structure of Norman society. ☑

6) Why was warfare important for the Normans? Give two reasons. ☑

7) Who were the three main claimants to the English throne after Edward died? ☑

8) Who did Harold Godwinson fight at the battles of Fulford and Stamford Bridge? ☑

9) Outline the events of the battle of Hastings. ☑

Resistance and Response (p.86-88) ☑

10) When was William crowned King of England? ☑

11) Who launched the rebellion in Mercia in 1068? ☑

12) Write a quick summary of what happened during the revolt in northern England in 1069. ☑

13) Give three reasons why the Anglo-Saxon resistance to the Normans was weak. ☑

14) Briefly describe the Harrying of the North. ☑

15) a) Who led the last Anglo-Saxon rebellion against the Normans?

   b) When were the rebels defeated? ☑

Norman Castles in England (p.89-91) ☑

16) What was a burh? ☑

17) a) What was the most common style of Norman castle?

   b) Give a quick description of what it was like. ☑

18) Why were castles important to the Norman military? Give three reasons. ☑

19) Describe the economic functions of castles. ☑

Conquest and Control (p.92-95) ☑

20) What information was recorded in Domesday Book? ☑

21) Outline the four stages of Domesday Book's creation. ☑

22) What changes did William make to the elite in England? ☑

23) Give two reasons why William changed patterns of landholding in England. ☑

24) Give two laws that William introduced when he became king. ☑

25) Describe three ways the Normans changed the Anglo-Saxon church. ☑

Elizabeth's Background and Image

Elizabeth I became queen in <u>1558</u>. She reigned for <u>almost 45 years</u>, until her death in <u>1603</u>.

Elizabeth I was Cautious, Intelligent and Powerful...

1) Elizabeth was <u>Henry VIII's</u> second child, the daughter of his second wife, <u>Anne Boleyn</u>. As a child, she was <u>third</u> in line to the throne, so <u>no-one</u> really <u>expected</u> her to become queen.

2) Elizabeth was <u>very cautious</u> and only trusted a few <u>close advisers</u>. She could also be <u>indecisive</u> — she was reluctant to make decisions without carefully considering their possible <u>consequences</u>.

3) She was <u>intelligent</u>, <u>confident</u> and very <u>well educated</u>. Despite having had little training in how to govern, she became a <u>powerful and effective</u> leader.

> **But some people didn't want her to rule...**
> * Because people believed women <u>couldn't rule effectively</u>, there was <u>pressure</u> for Elizabeth to find a <u>husband</u> who could rule for her.
> * There were also concerns about the <u>succession</u> (who would become king or queen after her death). If Elizabeth died <u>without an heir</u>, there would be a risk of <u>civil war</u>, with different groups <u>competing</u> for the throne.

> Elizabeth was <u>reluctant</u> to marry — women had to <u>obey</u> their husbands, so she would <u>lose</u> her <u>power</u> if she married. Because Elizabeth <u>never married</u>, she became known as the 'Virgin Queen'.

Elizabeth used Propaganda to maintain Public Support

<u>Public support</u> helped to make Elizabeth's position more <u>stable</u>, especially as some people doubted her. She and her councillors used <u>propaganda</u> to ensure she had a <u>positive</u> public image.

1) <u>Portraits</u> were commissioned showing Elizabeth as a <u>powerful</u> queen who was <u>pure</u> and <u>chaste</u> (a virgin) — they suggested that she was married to her <u>people</u> and was concerned with their <u>welfare</u> above <u>all</u> else.

2) <u>Plays</u> which emphasised Elizabeth's <u>wealth</u> and <u>power</u> were performed in court (see p.98). These helped to <u>combat</u> courtiers' fears that an unmarried woman was <u>too weak</u> to rule England properly.

3) Elizabeth was careful to make ordinary people feel <u>recognised</u> by the state. She often went on 'royal progresses' — she journeyed across <u>different parts</u> of England, allowing the public to <u>see</u> and <u>praise</u> her. Their public displays of <u>affection</u> helped her seem <u>popular</u> and <u>loved</u> by her subjects.

© Mary Evans / Iberfoto

> Elizabeth was often painted wearing symbols of <u>purity</u>. In this painting, her dress features <u>white roses</u>, which are associated with <u>chastity</u>. Elizabeth's portraits usually emphasised her <u>youth</u> and <u>power</u>.

Patronage helped to ensure Loyalty

1) <u>Patronage</u> involved handing out <u>titles</u> and <u>offices</u>, which gave men a source of <u>income</u>. Elizabeth had <u>lots</u> of these to give away, including high positions in the Church. Patronage was distributed at <u>court</u>.

2) Elizabeth's use of <u>patronage</u> helped to ensure <u>loyalty</u>. Those who received patronage became <u>dependent</u> on Elizabeth for some or all of their <u>income</u> and <u>status</u>, so they were likely to be <u>loyal</u> to her.

3) Elizabeth <u>distributed</u> patronage very <u>widely</u>. This helped to ensure political <u>stability</u> — all members of the elite felt they had a chance to be <u>rewarded</u> by the Queen, so they were <u>unlikely</u> to <u>rebel</u> against her.

> **Comment and Analysis**
>
> Traditionally, the <u>elite</u> was <u>dominated</u> by <u>noble families</u>. Their power mainly came from <u>land</u> that they <u>inherited</u>. By promoting men who <u>relied</u> on her for their wealth and influence, Elizabeth <u>limited</u> the power of the traditional <u>noble families</u> and made the new elite <u>more loyal</u> to her.

Elizabeth was very powerful, but her popularity helped...

Give one way the illustrator shows the power and purity of Elizabeth I in the picture above. [3]

Political Power in Elizabethan England

The main way to gain <u>status</u> and <u>power</u> in Elizabethan England was by having <u>good relations</u> with the Queen. For those who weren't part of court life, <u>local government</u> was a good option for getting on her good side.

Political Power relied on Access to the Queen

1) The Queen was the <u>centre</u> of <u>government</u>, and political power revolved around her. This meant that those <u>closest</u> to Elizabeth had the <u>greatest influence</u> and power.

2) The royal <u>court</u> was the centre of <u>political life</u>. It was a large group of people who <u>surrounded</u> the Queen at all times. More than <u>1000 people</u> attended the court, including Elizabeth's personal servants, members of the <u>Privy Council</u> (see below), members of the <u>nobility</u>, ambassadors and other foreign visitors.

3) Courtly <u>pastimes</u> included plays, concerts, hunting, jousting and tennis. There were also balls and grand meals.

> <u>Courtiers</u> had to <u>compete</u> with one another for the Queen's <u>attention</u> and <u>favour</u>. Towards the end of Elizabeth's reign, this <u>competition</u> led to growing <u>conflict</u> at court (see p.101).

4) Anyone who wanted to <u>get ahead</u> and increase their political power had to have a place at <u>court</u>. Courtiers didn't necessarily hold government positions — they became <u>powerful</u> through their <u>close relationship</u> with the Queen.

The Queen ruled with help from the Privy Council

The national government consisted of <u>Elizabeth</u>, the <u>Privy Council</u> and <u>Parliament</u> (see p.99).

1) The Privy Council was made up of around <u>twenty</u> men, all <u>chosen</u> by Elizabeth. Members of the Council were the Queen's <u>most trusted</u> advisors. Some <u>key ministers</u> served on the Council for <u>many years</u>.

> The council <u>oversaw</u> many different areas of <u>government</u>, including <u>religion</u>, the <u>economy</u>, the <u>military</u>, <u>foreign policy</u> and the Queen's <u>security</u>.

2) The Privy Council had <u>two</u> main <u>roles</u>. It gave <u>advice</u> to the Queen and managed the <u>administration of government</u>.

3) <u>William Cecil</u> became Elizabeth's <u>closest advisor</u> in <u>1558</u>, leading the Privy Council and making sure the government ran smoothly. Cecil continued to serve Elizabeth until his death in <u>1598</u>.

Comment and Analysis

Cecil was a <u>highly skilled</u> politician. Some historians argue that <u>Elizabeth's success</u> was as much due to <u>Cecil's remarkable skills</u> as it was to Elizabeth's own talents.

4) The Queen <u>didn't</u> have to follow the <u>advice</u> of the Privy Council. Councillors were expected to carry out her <u>instructions</u>, even when doing so went <u>against their advice</u>.

Local Government enforced National Laws

1) The role of local government was to <u>supervise</u> the running of each <u>county</u> and enforce the <u>law</u> there.

2) Most local government positions were <u>unpaid</u>. Members of the <u>nobility</u> and <u>gentry</u> (see p.106) often <u>volunteered</u> for them because being a part of the local government was a symbol of <u>status</u> and <u>power</u>.

3) An important local government position was <u>Justice of the Peace</u>. They were in charge of administering national policies like <u>poor laws</u> (see p.107) and <u>taxation</u> in their counties, and enforcing <u>law</u> and <u>order</u>. They also looked after local issues like maintaining <u>sewers</u>, <u>roads</u> and <u>bridges</u>.

4) Most counties had a <u>Lord Lieutenant</u>, appointed by the Queen. Lord Lieutenants were in charge of the Justices of the Peace, and had an important <u>military</u> role. For example, they maintained <u>defences</u> and managed the training of the <u>militia</u> (ordinary people called to fight alongside the army in an emergency).

5) Towards the end of the 16th century, the <u>number</u> of Justices of the Peace and Lord Lieutenants <u>increased</u>.

Comment and Analysis

After England went to war with Spain in 1585, there was a <u>higher demand</u> for Lord Lieutenants, as <u>military preparations</u> in each county became more important. Elizabeth also needed more Justices of the Peace to collect <u>extra taxes</u> to fund the war.

Being close to the Queen fast-tracked your career...

Write a short paragraph summarising Elizabethan local government.

The Role of Parliament

Unlike today, in the 16th century <u>Parliament</u> was only a <u>secondary</u> part of government.
Its sessions were <u>temporary</u> and <u>occasional</u>, and its <u>powers</u> were <u>limited</u>.

Elizabeth needed Parliament to Govern

© Mary Evans Picture Library

1) Elizabeth had the power to <u>summon</u> and <u>dismiss</u> Parliament. She
<u>disliked</u> working with Parliament and tried to use it <u>as little as possible</u>
— she only called <u>13 sessions</u> of Parliament during her 44-year reign.

Elizabeth <u>listened</u> to
Parliament, but <u>didn't</u>
have to take its advice.

2) Parliament's main roles were to grant Elizabeth <u>taxes</u> and
to help Elizabeth and her councillors to gauge the <u>mood</u>
of the country and levels of <u>support</u> for their <u>policies</u>.

3) Elizabeth also needed Parliament's approval to pass <u>new laws</u>.

4) But even when it was summoned, Parliament's powers were <u>limited</u>:

- Parliament <u>wasn't free</u> to decide what topics it debated. It had to have <u>permission</u>
  from the <u>Queen</u> to discuss <u>matters of state</u> (e.g. religion, the succession, foreign policy).
- If MPs (Members of Parliament) refused to pass a new law, Elizabeth could <u>bypass</u> Parliament by
  issuing a <u>royal proclamation</u> — this allowed her to make new laws <u>without</u> Parliament's consent.

The Privy Council helped Elizabeth to Manage Parliament

1) The <u>Privy Council</u> managed relations between Elizabeth and Parliament <u>very effectively</u>.
In particular, <u>Cecil</u> was <u>highly skilled</u> at convincing MPs to <u>support</u> the <u>Queen's policies</u> (see p.98).

2) Some members of the Privy Council sat in Parliament. They acted as
<u>royal spokesmen</u> and helped to <u>steer debates</u> in favour of royal policies.

3) The <u>Speaker</u>, who kept order in the House of Commons, was <u>chosen</u> by the <u>Queen</u>
and closely <u>monitored</u> by members of the <u>Privy Council</u>. This helped the Queen's
councillors to <u>control</u> Parliament and <u>convince</u> MPs to <u>support</u> royal policy.

Even when
Parliament did meet,
<u>Elizabeth</u> still had a lot
of <u>influence</u> over the
decisions that it made.

4) Elizabeth was a <u>strong public speaker</u>. She made a number of <u>powerful</u>
speeches in Parliament which helped to <u>persuade MPs</u> to obey her wishes.

There were some Disagreements, but Elizabeth stayed In Control

During Elizabeth's reign, Parliament <u>didn't</u> always agree with her policies:

1) Throughout her reign, MPs were <u>concerned</u> about who would rule England after Elizabeth's
death — they repeatedly tried to persuade her to <u>marry</u> or name an <u>heir</u> (see p.97).

2) Some <u>Puritan MPs</u> challenged Elizabeth's <u>religious settlement</u>
and tried to make England <u>more Protestant</u> (see p.100).

3) MPs were also <u>worried</u> about the threat from <u>Mary, Queen</u>
<u>of Scots</u>, and the <u>Catholic plots</u> surrounding her (see p.102).
They tried to convince Elizabeth to take <u>action</u> against Mary.

Occasionally, MPs tried to <u>force</u> the Queen to change her mind by threatening to
<u>refuse</u> to grant her <u>taxes</u>. Elizabeth <u>never</u> gave in to this kind of <u>parliamentary pressure</u>.
Effective <u>management</u> by the <u>Privy Council</u>, combined with Elizabeth's powers to <u>dismiss</u>
Parliament and <u>select</u> the <u>topics</u> it debated, meant that she remained firmly <u>in control</u>.

Comment and Analysis

Many people view Elizabeth's reign as a
'<u>Golden Age</u>', where Britain's wealth and
culture thrived, and the Queen was <u>well</u>
<u>liked</u>. But even though Elizabeth was
popular with many of her <u>subjects</u>, she still
faced some opposition in <u>government</u>. The
<u>worries</u> and <u>fears</u> of her MPs show that
her reign <u>wasn't always</u> straightforward.

The roll of Parliament — Elizabeth's least popular lunch...

EXAM
QUESTION

*Look at the picture of Parliament at the top of the page. Give one way that the
illustrator shows that the power of the Queen is central to Parliament's power.* [3]

The Elizabethans, 1580-1603

Puritan Opposition

Elizabeth tried to <u>reduce</u> religious tension during her reign, but the Puritans <u>didn't</u> make life <u>easy</u> for her.

Elizabeth's 'Religious Settlement' was a clever Compromise

1) Until the 1530s, England was a <u>Catholic country</u> and most people were Catholics. In the early 1530s, a period of <u>religious instability</u> began — between 1530 and 1559, England changed from a <u>Catholic</u> country to a <u>Protestant</u> country, and then <u>back again</u>. This caused <u>social</u> and <u>political turmoil</u>.

2) Elizabeth was a Protestant. When she came to power in 1558, she wanted to end religious instability by creating a <u>lasting religious settlement</u>. In 1559, Elizabeth <u>took control</u> of the English Church. She introduced <u>moderate</u> Protestant reforms, but she also let some elements of Catholicism <u>survive</u>.

3) This compromise became known as the '<u>middle way</u>' — it tried to satisfy as <u>many people</u> as possible.

The Puritans wanted to make the English Church More Protestant

The Puritans were <u>committed Protestants</u>. For them, the <u>religious settlement</u> of 1559 was only a <u>first step</u> in <u>purifying</u> the Church of England — they wanted <u>further reforms</u> that would make the Church <u>more Protestant</u>.

1) They were strongly <u>anti-Catholic</u> and wanted to <u>remove</u> all traces of Catholicism from the Church.

2) Some <u>Puritan MPs</u> resisted Elizabeth's religious settlement. Between 1584 and 1585, <u>Peter Turner</u> led a campaign demanding a more <u>Protestant</u> version of the Church of England's <u>Prayer Book</u>.

> The Prayer Book contained the <u>order of service</u> that all churches in England had to use.

3) Turner also tried to <u>get rid</u> of the <u>Church hierarchy</u> of archbishops, bishops, etc. This idea <u>threatened</u> Elizabeth because it questioned her <u>authority</u> as <u>Supreme Governor</u> of the Church — the head of the hierarchy. Elizabeth <u>rejected</u> the proposal and <u>stopped</u> it from being <u>discussed</u>.

4) In 1587, <u>Anthony Cope</u> tried to re-introduce Turner's reform. Elizabeth <u>banned</u> discussion of it in Parliament and <u>imprisoned</u> Cope.

5) Puritans opposed Elizabeth outside of Parliament, too. They held '<u>prophesyings</u>' — meetings of clergy (Church officials) where priests were taught how to preach. Elizabeth thought that the prophesyings would <u>encourage</u> more <u>Puritan opposition</u> to her religious settlement. In 1583, she <u>banned</u> all unlicensed preaching (see below).

Comment and Analysis

For Elizabeth, the <u>religious settlement</u> was <u>final</u> and <u>couldn't</u> be changed. She wanted <u>everyone</u> to <u>accept</u> it, so she saw <u>Puritan</u> demands for further <u>reforms</u> as a <u>serious threat</u>.

Archbishop Whitgift tried to Suppress Puritanism

1) In <u>1583</u>, Elizabeth made <u>John Whitgift</u> Archbishop of Canterbury. With Elizabeth's support, Whitgift launched an <u>attack</u> on Puritan clergy — all priests had to accept the <u>regulations</u> of the Church of England or face <u>suspension</u>. Between 200 and 300 Puritan priests were suspended.

2) Whitgift's campaign made some Puritans feel that there was <u>no hope</u> of <u>reforming</u> the Church of England. Instead, they decided to <u>break away</u> and form a <u>separate church</u>.

3) These Puritan <u>separatists</u> were seen as a <u>major threat</u> to the religious settlement. The government introduced <u>censorship</u> laws to prevent them spreading their ideas, and in <u>1590</u> several of their leaders were <u>arrested</u>.

Comment and Analysis

Whitgift's campaign faced some <u>opposition</u> from Protestants in the <u>Privy Council</u> and <u>Parliament</u>. Elizabeth <u>overcame</u> this by threatening to <u>dismiss</u> any Council members who opposed it, and <u>refusing</u> to let Parliament <u>discuss</u> the matter.

> The <u>threat</u> from Puritan separatists probably <u>wasn't</u> as <u>serious</u> as Elizabeth and her government thought. There weren't many separatists and they <u>didn't</u> have the <u>support</u> of any powerful members of the <u>elite</u>. <u>Most</u> Puritans were <u>moderates</u> who worked <u>within</u> the Church of England.

Sometimes the 'middle way' is the only way...

Write a paragraph explaining what Puritans did to oppose Elizabeth's religious settlement.

The Rebellion of the Earl of Essex

The last 15 years or so of Elizabeth's rule were so different to her early years that they're sometimes called her 'second reign'. One of the main differences was the growth of competing groups at court.

Elizabeth's Court split into Rival Groups in the 1590s

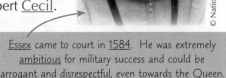

© National Museums NI / MARY EVANS

1) The make-up of Elizabeth's Privy Council changed towards the end of her reign. Several of her key ministers died around 1590. William Cecil (see p.98) died in 1598 and was succeeded by his son, Robert Cecil.

2) In 1593, Elizabeth made Robert Devereux, Earl of Essex, a member of the Privy Council. Essex's rise led to the growth of two conflicting groups at court, one around the Earl of Essex and the other around William and Robert Cecil.

3) The two groups were constantly competing for royal patronage and influence. They also disagreed over important matters, especially strategy in the war with Spain (see p.104). Elizabeth's inability to control this conflict undermined her authority.

> Essex came to court in 1584. He was extremely ambitious for military success and could be arrogant and disrespectful, even towards the Queen.

Essex launched a Rebellion in 1601

1) In 1599, Elizabeth sent Essex to Ireland at the head of a huge army. His task was to crush Tyrone's Rebellion, which had been going on since 1594 (see p.105). Essex made some limited attempts to fight the rebels, but when these were unsuccessful, he made a truce with them. He then abandoned his post and returned to England without the Queen's permission.

2) As a punishment, Elizabeth put Essex under house arrest for a time, banished him from court and took away most of his public offices. In November 1600, she also took away his monopoly on the distribution of sweet wines.

> Monopolies gave people the exclusive right to something, e.g. under his monopoly, Essex was the only one able to distribute sweet wines in England.

3) The loss of his political power and income drove Essex to revolt. On 8th February 1601, he launched a rebellion in London. Essex aimed to seize the Queen and force her to replace her closest advisers, especially Cecil, with himself and his followers.

4) Essex's rebellion failed within just a few hours. He received no support from ordinary Londoners, and most of his own supporters quickly abandoned him too. Essex was arrested, tried for treason and executed on 25th February 1601.

Comment and Analysis

In her later years, Elizabeth rarely appointed new men to the Privy Council. This created frustration among some courtiers who wanted government posts, so they encouraged Essex's rebellion.

The Conflict at court Undermined Elizabeth's Authority

1) The lack of popular support for Essex's rebellion shows that it wasn't a serious threat to Elizabeth's rule. She was still a popular and respected queen, and there was no desire to overthrow her or her government.

2) However, the rebellion does suggest that Elizabeth's authority over her court became weaker towards the end of her reign. By the 1590s, she was no longer using patronage as effectively as she had in the past.

3) Instead of balancing the different groups at court, she let the Cecils become too powerful, while failing to promote many others. This led to a build-up of resentment, which risked fuelling challenges to her authority — like Essex's revolt.

> The idea of a 'Golden Age' began to fade towards the end of Elizabeth's reign. Although propaganda still promoted the image of Elizabeth as a strong and powerful queen, the 1590s are often seen as her weakest decade in power.

4) The conflict at court in the 1590s also weakened Elizabeth's government and made it less effective. The constant competition and in-fighting between groups made it more difficult to make decisions than it had been earlier in Elizabeth's reign.

The end of Elizabeth's reign wasn't peaceful...

'The Queen's power remained strong from 1580 to the end of her reign.'
To what extent do you agree with this statement? [20]

EXAM QUESTION

Catholic Threats

Mary, Queen of Scots, lay at the <u>heart</u> of many Catholic plots to <u>overthrow</u> and <u>assassinate</u> Elizabeth.

Mary, Queen of Scots, had a *Strong Claim to the English Throne*

1) Mary, Queen of Scots, was the only child of <u>James V of Scotland</u>. She was Elizabeth's <u>second cousin</u>.

2) As a granddaughter of Margaret Tudor, Mary had a <u>strong claim</u> to the <u>English throne</u>. Mary became <u>queen of Scotland</u> in 1542 when she was just six days old.

3) Some believed Mary had <u>more right</u> to rule England than Elizabeth. They saw Elizabeth as <u>illegitimate</u> because she was born to Henry VIII's <u>second wife</u>, Anne Boleyn. Henry had divorced his <u>first wife</u>, but some people didn't think divorce was <u>possible</u>.

4) Mary was also a <u>Catholic</u>, so her claim was <u>supported</u> by many <u>English Catholics</u> who opposed Elizabeth's Protestant rule.

5) The threat Mary posed to Elizabeth <u>increased</u> in 1567, when Scottish nobles forced her to flee to <u>England</u>. She remained in England for the next <u>two decades</u>.

> Elizabeth still believed that Mary was the <u>rightful ruler</u> of Scotland, but was worried Mary would try to <u>overthrow</u> her if she <u>regained</u> the throne.

- Mary's claim to the English throne meant that there had been a <u>constant threat</u> of <u>invasion</u> from Scotland. If Elizabeth helped to reinstate Mary as queen, she'd be putting herself at risk. Instead, Elizabeth <u>imprisoned</u> Mary.
- However, Mary's <u>sudden appearance</u> in England and her <u>imprisonment</u> encouraged Catholic plots to <u>overthrow</u> Elizabeth and make Mary <u>queen</u>.

Walsingham *uncovered the Throckmorton Plot in 1583*

1) The <u>Throckmorton Plot</u> of <u>1583</u> aimed to <u>assassinate</u> Elizabeth and replace her with Mary. The conspirators planned for an <u>invasion</u> of England by <u>French troops</u>, financed by <u>Philip II of Spain</u> and the <u>Pope</u>.

2) A leading figure in the plot was <u>Francis Throckmorton</u>, a young Catholic man who carried messages between Mary and Catholic conspirators abroad. The plot was uncovered by <u>Walsingham</u>, who placed Throckmorton under <u>surveillance</u> for several months.

> <u>Francis Walsingham</u> was Elizabeth's principal secretary and <u>spymaster</u>. He established a large <u>spy network</u> in England and Europe. Walsingham <u>intercepted</u> the <u>letters</u> of Catholic conspirators and worked with an expert <u>cryptographer</u> to <u>decode</u> them. He also used <u>double agents</u> to infiltrate Catholic networks.

Walsingham *knew about Every Stage of the 1586 Babington Plot*

1) The <u>Babington Plot</u> was another conspiracy involving <u>France</u> and <u>Spain</u>. Again, the conspirators planned to <u>assassinate</u> Elizabeth and give the English throne to Mary, this time with the support of a joint <u>Franco-Spanish invasion force</u>.

2) <u>Anthony Babington</u> was one of the key conspirators. He was responsible for sending information to Mary from her <u>supporters</u> in England and Europe, and passing back her <u>replies</u>.

3) Through his <u>spy network</u>, Walsingham followed <u>every stage</u> of the plot. Using a <u>double agent</u>, he managed to secretly <u>intercept</u> all <u>letters</u> sent to and from Mary, and have them decoded.

4) One of Mary's letters <u>approved</u> plans to <u>assassinate</u> the Queen and <u>free</u> Mary from prison.

5) By <u>August 1586</u>, Walsingham had all the evidence he needed to break the plot. Babington and the other conspirators were <u>arrested</u>, tried and <u>executed</u> for <u>treason</u>.

Don't lose the plot, just learn this page...

Read this page through once more, then cover it up and scribble down the main features of the Throckmorton and Babington Plots. How serious a threat did these plots pose to Elizabeth's rule?

REVISION TASK

Catholic Threats

As Catholic threats continued to build, Elizabeth took more decisive action against Catholics in England.

The Babington Plot led to the Execution of Mary, Queen of Scots

1) Mary had been implicated in Catholic plots before, but Elizabeth had always been reluctant to take action against her. The evidence gathered by Walsingham finally persuaded her to put Mary on trial.

2) In October 1586, Mary was found guilty of treason. She was executed on the 8th February 1587.

3) Mary's execution removed the long-standing Catholic threat to Elizabeth at home. English Catholics now had no-one to rally around, and they lost hope of overthrowing Elizabeth and reversing the religious settlement. There were no more major Catholic plots during Elizabeth's reign.

4) However, the execution increased Catholic opposition abroad and made a foreign invasion more likely. In 1587, relations with Spain were at a low point — the two countries were at war over the Netherlands, and King Philip II had been preparing for an attack on England since 1585 (see p.104). Mary's execution made the situation worse. Philip was now even more determined to invade.

Some Catholics Continued to Practise their Faith

In the late 16th century, many people still practised Catholicism in England.

1) Some Catholics were 'recusants' — they refused to go to Protestant church services, even though they could be fined for doing so.

2) Others attended the Church services, but practised Catholicism secretly in their own homes. These Catholics were known as 'Church papists'.

> Many Catholic priests trained at special colleges called seminaries. The Jesuits were a separate group of Catholics who were dedicated to spreading Catholicism.

3) Jesuit and seminary priests began to arrive in England in the mid-1570s. Their aim was to help Catholics to keep their faith and encourage them to oppose the religious settlement.

- In 1568, William Allen founded a seminary college at Douai (now in France) to train English Catholic priests. Once trained, priests returned to England and secretly delivered Catholic services to English Catholics.
- In 1580, the priests Robert Parsons and Edmund Campion (who had trained at a seminary college in Rome) entered the country. Campion was executed for treason in 1581.

Comment and Analysis

The arrival of seminary and Jesuit priests made it seem unlikely that Catholicism in England would just fade away like Elizabeth had hoped. This strengthening of Catholicism threatened her religious settlement and prompted Elizabeth to introduce harsher measures against Catholics.

Elizabeth Enforced her Religious Settlement more Strongly

1) Two anti-Catholic Acts were passed in 1581 in response to the threat from Jesuit and seminary priests. They:
   - Massively increased the fines for recusancy, making them too expensive for most ordinary Catholics.
   - Introduced fines and prison sentences for people who said or attended Catholic Mass.
   - Made it treason (which was punishable by death) to convert to Catholicism or persuade others to do so.
   - Introduced prison sentences and the death penalty for anyone who encouraged rebellion.

2) In 1585, Parliament took further action against seminary and Jesuit priests. All English Catholic priests who had trained abroad were forced to leave England unless they swore allegiance to Elizabeth. Any English priests who were training abroad were also banned from returning home.

3) After Spain launched its Armada in 1588 (see p.104), fear of Catholicism got even worse in England. Recusants couldn't buy or sell land, and could have their property taken away if they didn't pay recusancy fines. In 1593, travel restrictions were also introduced for all Catholics.

Catholic opposition just wouldn't settle down...

'Elizabeth and her government overreacted to the threat Catholics posed to England during Elizabeth's reign.' To what extent do you agree with this statement? [20]

The War with Spain (1585-1604)

Neither England nor Spain particularly <u>wanted</u> conflict, but a dispute over the Netherlands kick-started war.

England and Spain went to War over the Netherlands

By the 1580s, <u>tensions</u> between England and Spain were already <u>running high</u>:

- King Philip II of Spain was a <u>devout Catholic</u> and disliked Elizabeth's religious settlement. He was accused of being involved in the <u>Throckmorton Plot</u> in 1583, which aimed to <u>overthrow</u> Elizabeth (see p.102). This <u>damaged</u> Elizabeth's <u>trust</u> in him.
- England had begun to build its <u>own empire</u>. Philip thought this would harm Spanish <u>trade</u>. English privateers had also been <u>trading illegally</u> with Spanish colonies and <u>raiding</u> Spanish ships.

1) In 1581, <u>Protestant rebels</u> in the Netherlands declared independence from Spain. In <u>1584</u> the rebel leader, <u>William the Silent</u>, was assassinated, and the revolt was in danger of being <u>defeated</u>.

2) Elizabeth decided to help the rebels — in <u>1585</u> she signed the <u>Treaty of Nonsuch</u>, which promised <u>military assistance</u>. <u>Religious</u>, <u>economic</u> and <u>military</u> factors influenced her decision.

- Elizabeth wanted to protect <u>Dutch Protestantism</u> and <u>prevent</u> Philip forcing <u>Catholicism</u> on the Netherlands.
- Many English goods were exported via Dutch ports, especially <u>Antwerp</u>. Elizabeth needed to <u>protect</u> English trade interests there.
- If the rebels were <u>defeated</u>, Philip might use the Netherlands as a base for <u>invading</u> England.

3) Philip saw the Treaty of Nonsuch as a <u>declaration of war</u> on Spain. In response, he began building a <u>huge fleet</u> (an <u>Armada</u>) that he planned to use to <u>invade England</u>.

The Armada was Launched in 1588

1) The Armada was a <u>huge fleet</u> of around <u>130 ships</u>, carrying an estimated <u>18,000 soldiers</u>. The Spanish had thousands more <u>soldiers</u> stationed in the <u>Netherlands</u> under the leadership of the <u>Duke of Parma</u>.

2) Philip's plan was for the Armada to meet Parma's army at <u>Dunkirk</u>. The <u>combined forces</u> would then sail across the Channel to England under the protection of the <u>Armada's warships</u>.

3) The Armada set out in <u>May 1588</u>. In <u>July</u>, the Spanish fleet was sighted off <u>Cornwall</u>.

4) Having sailed up the Channel, the Armada anchored at <u>Calais</u> to wait for Parma's troops. However, Parma and his men were being <u>blockaded</u> by <u>Dutch ships</u> and <u>weren't</u> able to reach the coast in time.

Things went from bad to worse for Spain...
- That night, England sent eight <u>fireships</u> (ships loaded with <u>flammable materials</u> and set alight) among the anchored Spanish ships. The Spanish sailors <u>panicked</u> and headed for the <u>open sea</u>. The weather made it <u>impossible</u> for them to return to their defensive position at <u>Calais</u>.
- The English advanced, and the following <u>battle</u> lasted for <u>many hours</u>. Five Spanish ships were <u>sunk</u>, and the rest of the fleet was forced to <u>sail away</u> from the French coast into the <u>North Sea</u>.

The Armada's Journey back to Spain was a Disaster

1) Spain decided to <u>call off</u> the attack on England and <u>return home</u> by sailing round <u>Scotland</u> and <u>Ireland</u>. The Spanish sailors were <u>unfamiliar</u> with this <u>very dangerous</u> route, and they encountered several powerful <u>Atlantic storms</u>.

2) Many ships <u>sank</u> or were <u>wrecked</u> on the Scottish and Irish coasts. Those ships that completed the journey ran short of <u>supplies</u>, and many men <u>died</u> of <u>starvation</u> and <u>disease</u>. <u>Less than half</u> the fleet and fewer than <u>10,000 men</u> made it back to Spain.

England and Spain — reluctant enemies...

The Armada was an important event in the war with Spain — you need to learn the story well.

The War with Spain (1585-1604)

The defeat of the Armada was a <u>great victory</u> for England, but the war with Spain <u>carried on</u>.

Spain gave Military Support to French and Irish Catholics

1) The English victory over the Spanish Armada <u>boosted</u> Elizabeth's <u>popularity</u> and <u>strengthened</u> the <u>Protestant</u> cause — it was seen as a sign that <u>God</u> favoured <u>Protestantism</u>.

2) But the defeat of the Armada didn't end the war — Catholic conflict in <u>France</u> and <u>Ireland</u> provided Philip with <u>new opportunities</u> to invade England.

French Catholics formed an Alliance with Spain

1) When Elizabeth became queen in 1558, France was a Catholic country. In 1584, the French heir to the throne died and a <u>Protestant</u> called <u>Henry of Navarre</u> became the next heir.

2) French Catholics didn't want a Protestant king so they made an <u>alliance</u> with <u>Spain</u>. Philip II promised to <u>prevent</u> Navarre from becoming <u>king</u>. In 1590, he sent troops to <u>invade</u> France and defeat Navarre.

3) Elizabeth <u>didn't want</u> Philip to succeed — if Spain controlled the French <u>coastline</u>, then Philip could sail directly across the English Channel and <u>invade</u> England more easily.

4) Between <u>1589</u> and <u>1595</u>, Elizabeth sent around 20,000 men to <u>help Navarre</u> fight against Philip's forces. In 1598, the Spanish finally <u>withdrew</u>.

Ireland helped Spanish Troops to attack England

1) During Elizabeth's reign, Ireland was ruled by England. Most people were <u>Catholic</u> and <u>opposed</u> the religious settlement.

2) In 1594, the Earl of <u>Tyrone</u> launched a <u>rebellion</u> against Elizabeth, demanding the <u>restoration</u> of the Catholic Church in Ireland. The rebellion lasted until 1603, and became known as the <u>Nine Years' War</u>.

> Elizabeth managed to <u>overcome</u> many threats from Catholic powers abroad, but the danger they posed was very <u>real</u>. The challenges reveal the <u>fragility</u> of her <u>religious settlement</u>.

3) Elizabeth was worried that Spain would offer to help Tyrone and then <u>invade England</u> from Ireland.

4) Sure enough, in 1601 a <u>Spanish fleet</u> sailed to Ireland with 4000 men on board. A <u>battle</u> between the English forces and the Spanish and Irish forces followed, and England <u>won</u>.

The war with Spain Continued until 1604

Continued tension between England and Spain helped to <u>sustain</u> the war.

1) Spain was determined to <u>end</u> the Protestant rebellion in the Netherlands and bring the country back under <u>Spanish control</u>. Elizabeth <u>carried on</u> supporting the rebels, which angered Philip.

2) England was still attacking Spanish <u>ships</u> off the coast of <u>Spain</u> and in the <u>Caribbean</u> (see p.111). Between 1588 and 1591, it carried out 300 raids and stole goods worth <u>thousands of pounds</u>.

3) Spain launched <u>two</u> more unsuccessful Armadas in <u>1596</u> and <u>1597</u>.

4) However, by the end of the 16th century, conflict was beginning to <u>drain</u> English and Spanish resources. In 1604, they signed a <u>peace treaty</u>, which brought an official <u>end</u> to the war.

Comment and Analysis

The war was a great <u>achievement</u> for Elizabeth. She successfully <u>defended</u> England from invasion and Spain <u>didn't</u> overpower English forces at <u>sea</u> or on <u>land</u>. However, the war itself wasn't a '<u>Golden Age</u>' for most English people. Catholics suffered <u>increased persecution</u> (see p.103) and it was a time of great <u>fear</u> and <u>uncertainty</u>.

Elizabeth had her fair share of neighbourly disputes...

Write two paragraphs explaining the part France and Ireland played in England's war with Spain. Include why Elizabeth felt threatened by the events in each country.

REVISION TASK

Rich, Middling and Poor Elizabethans

Elizabethan society was divided into three main groups and there was a big gap between the rich and poor.

The Gentry became Richer during Elizabeth's reign

1) Population growth and changes in farming practices (see p.107) were good for landowners, especially members of the gentry. More efficient farming, increased rents and rising prices for farm products like grain, meant they earned more money from their land.

> The gentry were part of the social elite, below the level of the nobility. They owned land and lived off the income it provided. They didn't have to do other work to survive.

2) As a result, the land-owning gentry became much wealthier during Elizabeth's reign, and members of the nobility also saw their incomes increase.

© Mary Evans Picture Library

The interior of Franks Hall, Kent — an Elizabethan mansion completed in 1591.

- From the 1570s, many members of the gentry and nobility improved their homes or built new ones.
- This allowed them to show off their wealth. New houses often had many large windows — glass was very expensive, so using a lot of it was a sign of prosperity. Large landscaped gardens were also a popular way to display wealth.
- It also improved living standards for the wealthy — the large windows made them lighter, and bigger chimneys and fireplaces meant they were better heated.

Some 'Middling' Elizabethans had New Opportunities

1) Below the gentry in the social hierarchy were 'middling' people — they had to work for their survival, but were rich enough to pay taxes. This gave them a higher social status than other workers.

> Yeomen earned their income by working their own land. They weren't rich, but had a comfortable life.

2) Some of the wealthiest middling people included yeomen and merchants. The growth of towns and the development of international trade (see p.113) allowed some merchants to become very rich. They often used their money to buy land and become part of the gentry.

3) Less prosperous middling Elizabethans included shop-keepers and small farmers. They had a modest lifestyle but they earned less and were at risk of slipping into poverty.

Comment and Analysis

The war with Spain (see p.104-105) made the position of some middling Elizabethans more difficult. Lower middling people struggled to afford taxes, which were increased after 1589 to help fund the war. Merchants were affected too, as some trade routes became restricted.

Elizabethan Attitudes towards the Poor

1) The majority of Elizabethans belonged to the 'lower sorts' of society, which were made up of craftsmen, unskilled labourers, apprentices, the unemployed and beggars. Most of these people lived in poverty.

2) The Elizabethans believed that the poor could be split into three categories:

- The helpless poor — those who couldn't support themselves, e.g. the elderly and the disabled.
- The deserving poor — people who wanted to work, but couldn't find a job in their area.
- The undeserving poor — Beggars, criminals and people who refused to work. Also migrant workers ('vagabonds') who left their homes and travelled around looking for work.

> The Elizabethans had little sympathy for the undeserving poor. They believed that they were often the cause of their own poverty.

The rich got richer, and the poor got poorer...

Look at the image of Franks Hall, Kent at the top of this page. Jot down as many bullet points as you can on how the illustrator shows it belongs to a rich Elizabethan family.

REVISION TASK

Poverty in Elizabethan England

The growing number of people living in poverty was a major problem in Elizabethan society.

Poverty Increased during Elizabeth's Reign

Poverty had several different causes, and not all of them were under Elizabeth's control.

Religious Changes meant there was Less Support for the Poor

1) In the past, monasteries had provided support for many poor, ill and disabled people. However, between 1536 and 1541, Henry VIII had closed down England's monasteries and sold off most of their land. This was called the dissolution of the monasteries.

2) Charity became the main source of support for the poor. But during Elizabeth's reign the problem of poverty became so bad that charitable donations by individuals were no longer enough.

Changes in Agriculture left many people Unemployed

1) Traditional farming wasn't very efficient — farmers rented small strips of land in large open fields to grow what they needed.

2) In the 16th century, landowners developed new techniques to make more money from their land. Instead of sharing open fields among many farmers, they enclosed these fields to create a few large farms.

3) These new farms required fewer labourers, so farmers who rented land were evicted, leaving them unemployed and homeless.

Comment and Analysis

These enclosures of farm land forced many people to migrate to towns or cities in search of work. The government viewed these migrant workers as 'vagabonds' and feared that they would encourage riots and rebellions.

Huge Population Growth pushed up Prices

1) In the 16th century, England's birth rate increased and the death rate fell. Food production couldn't keep pace with the growth in population. As a result, food prices rose.

2) Prices rose much more quickly than wages. Standards of living fell as ordinary people struggled to afford the necessities — many were forced into poverty.

3) There was also growing competition for land, and so rents increased.

As the poor couldn't afford to own the land they worked on, they were the hardest hit by higher rents.

The Government passed Poor Law Acts in 1597 and 1601

1) In the late 1580s and 1590s there was a poverty crisis. Several failed harvests led to food shortages and higher food prices. This pushed more people into extreme poverty — some people starved to death.

2) The government began to take more responsibility for the helpless and deserving poor (see p.106). It also introduced harsher measures for the undeserving poor, who were seen as a threat to law and order.

3) In 1597 it passed a Poor Law Act, which appointed 'Overseers of the Poor' in each parish. Overseers collected taxes for the poor, provided them with work and gave out aid like food and clothing. The Act also stated that prisons should be built in every town to house beggars, criminals and vagabonds.

4) In 1601, the government introduced another Poor Law Act. This Act outlined the role of the Overseers more clearly and informed parishes of the poor relief they were expected to provide.

Comment and Analysis

The 1601 Act was important because it created a national system of poor relief for the first time. Elizabeth hoped this would allow poor relief to be dealt out more fairly.

5) However, poverty was still a huge problem when Elizabeth died in 1603. Levels of poor relief also still varied widely from parish to parish, and the undeserving poor received very little help.

Social welfare was a little rough around the edges...

'Elizabethans were very unsympathetic towards the poor between 1580 and 1603.'
To what extent do you agree with this statement? [20]

Elizabethan Family Life

Families were at the <u>heart</u> of Elizabethan society, and were usually <u>positive</u> and <u>loving</u> environments. Family life taught children important <u>morals</u> and reinforced Elizabethan <u>social structures</u>.

Families played an Important Role in Elizabethan Society

1) Elizabethan families were usually <u>loving</u>, and <u>close relationships</u> with family members were <u>encouraged</u>.

2) Elizabethan family life was <u>hierarchical</u> — some members of the family had <u>more authority</u> than others. The father was the <u>head</u> of the family. The mother <u>assisted</u> him, and the children <u>obeyed</u> their parents.

Comment and Analysis

This hierarchical structure <u>reflected</u> the structure of larger organisations in society like the <u>Church</u> and the <u>state</u>. Elizabethans believed that families were essential for <u>maintaining</u> the idea of hierarchy, which helped to <u>strengthen</u> and <u>stabilise</u> the country.

3) <u>Wider kinship</u> (extended family) was also important. <u>Kin</u> formed part of a family's <u>social life</u> and could be called upon to provide <u>financial</u> help.

4) Having important or rich ancestors was a source of <u>pride</u> and <u>status</u>. Noble families would often hang <u>portraits</u> or <u>miniatures</u> (very small portraits) of their kin or ancestors in their homes.

5) Kin also provided useful <u>political</u> and <u>social</u> connections, particularly in wealthy families, e.g. children's education in other households (see below) was sometimes arranged using <u>wider family connections</u>.

People got Married for Different Reasons

1) In Elizabethan England, marriage could be a way of increasing a family's <u>wealth</u> or <u>social standing</u>. Husbands usually owned all of their wife's <u>money</u> and <u>property</u> once they were married.

2) For members of the <u>nobility</u> and <u>gentry</u>, the right marriage could <u>advance</u> a man's career at <u>court</u> or in <u>government</u>. But marriage wasn't always about money or status — many Elizabethans married for <u>love</u>.

3) A husband was the <u>head</u> of the household, and was responsible for providing an <u>income</u> for his family. He was expected to <u>care</u> for his wife and children.

4) A wife's main role was to run the <u>household</u> and look after her <u>children</u> and <u>husband</u>.

If their husbands went away, women were often left <u>in charge</u> of all household staff and servants. In some poor families, wives had to <u>work</u>. Women could help their husbands with <u>farm work</u> and sometimes even took on <u>separate jobs</u>, e.g. as midwives or shop assistants.

Children often Left Home to learn New Skills

1) Childbirth was extremely <u>dangerous</u> in Elizabethan times. Many women died giving birth, and infant mortality rates (the number of children who died) were <u>high</u>, especially amongst the <u>poor</u>.

2) The Elizabethans expected parents to <u>love</u> and <u>take care</u> of their children. Parents were also responsible for teaching children <u>morals</u> and <u>social expectations</u>.

3) <u>Richer</u> Elizabethan children were often <u>sent away</u> from the family home. Some went to <u>school</u>, but many became <u>skilled apprentices</u>. Children of the nobility were often sent to <u>noble households</u> to train for <u>knighthoods</u>.

Comment and Analysis

The <u>affection</u> between parents and children was demonstrated by the regular practice of giving a '<u>parental blessing</u>'. Every morning and evening children would <u>kneel</u> before their parents, who would reach out, place their hands on them and <u>bless</u> them.

4) Most <u>poor</u> and <u>middling</u> children stayed at home to work, but some were servants in other <u>households</u> or did an <u>apprenticeship</u>.

5) In poorer families, life was often a <u>struggle</u> for both parents, who had to work hard to <u>feed</u> and <u>clothe</u> their children.

The Elizabethans tried to create loving families...

If you had to investigate another aspect of Elizabethan family life, what would you research? Explain how this would help historians understand more about daily life in the Elizabethan era. [5]

The Elizabethans, 1580-1603

Elizabethan Theatre

The theatre became <u>incredibly popular</u> in the second half of Elizabeth's reign.

Theatres were attended by the Rich and the Poor

A performance at the Globe Theatre

© Mary Evans Picture Library/DOUGLAS MCCARTHY

1) At the start of Elizabeth's reign, England <u>didn't</u> have any <u>permanent theatres</u>. Instead, companies of actors <u>travelled</u> around, performing in <u>village squares</u> or the <u>courtyards of inns</u>. The first theatres were built in <u>London</u> in the <u>1570s</u>. They included <u>The Theatre</u> and <u>The Curtain</u>. <u>The Globe</u> was built in <u>1599</u>.

2) The theatre appealed to both <u>rich and poor</u>. Ticket prices started at just <u>1 penny</u>, so it was <u>affordable</u> for most people. However, different social groups sat in different parts of the theatre and <u>didn't</u> usually <u>mix</u>.

3) <u>Elizabeth</u> enjoyed plays — she <u>never</u> attended a <u>public theatre</u>, but often had plays performed at <u>court</u>. She also set up an <u>acting company</u>, The Queen's Men.

> Elizabeth <u>supported</u> the theatre during her reign, especially when it met with <u>opposition</u> (see below). This helped to <u>sustain</u> its popularity. Plays were also a useful form of <u>propaganda</u> (see p.97). Theatre celebrating the <u>power</u> and <u>importance</u> of the monarchy helped to develop a <u>positive image</u> of the Queen.

Elizabeth's reign was a 'Golden Age' for Playwrights

1) A huge number of <u>plays</u> were written during Elizabeth's reign, many of which are still performed <u>today</u>. Their <u>popularity</u> helps the Elizabethan era to be seen as a '<u>Merry England</u>' — the idea that <u>popular culture</u> created a <u>cheerful</u> and <u>enjoyable lifestyle</u> for most Elizabethans.

> <u>William Shakespeare</u> is the best-known Elizabethan playwright. He wrote <u>38 plays</u>. Other famous Elizabethan playwrights include <u>Christopher Marlowe</u> and <u>Ben Johnson</u>.

2) Plays were performed by <u>acting companies</u>. Two important Elizabethan companies were <u>The Admiral's Men</u> and <u>The Lord Chamberlain's Men</u> (Shakespeare's company).

3) Women <u>weren't</u> allowed to perform on stage, so actors were <u>all male</u> — boys played the female roles. One of the most famous actors was <u>Richard Burbage</u>. He was a member of The Lord Chamberlain's Men, and he played the <u>lead</u> in many of <u>Shakespeare's plays</u>.

The theatre was Very Popular, but it faced some Opposition

1) In medieval times (roughly 1000-1500), plays were put on by the <u>Church</u> to <u>educate</u> the public about <u>religion</u>. They would often act out stories from the <u>Bible</u> or show the struggles between <u>good</u> and <u>evil</u>.

2) During Elizabeth's reign, the purpose of plays <u>changed</u> — they became a form of <u>entertainment</u>. Plays <u>lost</u> their religious focus and were used by theatre owners to <u>make money</u>.

3) <u>Puritans</u> (see p.100) disagreed with this change, and believed that the establishment of theatres encouraged <u>immoral activities</u> like <u>gambling</u> and <u>dancing</u>. They also thought it was a <u>sin</u> for male actors to dress up as female characters.

> Puritans believed that Christians should live a <u>restrained</u> lifestyle. They opposed anything encouraging <u>playfulness</u> or <u>idleness</u>. This included <u>sports</u> and <u>popular pastimes</u>, like <u>cock-fighting</u> and <u>drinking</u>. They also disliked public <u>celebrations</u>, even for religious events like <u>Christmas</u>.

4) The <u>City of London</u> authorities thought theatres were <u>disruptive</u> and encouraged <u>crime</u>. The large crowds attracted <u>pickpockets</u> and were seen as a <u>threat</u> to public order. As a result, many theatres, including <u>The Globe</u>, were built just <u>outside</u> the City in <u>Southwark</u>.

5) Some members of Elizabeth's <u>government</u> worried that the theatre might be used to spread <u>pro-Catholic</u> or <u>anti-government</u> messages. As theatres grew in popularity, the government began trying to <u>control</u> what playwrights wrote.

Comment and Analysis

Although theatre brought a lot of <u>enjoyment</u>, the fact that many people <u>opposed</u> it suggests that popular culture in England during Elizabeth's reign <u>wasn't</u> always 'merry'.

The Puritans didth protest too much...

Grab a piece of paper and divide it in two. On one side, write down how theatre made Elizabethan England seem like a 'Golden Age'. On the other, write down its negative effects.

REVISION TASK

Persecution of Witches

The existence of witches was already <u>commonly accepted</u>, but fear of them reached a new level during Elizabeth's reign. People became <u>more suspicious</u> of witchcraft and the <u>persecution</u> of witches <u>increased</u>.

Witches were associated with Evil

1) Belief in power of witches began long <u>before</u> the Elizabethan era. People were <u>afraid</u> of witches because they believed that they acted on the <u>Devil's</u> orders and wanted to <u>cause harm</u> to others.

2) As a result, people often blamed their <u>personal misfortunes</u> on witches. Things like <u>storms</u>, <u>unexpected illnesses</u> and <u>bad harvests</u> were common accusations.

3) Those accused of witchcraft were usually older <u>women</u> who didn't <u>fit</u> in to society. These included mothers with <u>illegitimate</u> children, <u>spinsters</u> (unmarried women) and women who didn't follow social expectations by being <u>rude</u> or <u>outspoken</u>.

4) Elizabethans believed witches used '<u>familiars</u>' to help them cause harm — these were small <u>animals</u> like cats, dogs and toads that would follow their orders. Growths like <u>moles</u> and <u>warts</u> were also seen as common signs that a person was a witch.

> **Comment and Analysis**
>
> The Elizabethans didn't <u>always</u> see the supernatural as negative. '<u>Cunning folk</u>' were people who offered <u>useful services</u> using <u>supernatural methods</u>. These included <u>healing</u> and making <u>prophecies</u>. However, as witches were persecuted more, these practices were also <u>banned</u>.

Elizabethans became More Hostile towards Witches

During the Elizabethan era, people became <u>more concerned</u> about <u>witches</u> and the <u>supernatural</u>.

1) Elizabeth's reign coincided with the English <u>Renaissance</u> — a period of <u>new</u> and <u>creative</u> thinking in England. The Renaissance renewed people's <u>interest</u> in the <u>supernatural</u>.

2) Books had become more widely <u>available</u> thanks to the invention of the <u>printing press</u> in the middle of the 15th century. People could access <u>Bibles</u> and other <u>religious texts</u> which emphasised the <u>evil</u> of the Devil. New theories about <u>magic</u> and <u>witchcraft</u> were also published.

3) Elizabeth banned <u>Catholic rituals</u> like charms, blessings or <u>exorcisms</u>, which were used to cleanse someone of the Devil or evil spirits. This made some Elizabethans feel more <u>vulnerable</u>.

4) Witch-hunts became more popular <u>across Europe</u>. The Witchcraft Act of 1562 (see below) seemed to give <u>legitimacy</u> to people's fears, and <u>encouraged</u> the persecution of witches.

> Witch-hunts caused <u>mistrust</u> and <u>fear</u> in communities. Their <u>growing popularity</u> during Elizabeth's reign goes against the idea of a '<u>Merry England</u>'.

Accusations of witches Increased at the End of the 16th Century

1) In 1562, Elizabeth passed the Witchcraft Act, which made all acts of witchcraft a <u>crime</u>. Accused witches were given a <u>trial</u> in a court. Witches found guilty of <u>causing death</u> would be <u>hanged</u>. Less serious offences, like providing herbal remedies, carried a <u>prison sentence</u> of one year.

2) Many witch trials took place in the county of <u>Essex</u>. The first trials under the Witchcraft Act were held at <u>Chelmsford</u> in 1566. There were two more mass trials, in 1579 and 1589. In the 1589 trials, two boys testified against their own <u>mother</u> and <u>grandmother</u>.

3) Formal accusations against witches reached their <u>height</u> at the <u>end</u> of the 16th century. Between 1570 and 1609, <u>263</u> people were accused of being witches, but <u>only 64</u> were executed.

> Elizabeth treated witches more <u>leniently</u> than other European countries. <u>Torture</u> and <u>burning at the stake</u> were forbidden.

A woodcut of witches hanged after the 1589 Chelmsford trial.

© The Art Archive / Granger Collection

This page has left me pretty spellbound...

Witch-hunts are a good example of how Elizabethan popular culture could be unpleasant.

Elizabethan Adventurers

Elizabeth's reign saw an <u>increase</u> in exploration. Adventurers were driven by ambition and by new <u>economic incentives</u>, including the wealth that Spain gained from its <u>colonies</u> in the Americas.

Rivalry with Spain encouraged Exploration

1) As <u>tensions</u> between England and Spain grew in the run-up to war (see p.104), it became more and more <u>difficult</u> for English merchants to <u>trade</u> in Europe. This encouraged English merchants to make their international trade more <u>varied</u>.

> Spain controlled important <u>trading ports</u> like Antwerp (see p.113). In 1585, Spain also <u>banned</u> English ships from trading with <u>Spain</u>.

2) Elizabeth realised that England needed to <u>compete</u> with Spain <u>globally</u>. She encouraged English merchants to get involved in <u>long-distance trade</u> (see p.113).

3) <u>Spanish trade</u> with its <u>colonies</u> in the Americas was highly <u>profitable</u> — their <u>treasure ships</u> returned to Europe full of <u>silver</u> and <u>gold</u>.

4) The <u>wealth</u> of the region attracted <u>English sailors</u> who hoped to get rich by <u>trading illegally</u> with Spain's colonies and <u>raiding</u> Spanish settlements and treasure ships. Some also hoped to profit by establishing <u>English colonies</u> in the region (see p.112).

Comment and Analysis

<u>Privateering</u> (raiding ships and stealing their cargo) became <u>more common</u> after England went to war with Spain in 1585. This created <u>more opportunities</u> for Elizabethan adventurers.

Francis Drake sailed Around the World

1) Between <u>1577</u> and <u>1580</u>, Francis Drake, a leading English privateer, sailed around the world. This was only the <u>second global circumnavigation</u> (journey around the world) and the <u>first</u> by an English sailor.

> On his <u>way back</u> from South America, Drake was forced to go by a <u>different route</u> — this led to him sailing around the world.

2) Drake probably <u>wasn't</u> trying to sail around the world. It seems he was sent by <u>Queen Elizabeth</u> to <u>explore</u> the coast of <u>South America</u>, looking for opportunities for English <u>trade</u> and <u>colonisation</u>. He almost certainly planned to make money by <u>raiding</u> Spanish <u>colonies</u> and <u>treasure ships</u>.

3) On his return to England, Drake was <u>knighted</u> by Queen Elizabeth aboard his ship, the <u>Golden Hind</u>. This <u>royal recognition</u> and the <u>vast wealth</u> that Drake brought back from the journey <u>encouraged</u> more English sailors to set out on long-distance journeys.

John Dee helped Francis Drake to plan his voyage...
- John Dee was an Elizabethan <u>scientist</u> and an expert in <u>cartography</u> (analysing and making <u>maps</u>).
- He <u>personally advised</u> Elizabeth on British <u>colonisation</u> in <u>America</u>. He also advised the Muscovy Company (see p.113) on navigation and helped adventurers like Drake to <u>plan</u> their voyages.

Expeditions weren't always Successful

Other Elizabethan <u>adventurers</u> set out on <u>ambitious missions</u>, but not all of them succeeded.

1) <u>John Davis</u>, an English captain, led expeditions in <u>1585</u>, <u>1586</u> and <u>1587</u> to try to discover a new <u>trade route</u> to East and South East Asia via <u>Canada</u>.

2) Davis sailed around the coast of Greenland and Canada but <u>didn't</u> find a way through. (We now know that one <u>doesn't exist</u>.)

3) In 1594, <u>Richard Hawkins</u> sailed into the South Pacific and raided <u>Spanish colonies</u> on the west coast of <u>South America</u>. However, he was <u>captured</u> by the Spanish shortly after, and the goods he stole <u>never</u> made it back to England.

Comment and Analysis

Even though some expeditions <u>failed</u>, English exploration towards the end of the 16th century greatly improved <u>scientific</u> and <u>geographical</u> knowledge. It also provided new <u>trade opportunities</u> (see p.113), which gives support to the idea that Elizabeth's reign was a '<u>Golden Age</u>'.

Circumnavigation — taking the roundabout route...

Historians sometimes disagree over the success of Elizabethan adventurers. Jot down some arguments for and against their success, using the examples on the page to help you.

REVISION TASK

Raleigh and Virginia

In the 1580s, England tried to <u>challenge</u> Spain's dominance as an imperial power by establishing a <u>colony</u> in <u>North America</u>. But creating a permanent settlement turned out to be <u>pretty tricky</u>...

Walter Raleigh received Permission to Explore and Colonise

1) By the early <u>1580s</u>, England had claimed some territory in <u>North America</u>, but <u>hadn't</u> managed to establish a successful <u>colony</u> yet. During his journey around the world, <u>Drake</u> had claimed <u>New Albion</u> (in California) for England.

2) The English also claimed <u>Newfoundland</u> in eastern Canada. In <u>1583</u>, Sir Humphrey <u>Gilbert</u> set out to establish a <u>colony</u> in Newfoundland, but the expedition <u>failed</u>.

3) After Gilbert's failure, Elizabeth gave <u>Walter Raleigh</u> permission to explore and colonise unclaimed territories. She wanted Raleigh to establish a <u>colony</u> on the Atlantic coast of <u>North America</u>.

> **Comment and Analysis**
>
> An English colony would <u>challenge</u> Spain's <u>dominance</u> in the <u>Americas</u> and could be used as a <u>base</u> for attacking Spanish <u>treasure ships</u>. It was also hoped that the colony would provide opportunities for <u>trade</u> and be a source of <u>raw materials</u> that might be useful in future <u>wars</u> with <u>Spain</u>.

Raleigh's attempts to Colonise Virginia were Unsuccessful

1) In <u>1584</u>, Raleigh sent a <u>fact-finding</u> mission to North America. The fleet landed on <u>Roanoke Island</u>, explored the area and returned to England with two Native Americans. They gave a <u>glowing</u> report of the region, which encouraged Raleigh to organise a <u>second expedition</u>.

> Raleigh named his colony <u>Virginia</u> after Elizabeth, who was known as the '<u>Virgin Queen</u>'.

Roanoke Island, Virginia

2) The next year, Raleigh sent five ships to <u>Virginia</u>, led by Sir Richard <u>Grenville</u>. <u>108 settlers</u> (known as <u>planters</u>) tried to establish a <u>permanent colony</u> on Roanoke, while Grenville went back to England for <u>supplies</u>.

3) When <u>Francis Drake</u> visited Roanoke in <u>1586</u>, Grenville still <u>hadn't</u> returned and the planters were running <u>low</u> on <u>supplies</u>. Most of the planters decided to <u>return to England</u> with Drake, although a small group of men were left to maintain the colony.

4) A <u>third expedition</u> reached Roanoke in <u>1587</u> and found it <u>deserted</u> — it's thought that the men who stayed behind in 1586 were <u>killed</u> by <u>local people</u>. Around <u>100 planters</u> settled on the island and began to build a colony. They were expecting <u>supplies</u> from England in <u>1588</u>, but the fleet was <u>delayed</u> by the <u>Spanish Armada</u> (see p.104).

5) When the supply ships finally reached Roanoke in <u>1590</u>, all the planters had <u>disappeared</u>. They were <u>never found</u>, and Roanoke soon became known as the '<u>Lost Colony</u>'.

Several Factors led to the Failure of the Roanoke Colony

Bad Timing

If the <u>supply ships</u> hadn't been <u>delayed</u> by the <u>Armada</u>, the Roanoke colony might have <u>survived</u>.

Lack of Supplies

The planters <u>didn't</u> take enough <u>supplies</u> with them and found it <u>difficult</u> to <u>grow food</u> on Roanoke. This made them more <u>vulnerable</u> to problems like the delay of the supply ships in 1588.

Poor Planning

Establishing a colony thousands of miles from England was a major <u>challenge</u>, which required detailed <u>planning</u> and <u>organisation</u>. However, initial <u>exploration</u> of Roanoke was <u>inadequate</u> and the whole project was <u>poorly organised</u>. This was largely because Raleigh's <u>funds</u> were too <u>limited</u>.

As Raleigh learned, if you fail to plan, you plan to fail...

Make a timeline of Raleigh's attempts to colonise Virginia. Include all the expeditions to Roanoke Island between 1584 and 1590, and the key events of each expedition.

REVISION TASK

Foreign Trade

England's trade patterns changed <u>a lot</u> during Elizabeth's reign, which helped it <u>rival</u> its European competitors.

Elizabeth Strengthened Trade in Europe

England's <u>international trade</u> developed quite <u>slowly</u> compared to many of its European competitors.

- Portugal and Spain <u>dominated</u> the trade routes to the East (this included Asian countries like China and India). This gave them direct access to valuable items like <u>silk</u> and <u>spices</u>.
- English trade was <u>more restricted</u>, and a large part of the economy depended on <u>woollen cloth</u> exports to Europe. Most of this trade was done through <u>Antwerp</u> in the Netherlands, which was controlled by Spain. After Spain and England went to war in 1585 (see p.104-105), access to Antwerp became <u>more difficult</u>.

1) England wanted to build up her trade to compete with Spain and Portugal, but for most of the 16th century was <u>unable</u> to rival them at sea. Whilst attempts were made to break into Eastern trade, Elizabeth also tried to strengthen England's <u>European</u> trade.

2) Some looked for <u>new routes</u> into <u>Europe</u>, trading with <u>German towns</u> or through the <u>Baltic</u>.

The <u>Muscovy Company</u>, established in 1551, developed a trade route which sent goods like <u>cloth</u>, <u>lead</u> and <u>tin</u> on ships through the Baltic and White Seas, and then <u>overland</u> to Moscow. The traders were welcomed by the Russians, who allowed English exporters to pay <u>low rates of tax</u> on their goods.

Comment and Analysis

Although trade with Russia was a useful development for England, the <u>difficult nature</u> of the <u>route</u> to Russia meant that it <u>never</u> became a very important part of English trade.

3) Elizabeth also encouraged the development of England's international trade by giving <u>charters</u> to some <u>merchants</u>. Charters gave them <u>exclusive rights</u> to <u>trade</u> in a particular part of the world. For example, in 1600 she gave the <u>East India Company</u> a charter for trade with <u>Asia</u>.

England built Trade Links with Asia

Towards the <u>end</u> of the 16th century, England's situation began to <u>change</u>. New naval exploration (see p.111) and improved technology enabled England to compete <u>more successfully</u> against her rivals.

1) English merchants were keen to develop <u>trade</u> with <u>Asia</u>. In the past, trade in Asian luxuries like <u>silk</u> and <u>spices</u> had been dominated by merchants from <u>Venice</u>, who kept <u>prices</u> very <u>high</u>.

2) From the 1570s, English adventurers began to look for <u>new routes</u> which would allow them to trade <u>directly</u> with Asia. Some, like <u>John Davis</u> (see p.111), tried to find the so-called <u>North West passage</u> around the top of North America.

3) The <u>Levant Company</u>, formed in 1592, <u>bypassed</u> Italian merchants and traded directly with spice merchants in the <u>Ottoman Empire</u>. They brought large cargoes of <u>pepper</u> and <u>cloves</u> to England, which were highly prized for flavouring dishes.

Towards the end of the 16th century, the <u>Ottoman Empire</u> was made up of most of the <u>Eastern Mediterranean</u>, including countries like <u>Egypt</u> and <u>Syria</u>.

4) In 1583, two merchants, <u>John Newberry</u> and <u>Ralph Fitch</u>, sailed through the Mediterranean and went overland to India. They reported back to Elizabeth on the country's huge <u>wealth</u> and on prospects for <u>trade</u>.

5) In 1591, <u>James Lancaster</u> sailed to India around the <u>Cape of Good Hope</u> (the southern tip of Africa). Following Lancaster's success, the <u>East India Company</u> was set up in <u>1600</u> to trade with Asia. It sponsored successful <u>trading expeditions</u> to the region in <u>1601</u> and <u>1604</u>.

Comment and Analysis

England's trade patterns changed <u>dramatically</u> during Elizabeth's reign. By 1603, fleets of merchant ships were sailing <u>regularly</u> to the <u>Americas</u> and into the <u>Mediterranean</u>, and were beginning to break into the <u>Asian spice trade</u>.

England wanted to get a foothold in the East...

'England's foreign trade developed greatly during Elizabeth's reign.'
To what extent do you agree with this statement? [20]

EXAM QUESTION

The Elizabethans, 1580-1603

Revision Summary

You've polished off the Elizabethans — now it's time to test your knowledge with a quick revision summary.
- Try these questions and <u>tick off each one</u> when you <u>get it right</u>.
- When you've done <u>all the questions</u> for a topic and are <u>completely happy</u> with it, tick off the topic.

Elizabeth and Government (p.97-101) ☑

1) Describe Queen Elizabeth's character. ☑
2) What was the role of the Privy Council? ☑
3) What was patronage? ☑
4) Give two examples of local government positions in Elizabethan England. ☑
5) Describe three roles of the Elizabethan Parliament. ☑
6) Why did the Puritans oppose the religious settlement? ☑
7) Why did the Earl of Essex launch a rebellion in 1601? ☑

The Catholic Threat in Elizabethan England (p.102-105) ☑

8) Why did Mary, Queen of Scots, pose a threat to Elizabeth? ☑
9) Name two Catholic plots against Queen Elizabeth. ☑
10) Who was Francis Walsingham? ☑
11) Describe two ways that the persecution of Catholics increased in England between 1580 and 1603. ☑
12) Why were there growing tensions between England and Spain in the early 1580s? ☑
13) Give two consequences of the Spanish Armada for England. ☑
14) What was the Nine Years' War? ☑

Daily Lives in Elizabethan Society (p.106-108) ☑

15) Explain the differences in lifestyle between rich, middling and poor Elizabethans. ☑
16) Name the three different categories of poor people in Elizabethan England. ☑
17) Give three reasons why the problem of poverty was growing in Elizabethan England. ☑
18) Why was the 1601 Poor Law Act important? ☑
19) Give two reasons why family was considered important in Elizabethan society. ☑
20) Why was wider kinship important? ☑

Popular Culture in Elizabethan England (p.109-110) ☑

21) Name two theatres that were built in London during Elizabeth's reign. ☑
22) Name two types of people who opposed theatre in Elizabethan England, and give their reasons why. ☑
23) Give four reasons why people became more hostile to witches. ☑

Elizabethan England and the Wider World (p.111-113) ☑

24) Give two reasons why British exploration increased during Elizabeth's reign. ☑
25) Who was Richard Hawkins? ☑
26) Who organised the attempted colonisation of Virginia in the 1580s? ☑
27) Why is Roanoke Island known as the 'Lost Colony'? ☑
28) When was the East India Company set up? What was its aim? ☑

The Rise of the Nazis

The <u>desperation</u> caused by the economic <u>Depression</u> in Germany in the 1920s and 1930s meant that the German people were willing to consider any political party that <u>promised</u> something <u>different</u>.

The Great Depression caused Poverty and Suffering

1) After World War I, Germany was forced to accept the <u>blame</u> for starting the war. Germany was also forced to pay huge amounts of <u>reparations</u> — payments for the <u>damage caused</u> by the war. This caused huge <u>resentment</u> among ordinary Germans, who saw it as an attempt to <u>humiliate</u> Germany.

> It would have taken Germany until the <u>1980s</u> to pay off the reparations.

2) In 1923, Germany <u>couldn't afford</u> to pay the reparations, and so it looked to other countries, including the USA, for help.

3) With help from other countries, the German <u>economy</u> started to recover. However, in 1929 a massive <u>stock market crash</u> in the USA (the 'Wall Street Crash') started a global economic <u>depression</u>.

4) This Depression caused <u>massive unemployment</u> in Germany. In 1931, Germany's <u>biggest bank collapsed</u>.

As the state of the economy worsened, German money became almost worthless — here, it's being used as wallpaper. Within a few years, 1 US dollar went from being worth around 4 German Marks, to about 4000 billion German Marks.

© Photo Researchers / Mary Evans

The Nazis increased in Popularity during the Depression

1) The Nazis promised <u>prosperity</u> and to make Germany <u>great again</u>. *← Germans needed a strong leader like their past Kaiser*

2) Adolf Hitler, the Nazi leader, was a charismatic speaker and a <u>decorated soldier</u> from World War I. In 1923, he'd been <u>jailed</u> after trying (and failing) to <u>overthrow</u> the government. *← Gave him more time to change tactic / gained sympathy*

3) While in prison, Hitler wrote a book called <u>Mein Kampf</u> *← shows he's a clear leader* ('My Struggle') describing his <u>beliefs</u> and <u>ambitions</u>.

- <u>Mein Kampf</u> described Hitler's belief that Northern Europeans, including Germans, were members of a '<u>master race</u>' called the <u>Aryans</u>.
- It claimed that people of other <u>races</u>, <u>religions</u> and <u>political beliefs</u> (including Africans, Jews and communists) were <u>inferior</u> to Aryan Germans.
- It also described how he believed Germany had the right to <u>take over</u> other countries to provide <u>Lebensraum</u> (or 'space to live') for its people.

4) The Nazis promised a more prosperous and less humiliating future, which was <u>very popular</u> among the German people — it especially appealed to the <u>unemployed</u>, <u>businessmen</u> and <u>young people</u>. Some people also supported the <u>anti-communist</u> and <u>anti-Jewish</u> views held by the Nazi Party.

5) By 1930, Nazi membership had grown to over <u>300,000</u>.

Comment and Analysis

The Nazis' <u>patriotism</u> and <u>energy</u> seemed to offer a <u>way out</u> for the German people. The <u>unemployed</u> and the <u>young</u> were offered hope of a <u>better future</u>. <u>Businessmen</u> threatened with bankruptcy also hoped that the <u>future</u> would be brighter.

4) He was manipulating different audiences to win majority

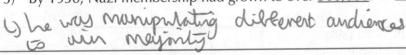

The Nazis — gaining popularity...

The graph on the right shows levels of unemployment in Germany in the early 1930s. How useful are this graph and the photograph above for a historian studying the reasons for Nazi popularity at this time? [15]

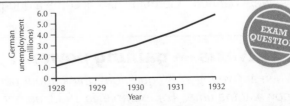

EXAM QUESTION

Establishing a Dictatorship

As the Depression got worse, political instability grew. Several elections were held in 1932 and 1933 to choose the president of Germany and the members of the German parliament (the Reichstag).

Hitler Gained Power in Elections... with the aid of a Political Deal

1) By April 1932, economic conditions had worsened. The country was desperate for a strong government.

2) Paul von Hindenburg had been President since 1925 and was due for re-election. Hitler decided to stand against him. Despite claiming he'd win easily, Hindenburg didn't win a majority in the first election, so a second vote was held. This time he won 53% of the vote, beating Hitler's 36.8%.

3) In July 1932, the Nazis won 230 seats in the elections for the Reichstag — more than any other party. Hitler demanded to be made Chancellor, but Hindenburg didn't trust Hitler and refused to appoint him.

4) Then in the election of November 1932, the Nazis seemed to be losing popularity — they lost 34 seats.

5) But Hitler struck a deal with another politician, Franz von Papen — if Papen would persuade Hindenburg to make Hitler Chancellor, Hitler would make Papen Vice-Chancellor.

6) Hindenburg agreed to Papen's suggestion, thinking that he could control Hitler. But Hitler used his new powers to call another election in March 1933, hoping to make the Nazis even stronger in the Reichstag.

> **Comment and Analysis**
>
> Hindenburg hoped that Hitler would be less extreme once he was actually in power. He also hoped that Hitler wouldn't be able to repair the economy — meaning he (Hindenburg) might be able to regain popularity and power.

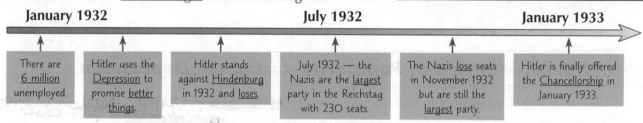

January 1932		July 1932			January 1933
There are 6 million unemployed.	Hitler uses the Depression to promise better things.	Hitler stands against Hindenburg in 1932 and loses.	July 1932 — the Nazis are the largest party in the Reichstag with 230 seats.	The Nazis lose seats in November 1932 but are still the largest party.	Hitler is finally offered the Chancellorship in January 1933.

The Nazis used Dirty Tricks to Win in 1933

1) In the elections of 1933, the Nazis took no chances:

- They controlled the news media, and opposition meetings were banned.
- They used the SA (the Nazi Party's large private army) to terrorise opponents.
- When a fire broke out in the Reichstag building, Hitler blamed the communists. He used the fire to claim that communists were a threat to the country and to whip up anti-communist feelings.
- Hitler was even given emergency powers to deal with the supposed communist threat. Many basic rights given to the German people under the Weimar constitution, e.g. freedom of speech, were suspended. Hitler used these powers to intimidate communist voters.

2) The Nazis won 288 seats but didn't have an overall majority. So Hitler made the Communist Party (which had 81 seats) illegal.

3) This gave him enough support in parliament to bring in the Enabling Act, passed with threats and bargaining in March 1933. This let him govern for four years without parliament.

4) Trade unions were banned in May 1933. Then in July 1933, all political parties, apart from the Nazi party, were banned. Germany had become a one-party state.

> **Comment and Analysis**
>
> The emergency powers granted to Hitler were a turning point — they mark the first step towards making Germany a dictatorship. Hitler justified them by saying that they were necessary to protect the German people. This meant he faced little opposition from the German public.

The Nazis — gaining power...

When answering exam questions, think about people's circumstances and what they could have known at the time. For example, in 1933, no one knew the horror that World War II would bring.

EXAM TIP

Achieving Total Power

Hitler was more powerful, but he still had <u>enemies</u>. He wanted to <u>remove</u> them to secure his <u>dictatorship</u>.

The SA was a Threat to Hitler

1) The <u>SA</u> had <u>helped</u> Hitler come to power, but Hitler now saw it as a <u>threat</u>.

2) Its members were very loyal to <u>Ernst Röhm</u>, the SA's leader. Hitler was worried that Röhm was becoming <u>too powerful</u> — by 1934, the SA had more members than the German army.

3) The SA was also <u>unpopular</u> with the leaders of the <u>German army</u> and with some <u>ordinary Germans</u>.

The 'Night of the Long Knives' — Hitler removes his enemies

1) <u>Ernst Röhm</u> was the biggest threat to Hitler, but Hitler was also worried about <u>other members</u> of the Nazi Party who <u>disagreed</u> with his views.

2) On the 29th-30th June 1934, Hitler sent men to <u>arrest</u> or <u>kill</u> Röhm and other leaders of the SA. Hitler also used this opportunity to remove some of his <u>political opponents</u>. Altogether, several hundred people were <u>killed</u> or <u>imprisoned</u>.

3) Hitler claimed that those who had been killed had been <u>plotting</u> to <u>overthrow</u> the government, so he declared that their murders were <u>legal</u>.

4) This became known as the '<u>Night of the Long Knives</u>', and was a triumph for Hitler.

5) It stamped out all potential <u>opposition</u> within the Nazi party and sent a powerful message to the party about Hitler's <u>ruthlessness</u> and <u>brutality</u>. It also showed that Hitler was now free to act <u>above the law</u>.

> **Comment and Analysis**
>
> Most Germans <u>wouldn't</u> have known exactly what had happened on the 'Night of the Long Knives' until a few days later, when Hitler declared the events legal. Even then, there was <u>little outcry</u>. It's likely that some people <u>believed</u> Hitler's claims that the violence was necessary to <u>protect</u> the country. Others were <u>too scared</u> to speak out.

Hitler took full control of National and Local government

1) In August 1934, <u>Hindenburg died</u>. Hitler used the opportunity to <u>combine</u> the posts of Chancellor and President, and also made himself Commander-in-Chief of the army.

2) He called himself <u>der Führer</u> (the leader) — this was the beginning of the <u>dictatorship</u>.

3) At this point, Germany was <u>reorganised</u> into a number of provinces. Each province was called a <u>Gau</u> (plural: Gaue), with a Gauleiter (a loyal Nazi) in charge of each.

4) Above them were the <u>Reichsleiters</u>, who <u>advised</u> Hitler, e.g. <u>Goebbels</u> who was in charge of propaganda, and <u>Himmler</u> who was chief of the German police.

5) At the top and in absolute <u>control</u> was the <u>Führer</u> — Hitler.

6) Every aspect of life was carefully <u>controlled</u>, and only <u>loyal</u> Nazis could be <u>successful</u>.

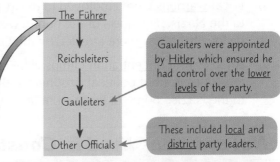

> Gauleiters were appointed by <u>Hitler</u>, which ensured he had control over the <u>lower levels</u> of the party.

> These included <u>local</u> and <u>district</u> party leaders.

> **Comment and Analysis**
>
> When the Nazis took over, some Germans were glad that someone was at last <u>taking control</u> after the chaos and political weaknesses of the Weimar years.

> The <u>army</u> had to swear an <u>oath of allegiance</u> to Hitler, instead of pledging to protect Germany. Some <u>German workers</u> were also forced to take an <u>oath of obedience</u>, promising loyalty to Hitler. Those who refused could lose their jobs.

The Nazis — eliminating opposition...

Make a timeline showing all the major events of Hitler's rise from being jailed to becoming the leader of his country. Include everything up to the point where Hitler becomes der Führer.

The Machinery of Terror

The Nazis aimed to make Germany a totalitarian state (where the government controls all aspects of life).

Germany became a Police State

1) The Nazis wanted complete control over the machinery of government and people's lives. Hitler's Enabling Act of 1933 (see p.116) allowed the government to read people's mail, listen in on their phone calls, and search their homes without notice.

2) This marked the beginning of Germany's transition into a police state — where a government uses a police force to supervise and restrict the activities of its citizens.

3) In April 1933, laws were introduced to sack civil servants who didn't support the Nazis and accept their rules. A year later, the Law for the Reconstruction of the Reich was introduced, which gave the Nazis total power over local governments.

4) The Nazis also made changes to the justice system. Judges didn't have to be 'fair' and unbiased. Instead, they were expected to make rulings that were in line with Nazi Party policy.

5) The Sicherheitsdienst (SD) was the Nazi intelligence service. It was initially run by Reinhard Heydrich — he aimed to bring every German under constant supervision.

> **The legal system was far from fair...**
> - In 1933, the Nazis set up special law courts where the basic rights of those accused were suspended — they couldn't appeal or question evidence given against them.
> - In 1934, Hitler established the People's Court in Berlin, which held trials for important political crimes. Defendants were nearly always found guilty.

People could be Terrorised into Conforming

The government was also prepared to use terror and even violence against the German people.

1) The SS (Schutzstaffel) began as a bodyguard for Hitler. It expanded massively under the leadership of Himmler during the 1930s. Its members were totally loyal to Hitler, and feared for their cruelty.

2) Himmler was also in charge of the secret police — the Gestapo. The Gestapo's job was to protect the German public, but their methods included harsh interrogations and imprisonment without trial.

3) Local wardens were employed to make sure Germans were loyal to the Nazis. Members of the public were encouraged to report disloyalty. Many were arrested by the Gestapo as a result.

4) After 1933, concentration camps were created across Germany and its territories to hold political prisoners and anybody else considered dangerous to the Nazis. Some of these were later turned into death camps (see p.130).

Security Police search a car in Berlin on the orders of the Gestapo.

© Mary Evans / Sueddeutsche Zeitung Photo

Not everyone lived in Constant Terror

1) Most Germans were prepared to go along with the new regime. Some people accepted the new rules out of fear.

2) Others went along with them because they believed in their aims, even if they didn't approve of the Nazis' brutal methods.

Comment and Analysis

For those that didn't fit in with the Nazi ideals (e.g. Jews), life under the SS and the Gestapo could be terrifying. But Hitler was supported, not feared, by many Germans.

The Nazis exercised control using any means necessary...

Make sure your answers include specific examples, as well as 'big ideas'. For example, don't just write that 'People were terrorised' — make sure you give examples of how they were terrorised.

EXAM TIP

Nazi Propaganda

The Nazis also used <u>propaganda</u> to help them control the German people's lives.

Propaganda aims to Control how people Think

1) Propaganda means spreading information that <u>influences</u> how people <u>think</u> and <u>behave</u>.

2) It gives only certain <u>points of view</u> and often <u>leaves out important facts</u>.

3) The <u>Nazis</u> used <u>powerful propaganda</u> to get the support of the German people. <u>Dr Joseph Goebbels</u> was in overall charge of the Nazis' 'propaganda machine'.

Nazi propaganda took Simple Ideas and Repeated them

1) Nazi propaganda was used to <u>unite</u> the German people and convince them that the Nazis would make Germany <u>strong</u>.

2) Germans were encouraged to <u>hate</u> the countries that signed the <u>Treaty of Versailles</u>. The Nazis said Germany should <u>fight</u> to get back the territory 'stolen' by the treaty.

> The Treaty of Versailles was a <u>peace treaty</u> forced on Germany after World War I. Many Germans hated it because they thought it was <u>unfair</u>. Germany had to pay heavy <u>reparations</u> (war fines) and accept <u>total blame</u> for starting the war.

3) Goebbels created the '<u>Hitler Myth</u>', which made Hitler seem like a god and the saviour of Germany. This was the '<u>cult of the Führer</u>'.

4) The Nazis' propaganda also said that <u>Jews</u> and <u>communists</u> were the biggest cause of <u>Germany's problems</u>. One Nazi paper claimed that Jews <u>murdered children</u> for the Passover Feast.

> A popular slogan was '<u>One people, one empire, one leader</u>'. Many Germans <u>devoted their lives</u> to Hitler.

5) The Nazis encouraged a return to <u>traditional</u> German <u>values</u> and a revival of <u>traditional</u> German <u>culture</u>.

The Government had to Approve all Artistic Works

1) Goebbels founded the <u>Ministry of Public Enlightenment and Propaganda</u> in <u>1933</u>. It had departments for <u>music</u>, <u>theatre</u>, <u>film</u>, <u>literature</u> and <u>radio</u>. All artists, writers, journalists and musicians had to <u>register</u>.

2) The Ministry would <u>only</u> approve works that were <u>in line</u> with <u>Nazi beliefs</u>.

The Nazis used the Media as a tool of Propaganda

1) The Nazis wanted to <u>surround</u> people with their propaganda. They used <u>censorship</u> to prevent Germans from seeing or hearing anything that gave a <u>different message</u>.

> According to Goebbels, radio was a '<u>weapon</u>' of the totalitarian state' — it was a way to <u>control</u> the German people.

2) They sold <u>cheap radios</u> and <u>controlled broadcasts</u>. By 1939 approximately <u>70%</u> of households had a radio, which gave the Nazis a <u>voice</u> in most people's <u>homes</u>.

3) In 1933, only 3% of German <u>daily newspapers</u> were controlled by the Nazis. By 1944, this had risen to <u>82%</u>. This meant the Nazis could decide what was published in the papers.

4) The Nazis also produced hundreds of <u>films</u>. Many films showed the <u>strengths</u> of the Nazis and Hitler, and the weakness of their opponents. An important German director was <u>Leni Riefenstahl</u>.

5) Another method of spreading propaganda was through <u>posters</u> showing the evil of Germany's enemies and the power of Hitler. Propaganda also let Germans know what was <u>expected</u> of them.

Nazi propaganda poster, 1935. It states that 'the German student' fights for the Führer and for the German people.

Radio Nazi — broadcasting to you wherever you are...

What can the above picture, which was aimed at German students, tell us about Nazi propaganda in the mid-1930s? Use your own knowledge in addition to the picture. [7]

Nazi Propaganda

Nazi propaganda was <u>sophisticated</u> and it was <u>everywhere</u>.

Nazi propaganda could involve Spectacular Displays

1) The Nazis used <u>public rallies</u> to spread their propaganda. The annual <u>Nuremberg Rallies</u> focused on speeches by leading Nazis, like Hitler and Goebbels. The 1934 Nuremberg Rally was recorded by Riefenstahl in her film '<u>Triumph of the Will</u>'.

2) One million people attended the 1936 rally. There were displays of <u>lights</u> and <u>flags</u> to greet the arrival of Hitler. These made him look <u>more powerful</u>.

3) Sporting events like the <u>1936 Berlin Olympics</u> were used to show off German wealth and power. But the success of non-Aryan athletes like African-American <u>Jesse Owens</u> (who won four gold medals) undermined Hitler's message.

4) Nazi power was also shown through <u>art</u> and <u>architecture</u>, and grand new buildings appeared in Nuremberg and Berlin.

Hermann Goering at a Nuremberg Rally, as shown in 'Triumph of the Will'.

Propaganda was used to change Culture and Society

1) The Nazis promised an empire that would last a <u>thousand years</u> — based on <u>traditional values</u>.

2) <u>Modern art</u> was banned, in favour of realistic paintings that fitted with Nazi ideology. Modern art was labelled '<u>degenerate</u>' and exhibitions were created to show people how 'bad' it was. The Nazis celebrated the works of <u>German composers</u>, such as Wagner, but much <u>modern classical music</u>, works by <u>Jewish composers</u>, and <u>jazz</u> were all attacked.

3) <u>School textbooks</u> were rewritten to make Germans look successful. Children were taught to believe in <u>Nazi doctrines</u> (see p.123).

4) The '<u>Strength through Joy</u>' programme sought to show ordinary workers that the Nazi regime cared about their living conditions (see p.122).

> During the <u>Weimar Republic</u> (the period of <u>democracy</u> in Germany between 1919 and 1933), artists began to use ideas that were <u>new</u> and <u>experimental</u>.

Propaganda was most Effective when Reinforcing Existing Ideas

1) It's quite <u>difficult</u> to tell how <u>effective</u> Nazi propaganda was. Some historians say Nazi propaganda was better at <u>reinforcing</u> people's <u>existing attitudes</u> than making them believe <u>something different</u>.

2) Many Germans felt angry and humiliated by the <u>Treaty of Versailles</u> (see p.119) so Hitler's promises to reverse the treaty and make Germany great again were very <u>popular</u>.

3) After the <u>political weakness</u> of the Weimar Republic, people found the image of Hitler as a <u>strong</u> leader appealing. So the '<u>Hitler Myth</u>' was very effective and made Hitler an extremely <u>popular</u> leader.

4) <u>Anti-Jewish</u> and <u>anti-communist</u> attitudes already existed in Germany <u>before</u> the Nazis came to power.

5) The <u>Weimar Republic</u> was seen as too <u>liberal</u> by many — they thought standards in Germany had slipped. These people liked the promise of a return to <u>traditional</u> German values.

6) The Depression had left many German people in <u>poverty</u>. This made them easier to <u>persuade</u>, and the Nazis' promises of help extremely <u>popular</u>.

> **Comment and Analysis**
>
> However effective their propaganda was, the Nazis' <u>control</u> of the media made it almost <u>impossible</u> for anyone to publish an <u>alternative</u> point of view.

Nazi spin — sophisticated, but probably not 100% effective...

'Propaganda was generally ineffective in influencing the German people during the Nazi era.'
How far do you agree with this view? [18]

Opposition to the Nazis

The Nazis had a tight grip on Germany, but some opposition remained.

The Political Left opposed Hitler, but was Divided and Weak

1) Once in power, the Nazis had banned other political parties, including those on the political left, such as the Communist Party and the Social Democratic Party (SPD).

2) But members of these parties formed underground groups to try and organise industrial unrest (e.g. strikes). These networks were often infiltrated by the Gestapo, and party members could be executed.

3) Their impact was also limited because the different parties of the left were divided and didn't cooperate.

Some members of the Church Opposed the Nazis

There was little opposition to the Nazis in Germany from Christian groups. But a number of Church members did oppose the Nazis, even though they risked being sent to concentration camps (see p.118):

1) Martin Niemöller was a Protestant pastor, a former U-boat (submarine) captain, and a one-time Nazi supporter. He objected to Nazi interference in the Church, and was one of the founders of the Confessing Church. He used a sermon in 1937 to protest against the persecution of Church members, and as a result spent several years in concentration camps.

> Hitler tried to unite the different Protestant Churches into one Reich Church. Some Church members split off in protest at this interference and formed the Confessing Church.

2) Another key member of the Confessing Church was Dietrich Bonhoeffer, a Protestant philosopher and pastor who opposed the Nazis from the beginning. He joined the resistance, helped Jews escape from Germany and planned to assassinate Hitler. He was caught and imprisoned, then executed just weeks before the fall of the Nazis.

3) Clemens August von Galen was the Catholic Bishop of Münster, who used his sermons to protest against Nazi racial policies and the murder of the disabled. His protests didn't stop the killing, but they did force the Nazis to keep them secret. Only the need to maintain the support of German Catholics stopped the Nazis from executing him.

The Edelweiss Pirates and Swing Kids were Youth Groups

1) The Edelweiss Pirates was the name given to groups of rebellious youths who rejected Nazi values.
   - They helped army deserters, forced labourers and escaped concentration camp prisoners.
   - At first the Nazis mostly ignored them, but cracked down after they started distributing anti-Nazi leaflets. Many members were arrested, and several were publicly hanged.

2) The Swing Kids (or Swing Youth) were groups of young people who rebelled against the tight control the Nazis had over culture, acting in ways considered 'degenerate' by the Nazi regime (e.g. listening to American music and drinking alcohol). They were mostly considered a nuisance rather than a threat, but some members were arrested and even sent to concentration camps.

Comment and Analysis

German opposition to the Nazis didn't really threaten their dominance, but it did mean the Gestapo was kept busy tracking down people who'd distributed anti-Nazi leaflets, held secret meetings, committed acts of sabotage, etc.

Comment and Analysis

Other Germans expressed their dissatisfaction with the Nazi regime in 'low level' ways — e.g. by grumbling about the government or spreading rumours. Not everyone considers this genuine opposition, but even this was probably risky.

If you weren't with the Nazis, you were against them...

Some people claim the Nazis faced little opposition from within Germany. To what extent do you think this claim is true? [18]

EXAM QUESTION

Work and Home

The Nazis encouraged <u>women</u> to be <u>homemakers</u> and tried to provide <u>jobs</u> for <u>men</u>.

Women *were expected to raise* Large Families

1) The Nazis didn't want <u>women</u> to have too much freedom. They believed their role was to provide <u>children</u> and support their families <u>at home</u>.

2) Women were <u>banned</u> from being <u>lawyers</u> in 1936, and the Nazis did their best to stop them following other professions.

> This didn't quite go to plan for the Nazis — after 1939, the war caused a <u>shortage of workers</u>, which meant lots of women had to <u>go back to work</u> (see p.127).

3) The <u>League of German Maidens</u> spread the idea that it was an honour to produce <u>large families</u>. The Nazis gave <u>awards</u> to women for doing this and encouraged them to marry by offering <u>financial aid</u>.

4) Women were expected to dress <u>plainly</u> and were <u>discouraged</u> from wearing make-up and smoking. At school, girls studied subjects like <u>cookery</u>. It was stressed that they should choose '<u>Aryan</u>' husbands.

Public Works *and Rearmament meant* Unemployment Fell

1) Hitler started a huge <u>programme</u> of <u>public works</u>, which helped to reduce unemployment — e.g. from 1933 jobs were created as a result of the construction of <u>autobahns</u> (motorways).

2) <u>All</u> men between 18 and 25 could be <u>recruited</u> into the <u>National Labour Service</u> and given jobs. Industrial output increased and <u>unemployment</u> fell.

3) Hitler also brought in <u>military conscription</u> and encouraged German <u>industry</u> to manufacture more <u>ships</u>, <u>aircraft</u>, <u>tanks</u> and <u>weapons</u> for the military. This <u>rearmament</u> meant further falls in <u>unemployment</u>.

4) Trade unions were banned (see p.116), and workers had to join the Nazis' <u>Labour Front</u> instead. The Labour Front acted like one big trade union, but it was controlled by the Nazis. Workers <u>couldn't</u> go on <u>strike</u> or campaign for better conditions, and <u>wages</u> were relatively <u>low</u>.

> **Comment and Analysis**
>
> Although <u>unemployment fell</u> after the Depression, the Nazis <u>fiddled</u> with the <u>statistics</u> to make it look lower than it really was — e.g. they didn't count <u>women</u> or <u>Jewish</u> people without jobs in the official unemployment statistics.

Many groups in society Felt Better Off

1) The Nazis made efforts to maintain the support of German <u>workers</u>. They wanted workers to feel <u>important</u> and believe that they were an essential part of the <u>Volksgemeinschaft</u>.

> '<u>Volksgemeinschaft</u>' means a <u>community</u> of people working hard towards the same <u>aims</u>.

- The Nazis introduced the <u>Volkswagen</u> (the 'people's car') as a luxury people could aspire to own.

- They also introduced '<u>Strength through Joy</u>' — a scheme which provided workers with <u>cheap holidays</u> and leisure activities.

- The '<u>Beauty of Labour</u>' scheme encouraged factory owners to <u>improve conditions</u> for workers.

© Mary Evans / SZ Photo / Scherl

2) Many in the <u>middle classes</u> also felt <u>better off</u>, e.g. small-business owners were able to advance more in society than previously.

3) But even though many people felt better off, workers and small-business owners had <u>lost out</u> in some ways.
- The cost of living rose by about <u>25%</u> — but wages didn't go up.
- Workers didn't have the <u>right</u> to <u>strike</u> or <u>resign</u>.
- <u>Small businesses</u> had to pay <u>high taxes</u>.

> **Comment and Analysis**
>
> During the <u>Depression</u>, one third of all workers had been <u>unemployed</u>. Many Germans had been <u>desperate</u>, so life under the Nazis did feel genuinely <u>better</u> for them.

Hitler reduced unemployment — and gained popularity...

You need to remember that a lot of ordinary Germans had been through some terrible times in the Depression — for a while the Nazis seemed to be making things better for them.

EXAM TIP

Young People

An important key to Nazi success was controlling the minds of German youth.

Youth Movements helped produce Committed Nazis

1) Hitler knew that loyalty from young people was essential if the Nazis were to remain strong.

2) Youth movements were a way of teaching children Nazi ideas —
so they would be loyal to the Nazi Party when they grew up.

The Hitler Youth seemed exciting...

- The Hitler Youth was founded in 1926. Boys aged fourteen and over were recruited to the movement. It became compulsory in 1936 and lasted until 1945.
- Boys wore military-style uniforms and took part in physical exercise preparing for war. High-achieving boys might be sent to Hitler Schools to be trained as loyal Nazi leaders.
- They also went on camping trips and held sports competitions. Some of those who took part said the organisation was fun, made them feel valued and encouraged a sense of responsibility.

The League of German Maidens was for girls...

- The League of German Maidens was the female branch of the Hitler Youth, aimed at girls aged between fourteen and eighteen.
- Girls were trained in domestic skills like sewing and cooking.
- Sometimes they took part in physical activities like camping and hiking. This gave girls new opportunities that were normally reserved for boys.

> **Comment and Analysis**
>
> After 1936, children were obliged to join the Hitler Youth and all other youth organisations were banned. However, towards the end of the 1930s, attendance actually decreased as activities became more military.

Education across Germany was 'Nazified'

1) Education in schools meant learning Nazi propaganda. Most teachers joined the Nazi Teachers' Association and were trained in Nazi methods. Children had to report teachers who did not use them.

2) Subjects were rewritten to fit in with Nazi ideas. Children were taught to be anti-Semitic (prejudiced against Jews) — for example, Biology courses stated that Jews were biologically inferior to 'Aryans'. History courses explained that the First World War was lost because of Jews and communists.

3) Physical education became more important for boys to prepare them for joining the army. They sometimes even played games with live ammunition.

4) In universities, students burned anti-Nazi and Jewish books, and Jewish lecturers were sacked. Jewish teachers were also dismissed from public schools.

> German children were always being bombarded with Nazi propaganda. Erika Mann, a German who opposed the Nazis, described Nazi education in Germany. 'Every child says 'Heil Hitler!' from 50 to 150 times a day...[it] is required by law; if you meet a friend on the way to school, you say it; study periods are opened and closed with [it]... [The Nazis'] supremacy over the German child...is complete.'

German Youth eventually became involved in Fighting the War

1) During the Second World War, members of the Hitler Youth contributed to the war effort — for example, helping with air defence work, farm work and collecting donations for Nazi charities.

2) Towards the end of the war, many Hitler Youth members ended up fighting alongside adults. They were known for being fierce and fanatical fighters.

> The Nazis' attempts to impose their ideology on children weren't always effective. See p.121 and p.126 for more about how unofficial youth movements resisted Hitler and the Nazis.

The Hitler Youth — not everyone's favourite youth group...

What can the above quotation (starting "Every child says 'Heil Hitler'..") tell us about Nazi propaganda? Use the source and your own knowledge to answer. [9]

Living Under Nazi Rule, 1933-1945

124

Nazi Racial Policy

The Nazi belief in the idea of a 'master race' caused a huge amount of harm.

Hitler wanted to 'Cleanse' Germany of 'Inferior' groups

1) Most Nazis believed that Germans were members of a superior ancient race called the 'Aryans'. Hitler thought people who were not pure Aryans (e.g. Jews) did not belong in Germany, and had no part to play in the new German Empire.

2) He wanted to 'cleanse' the German people by removing any groups he thought 'inferior'. Jews were especially targeted, but action was also taken against other groups.

> Hitler often claimed the Jews were responsible for many of Germany's problems.

- Many Romani (Gypsies) and Slavs (an ethnic group from central and eastern Europe) were sent to concentration camps (see p.118) The Nazis believed that they were racially inferior.
- The Nazis practised eugenics policies — they wanted to create a strong race by removing all genetic 'defects' from its gene pool. Many people with mental and physical disabilities were murdered or sterilised. Many people of mixed race were also sterilised against their will.
- Homosexual people were sent to concentration camps in their thousands. In 1936 Himmler, Head of the SS, began the Central Office for the Combating of Homosexuality and Abortion.

The Nazis Changed the Law to Discriminate against Jews.

1) In 1933, the SA organised a national boycott of Jewish businesses, which resulted in Nazi-led violence against Jews. The violence wasn't popular with the German people, so the Nazis decided to use the legal system to persecute Jews instead.

2) Over time, the number of jobs that Jews were banned from gradually increased.

3) The Nuremberg Laws of 1935 were based on the idea that Jews and Germans were biologically different. They removed many legal rights from Jews and encouraged 'Aryan' Germans to see them as inferior.

- The Nuremberg Laws stopped Jews being German citizens.
- They banned marriage between Jews and non-Jews in Germany.
- They also banned sexual relationships between Jews and non-Jews.

> Some Jews were given passports enabling them to leave Germany but preventing them from returning.

4) Jews were later forced to close or sell their businesses, and they were banned from all employment.

5) By 1938, all Jewish children had been banned from attending German schools and Jews were no longer allowed in many public places, including theatres and exhibitions.

> **Comment and Analysis**
> The Nazis' racial policies aimed to isolate Jews from the rest of society. 'Aryan' Germans were encouraged to avoid any contact with Jewish people.

Kristallnacht — The Night of the Broken Glass

1) In November 1938, a German diplomat was murdered in Paris by a Jew.

2) There was anti-Jewish rioting throughout Germany — thousands of Jewish shops were smashed and almost every synagogue in Germany was burnt down. In the days that followed, thousands of Jews were arrested and sent to concentration camps.

3) The Nazis claimed that the events of Kristallnacht were a spontaneous reaction by the German people to the Paris murder. In fact, they had been planned and organised by the Nazi government. Few ordinary Germans had participated.

> **Comment and Analysis**
> Kristallnacht was a turning point in the Nazi persecution of Jews — it was the first widespread act of anti-Jewish violence in Nazi Germany. After Kristallnacht, conditions for German Jews got even worse.

Nazi Germany — a climate of cruelty and fear...

Make a timeline showing how conditions in Germany worsened for Jews between 1933 and 1939.

Living Under Nazi Rule, 1933-1945

Germany's War Economy

Hitler had always planned a <u>war</u> to provide <u>Lebensraum</u> ('living space') for the German people.
But Germany <u>wasn't</u> at <u>full strength</u> when the <u>Second World War</u> broke out in 1939.

The Nazi Economy had to Prepare for War

1) Hitler transformed the German <u>economy</u> to prepare the country for war.

2) A <u>Four-Year Plan</u> was started in 1936, concentrating on <u>war preparations</u>. The Nazis needed to quickly
build up industries like <u>weapons</u> and <u>chemicals</u>, and increase Germany's <u>agricultural output</u>.

3) <u>Hermann Goering</u> was put in charge of the <u>economy</u>. He aimed to make Germany <u>self-sufficient</u> — so it
could produce enough goods and raw materials to not need imports.

> Supplies to Germany had been <u>blocked</u> during the First World War, causing severe <u>shortages</u>. By becoming self-sufficient, Hitler hoped to <u>avoid</u> this problem in future wars.

4) Many workers were <u>retrained</u> to do jobs that would help the war
effort, such as producing <u>weapons</u> and working in <u>chemical plants</u>.

5) But Hitler knew that ultimately Germany would need to <u>conquer</u> new
territories and <u>capture</u> their <u>resources</u> to become genuinely <u>self-sufficient</u>.

The Outbreak of War forced Changes in the Economy

1) When war broke out in 1939, the German economy <u>wasn't ready</u>. More changes were needed.

2) A <u>quarter</u> of the workforce was already working in <u>war industries</u>, especially
<u>weapons production</u>. Two years later this had become <u>three-quarters</u>.

3) A lot of German workers were <u>conscripted</u> into the army (made to join it), so the
Nazis had to use <u>foreign workers</u> to keep the economy going. This included <u>civilians</u>
from occupied territories, <u>prisoners of war</u> and <u>slave labourers</u> — see p.128).

4) Eventually, in <u>1942</u>, after several years of fighting, Hitler put <u>Albert Speer</u> in charge of the <u>war economy</u>.

- Speer focused the economy completely on the <u>war effort</u>.
- He improved efficiency and greatly <u>increased</u> weapons production.
- Germany also used <u>raw materials</u> from <u>occupied lands</u> to support its production.

Daily Life in Germany was Affected by the War

Germans had to make <u>sacrifices</u> to help the war effort:

1) Wages were <u>less</u> than they had been before the Nazis took control and working hours <u>increased</u>.

2) <u>Rationing</u> affected people's <u>quality of life</u>. <u>Food</u> and <u>clothes</u> rationing began in <u>1939</u>,
but while Germany was winning the war, most goods could still be bought easily.

- Rationing meant that some people ate <u>better</u>
than they had before the war, though it soon
became <u>impossible</u> to eat meat every day.

> <u>Toilet paper</u> and <u>soap</u> became difficult to get hold of too. And to save fuel, the use of <u>warm water</u> was restricted to two times per week. Germans also made use of 'ersatz' (or '<u>substitute</u>') goods. For example, <u>ersatzkaffee</u> ('substitute coffee') was made from acorns or other types of seed.

- Later in the war, things became <u>harder</u> for ordinary Germans.
By 1942, German civilians were living on rations of bread,
vegetables and potatoes — these rations <u>decreased</u> as the
war progressed (and were much less than British rations).

3) More <u>women</u> and <u>children</u> had to work, especially after 1941
when German forces suffered some heavy defeats in Russia.

> By 1944, <u>50%</u> of the German workforce were women (up from 37% in 1939).

Life under the Nazis got worse — even for Germans...

*In the exam, you'll need to think about the impact the Nazis had on life in Germany. On this page,
you could mention that heavy defeats meant more German women and children had to work.*

Growing Opposition

As the war went on, and especially as things started to go worse for Germany, opposition to Hitler grew.

There were some Anti-Nazi Protest Movements

1) The Kreisau Circle was an anti-Nazi movement led by Helmuth von Moltke and Yorck von Wartenburg.

- The group was against violence, so they didn't actively resist the Nazis. Instead they discussed how to make Germany a better country after the Nazis had fallen. Some members of the Circle tried to inform Allied governments about the dangers and weaknesses of Nazi control.
- In 1944, members of the Kreisau Circle, including Moltke, were arrested and executed.

2) The Rosenstrasse protest took place between February and March 1943 in Berlin, after the authorities arrested some of the last Jewish men left in the city. Many of them were married to 'Aryan' German women.

- When the men's wives discovered what had happened, they went to the building in Rosenstrasse ('Rose Street') where their husbands were being held.
- For several days, the women gathered outside the building and protested. Eventually Goebbels ordered the Jewish men to be released.

Comment and Analysis

This was one of the few public anti-Nazi protests that was successful. It's thought that the men were released because Goebbels saw it as the simplest way to quickly end the protest without attracting too much attention. He also thought the Jews would soon be killed anyway.

3) Underground networks of communists operated in Germany after 1941. They mostly gathered information about Nazi brutality and distributed leaflets.

Some young people joined the White Rose group

1) The White Rose group (active between 1942 and 1943) was an opposition movement of students and lecturers from Munich University. Among the leaders were brother and sister Hans and Sophie Scholl.

2) Some male members of the group had served in the army and had been horrified by the atrocities carried out by the German army, including the mass killing of Jews.

3) The group used non-violent methods to protest against Nazi discrimination against minorities — they wrote anti-Nazi graffiti and distributed anti-Nazi leaflets to encourage opposition. In 1943, the group organised the first public anti-Nazi demonstration.

Comment and Analysis

At her trial, Sophie Scholl stated that everything she had written in the leaflets was also known by many others, but they didn't dare to say anything about it.

4) Many of the group were later arrested by the Gestapo. Several were tortured and executed, including Hans and Sophie Scholl.

Resistance in the Army grew during the war

1) There had been plots against Hitler by army officers before the war. These became more serious when some became convinced Hitler was going to lead Germany to defeat.

2) One of the most famous army plots was the July plot of 1944. Claus von Stauffenberg (along with other German officers) planned to kill Hitler and install a moderate government, which would include members of the Kreisau Circle.

3) During a meeting, Stauffenberg left a bomb in a briefcase by Hitler's chair. However, someone moved the briefcase. The bomb exploded, but Hitler was unhurt.

4) Most of the plotters (including Stauffenberg) were quickly captured and executed.

It wasn't easy to stand against the Nazis...

'The success of the Rosenstrasse protest shows that protests by the German people could have forced the Nazis to stop their persecution of the Jews.' How far do you agree with this view? [18]

The Impact of Total War

Food rationing was one thing. But the impact of <u>total war</u> on German civilians went way beyond that.

'Total War' involves Soldiers and Civilians

1) A lot of wars are fought between two <u>armies</u>. The term '<u>total war</u>', on the other hand, is often used to describe conflicts where <u>all</u> of a country's resources are considered part of the war effort.

2) So total war is also a battle between countries' <u>economies</u>, their <u>scientists</u>, their <u>industries</u>, and their <u>civilians</u>. World War II is usually considered to have been a total war.

Germans were More Heavily Affected later in the war

1) After some <u>heavy defeats</u> in 1942, Germany prepared itself for <u>total war</u>. In a speech at the <u>Berlin Sportpalast</u> (sports arena) in February 1943, <u>Goebbels</u> stated:

> **Comment and Analysis**
>
> Hitler had hoped that the war he was starting would be <u>short</u> (i.e. a <u>quick victory</u>). This would have meant <u>less disruption</u> to normal life.

> 'Total war is the demand of the hour... The danger facing us is enormous. The efforts we take to meet it must be just as enormous... We can no longer make only partial and careless use of the war potential at home and in the parts of Europe that we control. We must use our full resources.'

2) This meant that <u>all</u> of Germany's resources had to be directed to help with the <u>war effort</u>.

- <u>Non-essential</u> production <u>stopped</u>, and small non-essential businesses were <u>closed</u>. Workers were instead used in <u>war-related</u> industries.
- <u>Civilian clothes</u> and <u>consumer goods</u> were no longer manufactured.
- <u>Rationing</u> was a fact of life in Germany from the very start of the war (see p.125). Food supplies for ordinary families became much more <u>restricted</u> later on.

  > German women never fought on the <u>front line</u> — they took mainly <u>clerical</u> and <u>administrative</u> roles. However, many women did help to operate Germany's <u>anti-aircraft</u> defences and served in <u>signals units</u> on the front line.

- More <u>women</u> were expected to <u>work</u> or join the <u>army</u>.
- Eventually, males between the ages of 13 and 60 who weren't already serving in the military had to join the <u>Volkssturm</u> — a part-time defence force (a sort of German 'Dad's Army').

Bombings Killed Thousands and left many more Homeless

1) From <u>1940</u> Germany <u>rapidly prepared</u> for <u>bombing</u>. Hundreds of community <u>air raid shelters</u> were built.

2) <u>Auxiliary hospitals</u> and emergency <u>first-aid stations</u> were also established to care for civilian injuries.

3) From <u>1942</u>, the British and American air forces began bombing German cities more <u>heavily</u>. Around <u>half a million</u> German civilians were killed, and many more were made <u>homeless</u>.

4) Germany was later flooded with <u>refugees</u> from other <u>German territories</u> and from cities like Dresden, Berlin and Hamburg, which were all <u>heavily bombed</u>.

5) Germany struggled to deal with the growing number of <u>refugees</u>. There was <u>little help</u> for people displaced by the war — most struggled to find <u>food</u> and <u>shelter</u>.

> German cities were attacked using <u>incendiary bombs</u> — these were designed to cause huge <u>fires</u>. Hamburg and Dresden were both fire-bombed.

Dresden, after an Allied air raid in February 1945.

© Mary Evans / Sueddeutsche Zeitung Photo

Germany had to throw everything behind the war effort...

Remember, total war wasn't what the Nazis had wanted. They had hoped for a short war and prepared accordingly. But things hadn't gone at all as the Nazis had planned.

EXAM TIP

Nazi Rule in Eastern and Western Europe

The Nazis conquered territory to the <u>west</u> and <u>east</u> of Germany, but <u>didn't</u> treat all areas <u>equally</u>.

Nazi rule in the West was Relatively Humane

1) Hitler had hoped to be able to <u>quickly</u> knock <u>western</u> European countries like France and Britain out of the war, <u>before</u> invading countries in the east to form Germany's <u>Lebensraum</u> (see p.115)

2) But the western countries <u>didn't</u> all surrender — e.g. Britain fought on.
   So a <u>long occupation</u> of Western countries followed.

3) Life in any Nazi-occupied country was far from pleasant, and <u>Jews</u> were especially <u>persecuted</u> in all territories under Nazi rule. But the Nazis <u>didn't</u> attempt to <u>exterminate</u> occupied countries' entire populations in the <u>west</u>.

> However, the Nazis would certainly <u>respond brutally</u> to any resistance, and arrests, detentions, and imprisonment in concentration camps were <u>common</u>.

4) It was the <u>resources</u> of these occupied countries in the west that Germany most wanted — <u>raw materials</u>, <u>agricultural produce</u>, and <u>industrial goods</u>. This led to <u>extreme shortages</u> for the inhabitants of those countries.

5) Germany also needed <u>manpower</u>. Citizens of occupied countries were <u>forced</u> to <u>work</u> for the Nazis in Germany. The work was hard, but conditions were generally <u>reasonable</u> for workers from <u>western Europe</u>.

6) There were also other <u>rules</u> that people in <u>occupied countries</u> had to live by:

   - Being <u>hostile</u> to <u>Germans</u> was forbidden.
   - Listening to <u>foreign propaganda</u> or <u>communicating</u> with Germany's enemies was forbidden.
   - Owning a <u>weapon</u> or a <u>radio</u>, <u>taking photographs outdoors</u>, <u>gathering</u> with other people without permission and displaying <u>flags</u> were all forbidden.

Nazi rule in the East was Brutal and Cruel

1) In occupied countries in <u>eastern Europe</u>, life could be <u>much harder</u>.

   - The Nazis thought of the east as <u>Lebensraum</u> for the 'Aryan master race' — it was intended eventually to become part of the <u>Greater Germanic Reich</u>.
   - This meant it had to be '<u>cleansed</u>' of non-Aryan populations. <u>Jews</u> and <u>Slavic</u> populations (e.g. Poles and Russians) were especially <u>targeted</u>.
   - Although the Nazis thought some members of these populations might be suitable for '<u>Germanisation</u>' (absorption into the German population), those considered <u>unsuitable</u> would be <u>killed</u>.

> In 1940, <u>Himmler</u> said, 'All Poles will disappear from this world. It is imperative that the great German nation considers the <u>elimination</u> of all Polish people as its chief task.'

> In 1939, <u>Hitler</u> told his commanders to kill 'without pity or mercy, all men, women, and children of Polish descent or language'.

2) When Germany invaded the Soviet Union in 1941, <u>Einsatzgruppen</u> (see p.129) followed the German army with orders to <u>kill</u> every <u>Jew</u> they found.

3) <u>Forced labourers</u> from the east were essentially <u>slaves</u>, and endured <u>terrible conditions</u>. About <u>2 million</u> non-Jewish <u>Poles</u> were forced into slave labour.

Comment and Analysis

The <u>different treatment</u> stemmed from the Nazis' belief that people in the <u>west</u> were of <u>Germanic</u> origin (they were 'Aryans', just like the Germans). People in the <u>east</u>, on the other hand, were thought to be '<u>biologically inferior</u>'.

The Nazis didn't treat everyone the same...

'Life in Nazi occupied countries was universally brutal and harsh.'
To what extent do you agree with this statement? [18]

The Holocaust

The Holocaust is the name given to the mass murder of Jews by the Nazis.
The Nazis called their plan to kill Europe's Jews the 'final solution'.

The Final Solution was the Genocide of Europe's Jews

1) Large numbers of German Jews had been sent to concentration camps since the Nazis came to power. After the conquest of countries in western Europe, many more Jews were deported to camps.

2) But the Nazis saw Europe's Jews as a problem that would eventually need a more 'complete' solution.

3) After the invasions of Poland and the Soviet Union, even more Jews came under Nazi control. Adolf Eichmann was put in charge of dealing with them.

> This was described as a 'territorial solution' to the Jewish question'.

4) The original plan was to deport all of Europe's Jews to a Jewish reservation in German-occupied Poland, where they could live far away from the German Reich.

5) Although many thousands of Jews were sent to this Polish reservation, it would have been impossible to put all of Europe's Jews there, and the plan was dropped.

> Or just the 'final solution'.

6) Instead the Jews were to be killed. This was described as the 'final solution to the Jewish question'.

Conditions in Ghettos were Terrible

1) As a temporary measure, Jews would first be made to live in ghettos — small areas of towns and cities where Jews could be gathered together away from the rest of the population.

2) Before entering the ghetto, Jews would have their possessions confiscated.

3) Inside the ghetto, conditions were terrible. Huge numbers of people died from disease or starvation. Some were used for slave labour — especially in weapons factories.

4) Jewish councils (the 'Judenrat') were made to oversee the ghettos. They were even forced to help organise the deportation of Jews to the death camps (see p.130).

5) Jews faced death for any resistance. Jewish authorities often decided the best way to save lives was to cooperate with the Nazis.

© Mary Evans / Imagno

The largest ghetto was in Warsaw. In this picture, Jewish police are separating different members of the population. The wall on the left separates the ghetto from the rest of the city.

Einsatzgruppen were mobile Killing Squads

1) After the Nazis invaded the Soviet Union, the Einsatzgruppen followed the German army. These were units of SS soldiers whose job was to murder people in occupied eastern Europe. They were a key part of the final solution and they killed in huge numbers, especially in Poland and the Soviet Union.

2) Their victims included those who were seen as racially impure (Jews in particular), enemies of Germany (e.g. officials of the Communist Party), and the physically or mentally disabled.

3) Some local communities helped the Einsatzgruppen to identify their victims by giving them information. Jews would be transported to execution sites to be killed and then buried in mass graves.

4) To speed up the rate at which people could be killed, trucks were converted into mobile gas chambers by having exhaust gases piped into the back where the victims were held.

5) But even these mobile gas vans were not felt to be efficient enough, and so a series of death camps was planned. The aim was that these should be able to kill on a genuinely industrial scale.

The 'final solution' — the ultimate madness...

'The Nazis always intended the destruction of Europe's Jews.' To what extent do you agree? [18]

EXAM QUESTION

The Holocaust

It's hard to believe, but this gets even <u>worse</u>.

Death Camps *were built to* Kill People *on an Industrial Scale*

1) To slaughter on the scale the Nazis required, <u>death camps</u> were built in eastern Europe. <u>Heinrich Himmler</u>, head of the SS, was in overall charge of this operation.

2) The camps included <u>gas chambers</u> to carry out the <u>mass murder</u>, and <u>crematoria</u> to burn the bodies.

3) The plan was to kill around 11 million people — <u>all</u> of the Jews living in Nazi-controlled territory.

4) People were transported to the camps from <u>all over</u> Nazi-occupied Europe. Jews were told they were being 'evacuated' to the east. They could take <u>luggage</u> with them and even had to <u>pay</u> for their own train tickets — the aim was to <u>hide</u> the fact that the Nazis intended to <u>kill</u> them and so prevent <u>mass panic</u>.

5) Mainly <u>Jewish</u> people were killed, but <u>other</u> groups were targeted as well, for example <u>Slavs</u> (e.g. Russians and Poles), <u>Romani</u>, <u>black people</u>, <u>homosexuals</u>, <u>disabled people</u> and <u>communists</u>.

Few People Survived *for Long* in the camps

1) On arrival at a camp, everyone would have their belongings and clothes <u>confiscated</u>. Items that the Nazis could use to help with the war effort (e.g. clothes, money) were sent back to Germany.

2) Most new arrivals were sent immediately to <u>gas chambers</u> disguised as <u>shower blocks</u> (to make people enter them more willingly). Their bodies were then <u>cremated</u>.

3) Some people would be selected for <u>forced labour</u>. Their <u>hair</u> was cut off, they were <u>tattooed</u> with a <u>registration number</u>, and they were issued with a striped <u>uniform</u>.

4) Others became the subjects of cruel 'medical' <u>experiments</u>.

5) For those not killed immediately, life in the camps was unbelievably <u>brutal</u>. Few people survived more than a <u>few months</u>. When someone was too <u>weak</u> or <u>ill</u> to work, they were <u>killed</u>.

The death camps were Auschwitz, Treblinka, Sobibor, Chelmno and Belzec. (The modern Polish borders are shown above.)

It's Hard *to understand* How this Mass Murder *happened*

1) By the end of the war, the Nazis had killed approximately <u>6 million Jews</u> and countless other people.

2) Before the war ended, orders went out to <u>destroy</u> the camps — but there <u>wasn't</u> time.

> Once it became clear that Germany would <u>lose</u> the war, Himmler wanted to <u>destroy</u> any <u>evidence</u> of the <u>genocide</u>. Special units were set up to visit mass graves and <u>burn</u> the <u>bodies</u> they contained. The corpses were usually removed by <u>Jewish prisoners</u>, who were then <u>murdered</u>.

3) After the war, people around the world found it <u>hard to believe</u> that this inhuman, cold-blooded extermination had taken place, and that <u>so many</u> soldiers were involved. It has been argued that they might have gone along with the Nazi leadership for various reasons:

- The Nazi guards felt they had to do their 'duty' and <u>obey orders</u>. They might have <u>feared</u> their leaders, or just felt that obeying orders was the <u>right thing</u> to do.

- Jews may not have been <u>regarded</u> as <u>fully human</u> — so killing them <u>didn't matter</u> to the guards.

Comment and Analysis

The world only discovered the horror of the death camps as the Allies advanced in <u>1945</u>. Some historians claim there's evidence leaders like Churchill were <u>told</u> about the camps — but didn't believe the facts.

Holocaust means 'Sacrifice' — Shoah means 'Catastrophe'...

Some Jewish people dislike the term Holocaust and prefer to use the word Shoah. It's important to learn about the Shoah / Holocaust. Cover this page and see how much you can write down.

Responses to Nazi Rule

People in Nazi-occupied countries <u>resisted</u> to some extent, but the <u>risks</u> involved were <u>huge</u>.

People Resisted or Collaborated in different ways

1) There was some <u>resistance</u> to Nazi rule in Nazi-occupied Europe. Other people <u>collaborated</u> with the occupiers, and a lot of people just <u>accommodated</u> them (put up with them).

2) The <u>types</u> of action people took can be grouped into different categories:

Acts of genuine resistance

> Minor acts of resistance are sometimes called <u>non-cooperation</u> (e.g. workers in a factory deliberately working slowly).

These are actions that tried to <u>hinder</u> the <u>Nazi war effort</u>, or <u>help Jews</u> or the <u>Nazis' enemies</u> — using either <u>violent</u> or <u>non-violent</u> methods.

- French and Polish <u>resistance movements</u> supplied <u>information</u> to the countries fighting Germany, and <u>disrupted</u> German communications by destroying train lines and cutting telephone wires.
- Some people offered to <u>hide</u> Jews from the Nazis. For example, in the Netherlands, <u>Anne Frank</u> and her family hid for over two years with the aid of several helpers. These helpers would have known how serious the <u>penalties</u> were for hiding Jews, but they still chose to help.
- In some countries there was <u>armed</u> resistance by guerrilla movements (e.g. '<u>partisans</u>' in eastern Europe).

> Penalties for resistance <u>varied</u> between countries — e.g. people in <u>Poland</u> could expect to be more harshly treated than those in <u>Denmark</u> (see p.128).

- In some <u>ghettos</u>, <u>underground movements</u> supplied <u>hot food</u> to help the Jews <u>survive</u> the harsh conditions.
- <u>Jews</u> themselves sometimes rose up against the Nazis. For example, in the <u>Warsaw ghetto</u> in 1943, Jews launched an <u>armed revolt</u> against the Nazis. It took almost a month for the Nazis to regain full control.

Acts of collaboration

These are actions that <u>helped</u> the Nazis.

- Whole <u>governments</u> could collaborate (e.g. the <u>Vichy government</u> in <u>southern France</u>, which <u>voluntarily</u> persecuted Jews, deporting tens of thousands of them to Nazi death camps), or it could be <u>individuals</u>.
- Acts of collaboration ranged from doing German soldiers' <u>laundry</u> and <u>denouncing</u> fellow citizens, through to taking part in <u>mass killings</u>.

Acts of accommodation

These are actions that <u>don't help</u> the Nazis, but <u>don't</u> do anything to <u>hinder</u> them or <u>help their victims</u> either. It's often called being a <u>bystander</u>.

People in occupied countries had a Difficult Choice

1) Given the <u>scale</u> of the crimes being committed by the Nazis, some people are surprised that more people <u>didn't resist</u> Nazi rule.

2) But <u>not everyone</u> would have been <u>aware</u> of what the Nazis were doing, and the <u>penalties</u> for resistance could be <u>extremely harsh</u>.

3) People faced a difficult choice — for example, they might have thought it more important to do what they could to <u>look after</u> their <u>family</u> than to resist the Nazis. Or they might just have wanted to <u>survive the war</u>.

> <u>Primo Levi</u>, a <u>survivor</u> of Auschwitz, has explained that resistance was especially difficult for <u>Jews</u>, partly because the Nazis had taken away any <u>hope</u> of rescue or of finding a place of <u>safety</u>.

Resistance was extremely risky, and often futile...

This course is partly about understanding people's lives and experiences — using what you've learnt, jot down a list of reasons for why some Germans might have accommodated the Nazis.

Revision Summary

You've finished the section, which can only mean one thing — it's time for a lovely revision summary.
- Try these questions and <u>tick off each one</u> when you <u>get it right</u>.
- When you've done <u>all the questions</u> for a topic and are <u>completely happy</u> with it, tick off the topic.

The Nazi Dictatorship (p.115-117) ☑

1) Give three reasons why the Great Depression helped the Nazis to become more popular. ☑
2) Describe how Hitler rose to the position of Chancellor. ☑
3) What was the Enabling Act? When was it introduced? ☑
4) Give two examples of legislation that the Nazis passed shortly after the Enabling Act, which helped the Nazi Party to consolidate its power. ☑
5) What happened on the 'Night of the Long Knives'? ☑

Control and Opposition, 1933-1939 (p.118-121) ☑

6) Describe three powers the Nazis had that suggested Germany had become a police state by 1934. ☑
7) Who was in charge of the Nazi Party's 'propaganda machine'? ☑
8) What were the aims of Nazi propaganda? ☑
9) What was the 'Hitler Myth'? ☑
10) Name two members of the Church who opposed the Nazis. ☑
11) Who were the Swing Kids? ☑

Changing German Lives, 1933-1939 (p.122-124) ☑

12) What expectations did the Nazi Party have of women? ☑
13) Describe one measure the Nazis used to reduce German unemployment. ☑
14) What was the Hitler Youth? ☑
15) How was education in Germany affected while the Nazis were in power? ☑
16) What were the Nuremberg Laws? ☑
17) Describe the events of Kristallnacht. ☑

Germany during the Second World War (p.125-127) ☑

18) Describe one way in which daily life was affected in Germany after the outbreak of war. ☑
19) What was the White Rose Group? ☑
20) Who was Claus von Stauffenberg? What did he do to oppose Nazi rule? ☑
21) Describe what's meant by 'total war'. How did total war change Germany's economy? ☑

Nazi Occupation (p.128-131) ☑

22) Describe three differences between Nazi rule in occupied countries in western Europe and those in eastern Europe. ☑
23) What is a ghetto? Describe their role in the Holocaust. ☑
24) What was the role of the Einsatzgruppen? ☑
25) Name four groups of people who were targeted for execution in the Nazi death camps. ☑
26) How did people in Nazi-occupied countries resist the occupation? ☑
27) Give two reasons why someone may have chosen not to resist the Nazis. ☑

Skills for the History Around Us Exam

This page is full of <u>great advice</u> on how to prepare for your <u>History Around Us</u> exam.

You've got to answer *Two Questions* in the exam

1) In the exam, you'll have an hour to answer <u>two</u> questions from a choice of <u>three</u>.

2) The questions will be based on issues to do with the <u>physical features</u> and <u>historical context</u> of the site you've studied, as well as how we can use the <u>historic environment</u> to learn about history.

3) For every question, you'll have to write about the <u>features</u> of your site as well as your own <u>historical knowledge</u>.

4) Don't just include <u>everything</u> you know, though. Make sure all the details you include are <u>relevant</u> to the <u>question</u> you've been asked.

5) As you write your answer, you must tell the examiner which <u>periods</u> of history you're writing about. Use <u>dates</u> or <u>terms</u> such as 'in the <u>eighteenth century</u>' or 'during the <u>Iron Age</u>'.

The Physical Features *of a Site* can tell you a lot about its History

1) In the exam, you'll have to <u>write</u> about what your site's <u>physical features</u> tell you about its <u>history</u>.

2) This means you'll need to know your site pretty <u>well</u>. 'Physical features' could be <u>anything</u> about the site — from its <u>structure</u>, to <u>materials</u> used to build it, to small <u>design</u> details.

3) The <u>questions</u> below are things that you may have to write about in the <u>exam</u> — keep them in <u>mind</u> as you study your site. <u>Before</u> the exam, go through them <u>all</u> and make sure you can answer each one <u>fully</u>.

Physical Features
• <u>Where</u> is the site located? <u>Why</u> is it located there?
• <u>When</u> was the site created? <u>Why</u> did people create the site?
• <u>Have</u> the site and its uses <u>changed</u> over time? If so, <u>why</u>?
• Does the site have any <u>particular</u> features which are <u>significant</u>?

Think about which features of your site <u>changed</u> and when, and whether this reflects changes in <u>society</u> and <u>culture</u>.

Some sites may have features which show you something <u>important</u> about the site and its history. Make sure you can <u>identify</u> these features and <u>explain</u> their importance.

Talk about *Relevant* physical features in the Exam

1) Your site will probably have <u>a lot</u> of physical features that you could write about in the exam.

2) Only talk about <u>features</u> of your site that are <u>relevant</u> to the <u>question</u> and the <u>points</u> that you're making in your answer. You need to <u>select</u> pieces of information that <u>support</u> your arguments.

For example, if you get a question about the <u>location</u> of your site, think about the physical features which help you explain <u>why</u> the location was chosen.	If the location of a <u>castle</u> was chosen because it was easy to <u>defend</u>, you could talk about the physical features of the site which are <u>related</u> to its defence, such as a <u>moat</u> and <u>thick walls</u>.

The exam is in site, so make sure you know your stuff...

Make sure you know your site from top to bottom and you won't have anything to worry about in the exam. Remember to consider how the site has changed, how it's stayed the same, why this happened, etc.

Skills for the History Around Us Exam

Here's some more <u>advice</u> about how to do well in that tricky <u>History Around Us</u> exam.

You need to know about the Historical Context of your Site

1) Your site won't be <u>directly linked</u> to any of the <u>topics</u> you've studied.

2) You need to know what was <u>happening</u> at your site at <u>different points</u> in time — its <u>historical context</u>.

3) You'll also need to know how your site <u>fits in</u> with <u>other similar sites</u> around the country.

Historical Context

- Have there been significant <u>events</u> or <u>developments</u> in your site's history?
- What different <u>activities</u> took place and what different <u>groups</u> of people were present at your site at <u>different times</u>?
- What does the site tell you about people's <u>lives</u> and <u>attitudes</u> in different periods of history? How much have these <u>varied</u> over time?
- How does this site <u>compare</u> with other sites of the same type?
- Does this site have <u>importance</u> on a <u>local</u> or <u>national</u> level?

> Think about how <u>changes</u> at your site might have been <u>affected</u> by its historical <u>context</u>.

> Is your site <u>typical</u> of this type of site (e.g. a typical Elizabethan manor house), or is there anything which makes it <u>unusual</u>?

Use your Own Knowledge to put physical Features into Context

1) <u>Back up</u> your answers in the exam by using your own <u>knowledge</u> of the context of your site.

2) This isn't the place to write down <u>everything</u> you know about history — select the most <u>relevant</u> bits of your knowledge to back up your answer.

> The <u>number</u> of <u>windows</u> a Georgian property has could be a sign of the <u>wealth</u> of the owner. A <u>window tax</u> was brought in just before the Georgian period in <u>1696</u>, and a <u>glass tax</u> was introduced in <u>1746</u>. This meant that windows were <u>expensive</u> — some people bricked up or covered up their windows. Therefore, it is likely that the <u>more</u> windows a building had, the <u>richer</u> its owners were. Including lots of windows was an opportunity to <u>show off</u> their wealth and assert their <u>elite status</u>.

Think about how sites can help you Understand History

1) Some questions might ask you about the <u>challenges</u> and <u>benefits</u> of studying the <u>historic environment</u>.

2) Think about the <u>difficulties</u> of studying sites that might have <u>decayed</u> or been <u>rebuilt</u> or <u>restored</u> over time.

3) You might also need to think about how <u>difficult</u> it would be to create an <u>accurate</u> <u>interpretation</u> (e.g. a painting or a piece of fiction) of your site, or of daily life there.

4) Think about what you can <u>tell</u> from the <u>remains</u> of your site, and what information has been <u>lost</u>.

Studying the Historic Environment

- What are the <u>advantages</u> and <u>difficulties</u> of studying this particular site?
- How are <u>modern interpretations</u> (e.g. paintings) shaped by what <u>remains</u> of the site today?
- What <u>questions</u> could be asked about the site? How can these be turned into <u>historical enquiries</u>?

In 2008, a man broke 46 toilet seats with his head in one minute...

Random facts are fun, but they're also pretty useless if you're trying to pick up marks in the exam. Study all of the features of your site — it'll help you to answer the questions with the most relevant examples.

Skills for the History Around Us Exam

This page'll give you a few tips on how to use your knowledge of your site's features to write a good essay.

You'll need to use your Knowledge of Features in the Exam

The exam questions will deal with the issues from the last two pages.
They will each link at least two of them together. Here's an example:

This question asks you to link a turning point in history with changes to your site and how people used it.

Choose a turning point in your site's history. Explain how and why this changed the site and the way it was used. Use physical features of the site as well as your knowledge to support your answer. [25]

The question won't name a specific site. You'll write about the one you've studied.

Link historical Events to the Features of your site

This extract from an answer links an event in the site's history (the arrival of a particular group of immigrants) with a physical change to the site (the construction of a distinctive type of building).

A major turning point in the history of Spitalfields was the arrival of Huguenot immigrants from France between 1670 and 1710. The Huguenots helped to create a thriving textile trade in Spitalfields, setting up numerous workshops in the area. They constructed impressive buildings designed to house their families as well as the weavers who worked for them. These houses had large windows on their upper floors to let in light for weaving and can still be seen today, for example on Fournier Street.

This describes the event and gives details of when it took place.

This explains why the site changed, and describes which features can still be seen today.

Some Details about your site might have been Lost

This extract talks about the difficulties of using a historical site in the present day to investigate events or changes that happened a long time ago.

One of the difficulties in studying Carisbrooke Castle results from the fact that the site has changed a great deal throughout its history, with new features added and old ones altered. The main function of the castle changed when Isabella de Fortibus made it more of a residence than a military outpost in the 13th century. However, most features that she added, such as a large hall and a chapel, have been extensively rebuilt and restored since this time, so it is difficult to learn about this change from studying the physical remains of the castle.

Sites that have been through lots of changes of purpose and ownership often look very different in the present day from how they looked in the past.

Remember to use specific examples of the physical features of your site.

Who knew features could be so revealing...

The questions might seem a bit daunting, but if you learn the features of your site inside-out and know how to use them to support your argument, then you'll be off to a great start in the History Around Us exam.

Exam Hints and Tips

These pages will show you how to <u>use</u> your knowledge to get those <u>all-important marks</u>.
Make sure that you read <u>all</u> of this very very <u>carefully</u>.

You will take 3 Papers altogether

1) <u>Paper 1</u> is <u>1 hour 45 minutes</u> long. It's worth <u>80 marks</u> — <u>40%</u> of your GCSE. This paper will be divided into <u>2 sections</u>:
   - Section A: <u>Thematic Study</u> (see pages 3-4).
   - Section B: <u>British Depth Study</u> (see pages 78-79).

> The Thematic Studies covered in this book are <u>The People's Health, c.1250 to present</u> (on pages 5-32) and <u>Migrants to Britain, c.1250 to present</u> (on pages 33-53). The British Depth Studies covered in this book are <u>The Norman Conquest, 1065-1087</u> (on pages 80-96) and <u>The Elizabethans, 1580-1603</u> (on pages 97-114).

2) <u>Paper 2</u> is <u>1 hour</u> long. It's worth <u>50 marks</u> — <u>20%</u> of your GCSE. The paper is about <u>History Around Us</u>. You'll need to answer <u>two essay questions</u> from of a choice of three.

> See pages 133-135 for tips on how to answer questions about the <u>site</u> that you've studied for <u>History Around Us</u>.

3) <u>Paper 3</u> is <u>1 hour 45 minutes</u> long. It's worth <u>80 marks</u> — <u>40%</u> of your GCSE. This paper will be divided into <u>2 sections</u>:
   - Section A: <u>Period Study</u> (see pages 3-4).
   - Section B: <u>World Depth Study</u> (see pages 78-79).

> The Period Study covered in this book is <u>The Making of America, 1789-1900</u> (on pages 54-77). The World Depth Study covered in this book is <u>Living Under Nazi Rule, 1933–1945</u> (on pages 115-132).

> **Make sure you know which <u>Thematic Study</u>, <u>Period Study</u> and <u>Depth Studies</u> you're studying. They might <u>not</u> be the ones we've covered in this book. And remember... some of your exam papers will contain questions on topics you <u>haven't studied</u> — <u>IGNORE THOSE</u>. Only answer questions <u>on the topics you've studied</u>.**

Remember these Four Tips for Answering Questions

1) Don't spend Too Long on Short Questions

1) <u>Learn the rule</u> — the <u>more marks</u> a question is worth, the <u>longer</u> your answer should be.
2) Don't get carried away writing loads for a question that's only worth 5 marks — you need to <u>leave time</u> for the higher mark questions.

2) Plan your Essay Answers, but not the others

1) You <u>don't</u> need to plan answers to the <u>shorter source questions</u> in the exam. That will <u>waste time</u>.
2) For <u>longer essay questions</u>, it's very important to make a <u>quick plan</u> before you start writing.
3) Think about what the <u>key words</u> are in the question. Scribble a <u>quick plan</u> of your <u>main points</u> — <u>cross through this neatly</u> at the end, so it's obvious it shouldn't be marked.

3) Stay Focused on the Question

1) Make sure that you <u>directly answer the question</u>. <u>Back up your points</u> with <u>relevant facts</u>. Don't just chuck in everything you know about the period.
2) You've got to be <u>relevant</u> and <u>accurate</u> — e.g. if you're writing about the rise of the Nazi Party, don't include stories about a London camel called George who moved rubble during the Blitz.
3) It might help to try to write the <u>first sentence</u> of every <u>paragraph</u> in a way that <u>addresses</u> the question, e.g. 'Another way in which Normans took over the roles of Anglo-Saxon elites is...'

4) Use a Clear Writing Style

1) <u>Essay answers</u> should start with a brief <u>introduction</u> and end with a <u>conclusion</u>.
2) Remember to start a <u>new paragraph</u> for each new point you want to discuss.
3) Try to use <u>clear handwriting</u> — and pay attention to <u>spelling</u>, <u>grammar</u> and <u>punctuation</u> (see next page).

Exam Hints and Tips

In Paper 2, the examiner will be marking you partly on your <u>spelling</u>, <u>punctuation</u> and <u>grammar</u> (SPaG). SPaG is worth <u>nearly 5%</u> of your overall mark, so don't forget to write nicely (as my mum would say).

Remember to Check your Spellings

1) You should leave about <u>five minutes</u> at the end of the exam to <u>check your work</u>.

2) Check as <u>many</u> questions as you can, but make sure you read over the questions which award <u>SPaG marks</u> especially <u>carefully</u>. (Marks are shown very clearly at the end of each question.)

3) There <u>won't</u> be time to check <u>everything</u> thoroughly, so look for <u>obvious</u> spelling <u>mistakes</u>...

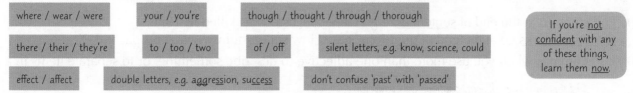

where / wear / were	your / you're	though / thought / through / thorough
there / their / they're	to / too / two	of / off	silent letters, e.g. know, science, could
effect / affect	double letters, e.g. a<u>gg</u>ression, su<u>cc</u>ess	don't confuse 'past' with 'passed'

If you're <u>not</u> <u>confident</u> with any of these things, learn them <u>now</u>.

4) Make sure you haven't <u>repeated</u> words like '<u>and</u>', '<u>but</u>' and '<u>because</u>':

> Cholera became an epidemic in 1832 <u>and</u> it killed thousands of people <u>and</u> it eventually declined.

Using 'and' both times sounds really <u>boring</u>.

> Cholera became an epidemic in 1832 <u>and</u> it killed thousands of people, <u>but</u> it eventually declined.

This <u>doesn't</u> sound so <u>repetitive</u>.

5) <u>Don't worry</u> if you find a mistake when you <u>check</u> your work. As long as you make your corrections <u>clearly</u>, the examiner <u>won't</u> mark you down.

6) If the mistake is just <u>one word</u> or a <u>short phrase</u>, cross it out <u>neatly</u> and write the correct word <u>above</u> it.

> believed
> Many settlers falsely b̶e̶l̶e̶i̶v̶e̶d̶ that Native Americans were inferior and savage.

Spell Technical Words correctly

1) There are a lot of <u>technical words</u> in history. You need to be able to <u>spell</u> them <u>correctly</u>. <u>Learn</u> these examples to start you off. The <u>underlined letters</u> are the tricky bits to watch out for.

| <u>a</u>lli<u>a</u>n<u>ce</u> | ar<u>gu</u>ment | bi<u>a</u>s<u>ed</u> | contro<u>v</u>er<u>si</u>al | con<u>se</u>qu<u>e</u>n<u>ces</u> | defen<u>ce</u> | d<u>e</u>mocr<u>a</u>cy |
| fas<u>c</u>ism | for<u>ei</u>gn | govern<u>m</u>ent | interpr<u>e</u>tation | parli<u>a</u>ment | sour<u>ce</u> | su<u>cc</u>e<u>ss</u>ful |

2) You'll also have to learn how to spell <u>names</u> and <u>technical terms</u> from the <u>topics</u> you're studying. Go back through them and <u>make a list</u> of tricky names and words. Here are some to look out for:

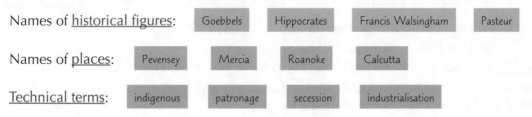

Names of <u>historical figures</u>: Goebbels | Hippocrates | Francis Walsingham | Pasteur

Names of <u>places</u>: Pevensey | Mercia | Roanoke | Calcutta

<u>Technical terms</u>: indigenous | patronage | secession | industrialisation

---

Learn this page and make spelling errors history...

Mnemonics can help you remember how to spell tricky words. For example, you can remember 'biased' with the phrase '<u>B</u>leary <u>I</u>nsomniacs <u>A</u>void <u>S</u>leep <u>E</u>very <u>D</u>ay'. Or something similar...

Exam Hints and Tips

How do you spell 'industrialisation'? That's no problem for you. You've got all the tricky words down — now you just need to make sure your ideas are presented well by using correct <u>punctuation</u> and <u>grammar</u>.

You need to Punctuate Properly...

1) Always use a <u>capital letter</u> at the start of a <u>sentence</u>.
Use capital letters for <u>names</u> of <u>particular people</u>, <u>places</u> and <u>things</u>. For example:

<u>All sentences</u> start with capital letters. → *In 1933, Hitler was made Chancellor of Germany.*

The name of a <u>person</u>.   A <u>title</u>.   The name of a <u>country</u>.

2) <u>Full stops</u> go at the end of <u>sentences</u>, e.g. 'General Custer was killed in 1876.'
<u>Question marks</u> go at the end of <u>questions</u>, e.g. 'How successful was Nazi propaganda?'

3) Use <u>commas</u> when you use <u>more than one adjective</u> to describe something, or to separate items in a <u>list</u>:

Elizabeth I was <u>intelligent, cautious</u> and <u>powerful</u>.

4) <u>Commas</u> can also <u>join two points</u> into one sentence with a joining word (such as '<u>and</u>', '<u>or</u>', '<u>so</u>' or '<u>but</u>'):

Water supplies were poor in medieval English towns, <u>so</u> many people were forced to drink dirty water.

5) <u>Commas</u> can also be used to separate <u>extra information</u> in a sentence:

Edward I, <u>who was King of England in the late 13th century</u>, put restrictions on Jewish people who lived in England.

...and use Grammar Correctly

1) Make sure your writing <u>isn't too chatty</u> and doesn't use <u>slang words</u>. It should be <u>formal</u>.

Robert Koch's discovery about cholera was <u>well</u> useful.   *Robert Koch's discovery about cholera was <u>very</u> useful.*

This language is <u>too informal</u> for an exam.   This is <u>more appropriate</u>.

2) <u>Don't change tenses</u> in your writing by mistake:

The mountain men <u>explored</u> the West first — they <u>hunted</u> animals for their skins.

<u>Both</u> verbs are in the <u>past tense</u> — which is correct. Writing '<u>hunt</u>' instead of '<u>hunted</u>' would be wrong.

3) Write your longer answers in <u>paragraphs</u>.
   - A paragraph is a <u>group of sentences</u> which talk about the <u>same thing</u> or <u>follow on</u> from each other.
   - You need to start a <u>new paragraph</u> when you start making a <u>new point</u>.

You show a <u>new paragraph</u> by starting a <u>new line</u> and leaving a <u>gap</u> (an <u>indent</u>) before you start writing:

From 1933, Hitler started a programme of public works, such as the building of huge new motorways. This gave jobs to thousands of people.
   Even though there was increased employment, the Nazis altered the statistics so that things looked better than they were. Wages were also poor.

If you've <u>forgotten</u> to start a <u>new paragraph</u>, use a <u>double strike</u> (like this //) to show where the new paragraph should <u>begin</u>.

4) Remember — '<u>it's</u>' (with an apostrophe) is short for '<u>it is</u>' or '<u>it has</u>'.
'<u>Its</u>' (without an apostrophe) means '<u>belonging to it</u>'.

5) It's always '<u>should have</u>', not 'should of' (and also 'could have' and 'would have' too).

6) If you know that you <u>often</u> confuse two words, like 'it's' and 'its', <u>watch out</u> for them when you're checking your work in the exam.

That's that, then — all that's left to do now is to sit the exams...

Good SPaG is a great way to get marks in the exam. So make sure you've learnt all the stuff on this page, and also everything about anything that's ever happened in all of history, and you should be okay.

Index

Index